A New Education Politics

Bob Rae's Legacy and the Response of the Ontario Secondary School Teachers' Federation

George Martell

An Our Schools/Our Selves Title

James Lorimer & Company Ltd., Publishers
Toronto, 1995

For subscribers to *Our Schools/Our Selves: a magazine for Canadian education activists*, this is issue #42, the Sixth of Volume 6.

The subscription series Our Schools/Our Selves (ISSN 0840-7339) is published six times a year. Publication Mail Registration Number 8010. Mailed at Centre Ville, Montreal, Quebec.

Canadian Cataloguing in Publication Data

Martell, George, 1940–
A new education politics : Bob Rae's legacy and the response of the Ontario Secondary School Teachers' Federation

(Our schools/our selves monograph series ; no. 19)
Includes bibliographical references.
ISBN 0–55028–488–6

1. Education and state – Ontario. 2. New Democratic Party of Ontario. 3. Ontario Secondary School Teachers' Federation. I. Title. III. Series.

LC91.2.06M3 1995 379.713 C95–931828–3

Design and typesetting: Tobin MacIntosh.

Front Cover Design: Nancy Reid.

Our Schools/Our Selves production: Keren Brathwaite, David Clandfield, Lorna Erwin, John Huot, Doug Little, Bob Luker, George Martell, Satu Repo (Executive Editor), Bairy Sium, Harry Smaller.

James Lorimer & Company Ltd., Publishers
35 Britain Street
Toronto M5A 1R7

Printed and bound in Canada by La maîtresse d'école inc., Montreal, Quebec.

Dedication

For all those NDP education activists
who knew it didn't have to turn out this way.

Preface

I began this book out of the experience of Bob Rae's Social Contract. I wanted to show its impact on Ontario schools and the response of the Ontario Secondary School Teachers' Federation (OSSTF), which took the lead in resisting this extraordinary assault on the province's school system. I initially hoped the book might contribute to a debate on the future of Ontario education which would eventually come to a head in the past provincial election. I had, of course, no expectation that any of the three major political parties might be persuaded to carry the banner of progressive education reform. They had by this time become largely indistinguishable on most education policy issues, the NDP having largely built on the policies of earlier Tory and Liberal administrations. But the run-up to the election seemed a good opportunity to raise an alternative vision to the increasingly right-wing thrust in our schools, particularly as it emerged in the Social Contract process and its implications for the future. That was OSSTF's position as well. It reflected the general strategy of the Public Services Coalition and their union allies in the private sector who had been traditional NDP supporters: "Use the election to raise issues. Back off partisan NDP politics — we don't know what to do with the party now." With this decision, it seemed to me, the political landscape of the province had irrevocably changed, and nowhere more so than in education, which had seen a complete breakdown in the relationship of the Ontario teacher federations and their provincial government. The election process could at least help make that clear: to say what had been lost and to begin the task of rebuilding an opposition on stronger foundations. In setting out the Social Contract struggle between OSSTF and the provincial government — this book was originally titled *Bob Rae vs. the Teachers* — I had hoped to contribute to both of these goals.

With the Report of the Royal Commission on Learning in February of this year, the necessity of opposing NDP initiatives and developing an alternative program became even more pronounced for teacher unionists and education activists. The commissioners articulated what the Education Ministry now calls its "New Foundations" for the future, and these foundations went much deeper than the slash and burn of the Social Contract. It became even clearer that the shape of education politics in Ontario had been fundamentally altered. The hidden agenda of deficit-led restructuring — a corporate and bureaucratic vision of school governance and educational purpose — had now been placed formally on the table. OSSTF was obliged to nail down the terms of its opposition, in circumstances quite unlike anything the organization has previously experienced and which involved a major rethinking of Federation policy. I had no option but to include this response — at least in its first expression — in the final section of this book. The result was that the writing had to be extended way beyond the time it might have been of any use during a sustained issues campaign in the spring of 1995.

As it turned out, of course, such a campaign failed to materialize. The three parties and the media made sure of that. All that came to matter — in what passes as a public arena on such questions — were different political spins on the deficit issue, taken largely from the same perspective of neo-conservative economics. The Public Services Coalition and its allies had yet to build an organization that might have insisted that an alternative perspective be given equal weight.

At one point, however, it seemed that the Our Schools/Our Selves editorial team might get the book out a week or so before election day, pressing hard on the good will of our typesetter and printer. And, for a moment, that seemed a tiny gesture worth making. It would have no effect on the outcome of the election, but it would make us feel better — joining hands with those who did try to raise their voices in this election, even if there was almost no one running who wanted to hear them. In the end, though, it seemed preferable to wait a little, let the election take place and its coverage subside. Whatever government took office after June 8 would now follow the pattern laid down by the Rae administration in educational restructuring. The resistance to this pattern, opened up by OSSTF, would move forward on positions already staked out in the Federation's early days of opposition. It promised an explosive series of conflicts in the years to come. In the end, that seemed the most important thing to stress: the continuing destructiveness of the NDP legacy in Ontario education and the growing resistance to this legacy by a teacher's organization and its allies. The book is as much a study of how we face up to where the government of Mike Harris begins in education as it is a history of how Bob Rae got them there. Plunging into the last days of the Ontario election might well have obscured this point.

A new education politics in Ontario had been been born.

Acknowledgements

First of all, I want to thank the members of the Ontario Secondary School Teachers' Federation who took the trouble to make their views known to me, not only concerning the Rae government's assault on public schooling in Ontario but also on the larger economic and political context in which it took place. I hope I have caught both the spirit and the substance of what they told me. OSSTF would want to me to say, however, that the governing opinions of this book are entirely my own; they do not represent an official federation position. OSSTF's more considered judgement of the NDP's legacy in education will come in due course, as much in action as in analysis. I also want to thank the organization for a grant that helped make the writing of this book possible.

There were a number of officials and politicians who spoke at length with me, largely off the record. We did not always concur on our interpretation of the issues we discussed. We did, however, share a good deal of agreement about what actually happened in Ontario education during this NDP administration, and I have tried hard to hold on to these facts as we all understood them. My thanks for these conversations and for the patience and kindness these people showed to me in explaining a number of complex policy areas, particularly since they did so knowing that my conclusions were likely to run counter to their own.

I am also grateful to the press corps at Queen's Park for their detailed and remarkably even-handed coverage of the Social Contract process. They made this story much easier for me to tell. Among these reporters, I want especially to thank three chroniclers of the Rae regime: George Ehring and Wayne Roberts for their book *Giving Away A Miracle: Lost Dreams, Broken Promises & The Ontario NDP* and Tom Walkom for his book *Rae Days: The Rise and Follies of the NDP* and his daily column in *The Toronto Star*. Without this writing and the context it provided, the educational struggle I have outlined here would have had far less meaning.

In the last few weeks, with almost no notice, a number of friends agreed to read and comment on a draft of this book. They include John Calvert, Bob Davis, Lorna Erwin, Larry Kuehn, Loren Lind, Doug Little, Tim Little, David Livingstone, Satu Repo, Bob Spencer and Jim Turk. Not only did they substantially improve what I had written, but they saved me from a number of errors of both fact and interpretation. They could not, of course, save me from whatever faults the main line of my argument may include. Nor could my editors David Clandfield and Cy Strom. They have, nevertheless, struggled with me to incorporate as much clarity and balance as time and my own limitations would permit. I offer what thanks I can to all of these readers and editors for their grace under pressure and their commitment to telling this story as accurately as possible. In the same spirit, I also offer my thanks to Tobin MacIntosh, our typesetter and designer, for his grace under pressure and his commitment to getting the manuscript right.

Finally, I want to thank my partner Elaine MacIntosh, whose work as a classroom teacher continues to remind me how important it is to resist and to continue to resist the Ontario government's on-going attack on the province's public schools.

G.M.
Toronto, June 1995.

Contents

PART II

TOWARDS A NEW EDUCATION POLITICS: A REPONSE TO THE ROYAL COMMISSION ON LEARNING

Introduction

The Politics of Money

This book focuses on a particular moment in the increasingly pervasive corporate assault on Canadian education: the period between 1993 and 1995, when Bob Rae's Social Contract and the Royal Commission on Learning combined to form two prongs of a major new offensive against public schooling in Ontario. In coming to grips with this offensive, I want to look at the resistance mounted against it by the Ontario Secondary School Teachers Federation (OSSTF), the province's most powerful teachers' union.

We enter this moment, which officially began in the spring of 1993, by concentrating on the two major government initiatives which dominated public perception of the Social Contract: The first of these was the imposition of financial cutbacks (expressed in the education sector, as it was throughout the broader public sector, in job loss, a smaller tax base, wage reductions, diminished services, and poorer working conditions). The second was the frontal attack on a system of collective bargaining built to resist such cutbacks.

For a good part of the book, we examine a struggle over how much money is to be raised and spent for public services and jobs, particularly in the province's school system. This is no small issue, of course, but the Social Contract was about a lot more than the extent of government spending. It was also about who spends that money and what they spend it on —

about power and what people do with it. At the heart of this issue lay a fundamental struggle over the purposes of the state system and its schools. Both the Ontario government and its opponents in the Public Services Coalition (including OSSTF) seemed to understand this quite clearly, though such a broad perspective rarely surfaced at the various bargaining tables over which they met. Where many of these larger issues did become explicit, however, was in the recent Royal Commission on Learning, which former OSSTF vice-president Bob Garthson has called "Social Contract II." We will deal with the Royal Commission and OSSTF's resistance to it in Part 2 as part of the broader Social Contract struggle.

In future Our Schools/Our Selves books, we want to look more thoroughly at the larger corporate agenda for a "restructured" public sector and popular resistance to it, especially in education. In focusing now on this battle over public finance, and its extension into governance and curriculum questions by the Royal Commission, I hope to clear a little ground for this larger work.

What I especially want to isolate are a few strategic fundamentals for education activists who hope to resist the corporate assault on our schools, particularly when it is carried out by a social democratic party and a leader like Bob Rae. If we don't get these fundamentals straight, we will remain unable to respond effectively to such assaults on education and on the state system as a whole.

It is a search, I think, which is now shared broadly among teacher leaders and rank-and-file activists throughout Ontario.

Such fundamentals are not easily captured. They are not a detached body of knowledge, kept in a strategic policy archive, to be brought out in a time of political crisis. They emerge, instead, out of the whole lived practice of a society (and of organizations like OSSTF within it). They change with this practice, and they can get lost in it as well, as both leaders and their membership come to neglect the forest for the trees. What I want to do here is to try to extract these fundamentals from the practice of OSSTF as it attempted to mobilize against Bob Rae's Social Contract: to learn from its strategic mistakes, as the organization is itself doing, but also, perhaps more importantly, to learn from its successes and to build on what has already been accomplished.

If the cover of this book had room for another subtitle, it might have read "Where do we stand and fight?" This is the question asked in Part 2, the final section of this book, in which I hope to integrate OSSTF's experience of the Social Contract with its response to the Royal Commission on Learning. "Where do we stand and fight?" is an honest question for OSSTF. The Federation is now in the process of preparing strategies on key initiatives flowing from the Royal Commission. The issues that all teachers face are now pressing hard. Major funding and service cutbacks along with a widespread attack on collective bargaining rights are only the most obvious. In the NDP government's response to the Royal Commission on Learning we saw more centralization of decision-making, curriculum and education funding and far more influence for the corporate sector. We can also anticipate a more inflexible streaming system than currently exists, as more high-tech mechanisms for standardized testing and corporate job-slotting are put into place. All in all, it adds up to an unremitting assault on the province's schools. It is unlikely that the newly elected Conservative government under Mike Harris will change direction. Rather it will push even further in the same direction.

OSSTF is moving towards an answer to this assault, one I believe can serve as a basis for future action. Part of this answer (which the Federation holds alongside its partners in the Public Services Coalition and much of labour generally) lies in building an economic vision for Canada and Ontario and making it central to public sector collective bargaining. The other part of the answer (increasingly shared with a much broader spectrum of progressive organizations across the country) integrates this economic vision into a more inclusive view of a democratic and caring society. For OSSTF this means a socially purposeful school system made practical through a powerful alliance of teachers, students, parents, community groups and the labour movement as a whole.

On all these fronts — whether dealing with money, power or the quality of curriculum and the purposes of schooling — OSSTF is gradually concluding that teachers and their allies must finally take hold of the educational reform agenda. A kneejerk defence of the public schools doesn't work anymore, even though the public school system must be strongly defended. Teachers not only have to say what's right with the education they provide, they also have to say what's wrong and spell out what to do about it.

For OSSTF and its allies, however, there is another question to be asked: Whom, in fact, are they fighting? In Part 1, an analysis of the Social Contract struggle as OSSTF experienced it, I make the argument that they are not only fighting a corporate/bureaucratic assault on the school system, but a social-democratic assault as well — and that the two have essentially become one. The NDP, as a result of its actions in office, became an enemy of the Ontario school system.

With the collapse of a social democratic alternative, a complete rethinking of the political landscape now seems to be in order. Alongside a revamped movement for social activism, a new political party of the democratic left has to emerge. Among its policies it must carry a progressive education agenda to Queen's Park and to the province's local school boards. My hunch is that most Ontario teacher activists would be sympathetic to such a party, if presented with a realistic proposal for its creation. It may be, of course, that an alliance of teachers, labour and community groups could so effectively take over the NDP that for all intents and purposes it could become, once more, a "New Party." I am less optimistic about this option, but it is clearly a realistic alternative. What is no longer an alternative is a middling reform of the NDP, although this remains the hope of a good many Ontario teachers, unionists and community activists. I would like to think this small history of the Social Contract struggle will help them change their minds.

As we move into this history, I want to briefly describe OSSTF's evolving politics as the organization entered the Social Contract process. These politics help explain the Federation's leading role in building an opposition to the Rae government. They also help us understand the difficulties OSSTF faced in transforming that opposition into fully successful resistance. Essentially, these are the politics of money: the politics of most union negotiations, the politics of wealth and its distribution. They are sometimes called the politics of social democracy. OSSTF cut its teeth on these politics, and because of them achieved some remarkable successes and a solid organizational base. As we shall see, however, they were not enough to withstand the neo-conservative juggernaut that Bob Rae eventually turned their way.

But first, though, a few words about the Social Contract itself.

More than anything else it involved a profound shift in what the politics of money are supposed to be for social democrats.

The Social Contract Package

The Money Question: Public Cutbacks, Private Profits

OSSTF did not expect Bob Rae's assault on the public sector and its schools.

What the Federation did expect (like most people in Ontario) were the policies of a social democratic government — policies directed to mitigating the excesses of capitalism, rather than exacerbating them. There would, of course, be no messing with private production or any serious expansion of public ownership. A few years back the Federation had watched Jim Laxer, the NDP's chief federal researcher, get fired for proposing less focus on consumer spending and more on the creation of wealth; it knew that Ontario's NDP premier was among Laxer's opponents in that argument. With this government, OSSTF understood that General Motors and Xerox Corporation could look forward to business as usual, but business with a human face.

The Federation expected the NDP, in other words, to behave like Keynesians — to maintain a balance between domestic levels of production and consumption and, in a time of recession, to focus on getting money into workers' pockets to increase consumer demand and help kickstart the economy. Such a focus would also mean greater equity across the population, a better life for all. This was the NDP position. OSSTF figured they meant it. Whatever cynicism the Federation kept in reserve for the government, Keynesian pump-priming was something they took for granted. It was the meaning of social democracy in the post-war era. Even Tory administrations took it seriously.

In this context, OSSTF expected that "social wages" — the savings for working people that come with public provision of education, health, social services and welfare — would be solidly protected and that a jobs strategy — encouraging investment in industry and infrastructure — would be the number one priority for the NDP. More generally, they anticipated a slight shift in the direction of the state system to focus on the "social fabric" of the society. The state's job, the NDP had said and OSSTF's leadership agreed, was to even things up somewhat between labour and capital. Government was about "fairness".

To put this another way, OSSTF expected government initiatives to go against the grain of immediate corporate interests on a whole range of issues — from welfare rates to school funding to levels of corporate taxation. Then, after a hammering in the press and the business community, these initiatives would end up in a series of legislative compromises, whose reasonableness the corporations would eventually accede to and which would, presumably, benefit everyone.

What OSSTF and the province got instead was a set of policies diametrically opposed to this position. For all intents and purposes, it amounted to a neo-conservative[1] revolution in Ontario — a major restructuring of government wages, services, employment and tax polices which was focused on the needs of foreign bond holders and international corporations, who threatened the province with the consequences of global economic restructuring. Central to this revolution was the imposition of a "Social Contract" upon Ontario's public sector employees. And surrounding it was a package of economic policies which changed the face of Ontario politics.

With Bob Rae's government, Ontarians ended up with a program for slashing public sector jobs, services and wages and raising individual taxes that exceeded anything done by any administration anywhere in Canada. As Tom Walkom writes, it was "more than Brian Mulroney's Conservatives had ever done, more than Jean Chrétien's Liberals ... more than [Ralph] Klein has done in absolute or relative terms." In its 1993 Social Contract budget alone, the Ontario NDP took $8 billion out of the Ontario economy, "the largest single cut-back," says Walkom, "ever made by any Canadian government."[2] The Ottawa-based research firm Informetrica estimated that the jobs lost directly or indirectly as a result of this cutback could total 85,000. (It was the same firm Rae was pleased to quote some months later, when it estimated that federal high-interest policies between 1989 and 1992 cost Ontario an additional 75,000 jobs.[3])

When inflation is taken into account, Walkom says, Queen's Park spent "less on job creation [in 1993] than it did [under the Liberals] in 1989 when the economy was booming."[4] In 1995, job creation remains at much the same level.[5]

From 1991 to 1995, the number of full-time jobs in the Ontario public service declined by 6.4 percent, a loss of some 5,500 jobs.[6] And this does not include public service jobs that would have been gained, in pre-Social-Contract days, through population or client growth of one kind or another. In the first year of the Social Contract, for example, OSSTF estimates that, despite enrolment growth of 2 percent, 1,255 teaching positions were lost to Ontario public high schools alone.[7]

In the private sector, over approximately the same time span, the combination of the recession and the policies of Bob Rae, Jean Chrétien and Brian Mulroney has resulted in 72,000 fewer people officially working in Ontario in December 1994 than in December 1990.[8] Whatever the rhetoric of the "Jobs-Ontario program," the province lost 72,000 jobs more than it created. And the jobs lost were much better paid than the jobs created.[9]

Welfare recipients almost doubled during Rae's five years. The number of people receiving assistance went from 730,000 to 1.3 million — one in every nine Ontario residents, one in every five of the province's children. In 1990 welfare cost the province $3.5 billion. By 1995 the bill had risen to $6.8 billion. At the same time, the gains in welfare rates achieved by poverty activists in the first years of the NDP government were substantially stripped away by a variety of more recent rule changes,[10] and then through cuts in the rates themselves.[11]

By 1995, 1,400,000 Ontario residents, 14 percent of the population, could be considered poor.[12]

Some job sectors did improve somewhat. Unionized workers experienced a rise in real wage rates rise of three-quarters of a percent each year on average.[13] The minimum wage rate climbed from $5.00 to $6.85, or 37 percent, three times the rate of inflation for the period. People working for these wages, however, are still not living off the fat of the land. An individual working a "normal" month in industry (162.5 hours) for this pay would take home $1,113.13. If that person were looking after a spouse and two kids on this amount, he or she would do $300 a month better on welfare.[14]

In contrast, Ontario-based corporations grew rich over these five years. Corporate profits more than doubled over the last decade, and rose even faster over the last three years of the Rae government.[15] At the same time, their head offices paid increasingly fewer dollars into public coffers. In the May 1994 NDP budget, Ontario corporations contributed only 8 percent of the province's taxation revenue. Only ten years ago this corporate contribution stood at 20 percent. The 1992 Fair Tax Commission reported that in 1989 over 23,300 corporations that filed Ontario income tax returns paid no income tax on combined profits of $18.5 billion. After eliminating all possible deductions for these corporations (losses in previous years, income tax paid in other provinces, inter-corporate dividends, etc.), there remained 6,700 corporations doing business in Ontario that paid no tax on profits amounting to $3.3 billion.[16] The same pattern continues to the present day. In Canada as a whole the corporate share of public revenue is now less than in any G-7 country.[17] Personal income tax, on the other hand, rose steadily over this period. Individual taxpayers currently contribute some 50 percent of provincial government revenue, up from 30 percent some 30 years ago.[18] The same pattern exists at the federal level. And it is not the rich who are being hurt by this focus on personal income tax. The tax rate on our top income earners has declined from a high of 80 percent in the 1960s to about 50 percent today. Across the country (and Ontario would follow this trend) the wealthiest 1 percent of our citizens now own more than the bottom 80 percent.[19]

At the end of five years of Bob Rae, Brian Mulroney and Jean Chrétien, then, what we had was a lot less money in working people's pockets and a lot more in corporate bank accounts. (In 1994 the purchasing power of the average income in Ontario was estimated at 8 percent less than it had been in 1989.[20]) We also had a situation in which the provincial government collected less taxes, spent more on welfare, and had less to contribute to social service, education and health costs. These, in turn, had to be covered by individuals out of their own resources or through increased local taxation. The result was even less money for consumers to spend. It was a recipe, as OSSTF and its allies consistently argued, for continued recession.

It is also a policy we can expect to blossom fully over the next four or five years. Mike Harris has promised to slash thirteen thousand more government jobs, get even tougher on welfare recipients (beginning with a 20 percent cut in benefits), and provide a business climate even more hospitable to franchise operations and branch plants and more acceptable for foreign bond holders and international corporations.[21]

It is very difficult to estimate the decline in Ontario public services already due to this package of economic policies surrounding the imposition of the Social Contract. Their destructive implications are still being worked out in a thousand different ways across public agencies and institutions.

In education, we are just starting to realize the full nature of their impact.

A recent staff report to the Metropolitan Toronto School Board,[22] for example, estimated that the recession and the province's economic and taxation policies reduced the Board's tax base by $250 million since 1991. By 1998, the Metro board expected to lose an additional $50 million from property taxes. It also suffered major reductions in provincial transfer funds and was obliged over the preceding few years to raise local property taxes significantly. In 1994, however, the Metro board had frozen its tax rates and cut $62 million from local board budgets and $38 million from its own allocation. In 1995 Metro staff not only recommended an additional increase in the education mill rate of 3 percent and a debenturing of $70 million to fund previously approved capital costs, but they also insisted on another $64.3 million reduction in local board budgets.

For the City of Toronto this new Metro cut came to $19 million. Almost three-quarters of that money was taken from areas that directly affect students and classroom teachers: continuing education, teacher release time, curriculum program, local levy teachers,[23] educational assistants, students' assistance, and student support services. For a local board already stripped to the bone — 1994's Metro cut for Toronto was $25.6 million to which another cut of $7 million was added due to local revenue shortfall — this new level of cuts promises a real savaging of its classroom base.[24] And next year it could well be worse.

The years previous to these cuts weren't so great either. The extent to which the City of Toronto's board was hurt can be seen in the continuing decay of its physical plant. Forty percent of the board's 154 properties are more than 50 years old. A 1985 report said that "$7 million a year should be added to Toronto's maintenance budget 'to maintain the integrity and safety of school buildings' and deal with the backlog of problems." The trustees agreed, but added a total of only $3.2 million to the maintenance budget in the eight years following that report. As 1993 came to a close, the Metro board cancelled most future school building projects, and ended up borrowing $137 million in 1993 and 1994 just to finance existing construction commitments.[25]

The local boards of Metropolitan Toronto aren't alone in facing the problem of decaying schools. A 1993 survey sponsored by the Ontario Association of School Business Officials concluded that "more than 400,000 Ontario students ... attend schools deemed to be 'inadequate' because of their poor physical condition." The survey canvassed 358 school boards about the age and condition of their schools. It found that "73 percent of schools have outlived their 30-year life expectancy. And 20 percent of schools were deemed by board officials themselves to be 'inadequate places' for students to learn."[26]

Control For The Future: The Attack On The Rights Of Labour

The second surprise attached to the Social Contract package — in addition to its disavowal of social democratic principles and the severity of the cuts involved — was the government's determination to insure that this package of neo-conservative reforms would be extended effectively into the future.

No area was exempt, not even the smallest.

On a number of low-cost issues, the government was prepared to take exceptionally mean-spirited action to nail down the larger logic of its vision for a restructured Ontario. Very little money was at stake, for example, in its decision to push publicly-supported childcare into a welfare ghetto,[27] to turn down proposals for a real breakfast and lunch program in Ontario schools,[28] to impose a new cadre of welfare officials to catch "cheaters" in the system,[29] or to insist on more rigorous welfare criteria for certain classes of needy immigrants. What was at stake, however, was the principle of undercutting universal programs and offering fewer government handouts. It was a principle, the government figured, that was worth the public relations damage attached to such decisions. A restructured future depended on it.

As we shall see, the government proved itself equally determined in carrying out its much larger ("historic") contribution to a neo-conservative future for Ontario — the imposition of Bill 48, which not only brought the Social Contract package to bear on the broader public service, but more importantly, stripped its unions of their collective bargaining rights as part of a broader government assault on the legal framework of labour relations.

The analysis by Sack Goldblatt Mitchell, Bob Rae's old law firm, makes it clear, as Thomas Walkom writes, that Bill 48 provided extraordinary new powers to government and public employers:

> Employers would be allowed to override human rights laws and even the government's proposed employment equity legislation to save money.
>
> As for the government, it has virtually the power to decertify unions.

> For instance, the bill would allow the government to arbitrarily decide that a troublesome union, such as the Canadian Union of of Public Employees, which has refused to play ball with Rae, no longer has the right to bargain for its members under the social contract.
>
> Instead, the government could designate any other group it wished — such as a tame company union — to represent CUPE members at these talks.
>
> Legal safeguards allowing judicial review of administrative decisions have been removed.
>
> And in an unprecedented move, the cabinet would have the right to unilaterally redefine what all the words used in the bill mean, after the bill has passed.[30]

As this analysis was becoming clear, OSSTF's lawyers informed it that Bill 48 breached a number of international labour conventions to which both Canada and Ontario are bound. In response, the Federation launched a complaint with the International Labour Organization in Geneva, claiming that the NDP legislation infringed upon "international obligations to permit freedom of association in the truest sense."

OSSTF did not beat about the bush in setting forth its reasons for this complaint. "Bill 48," it declared, "imposes penalties upon the members of any public sector union that refuses to come to the negotiating table, by refusing access to the public job security fund; imposing a minimum three-year compensation freeze; and threatening forced wage reductions by requiring leaves of absence without pay."

"Such punitive measures," the Federation continued, "literally blackmail and coerce the members of every public service union, and the unions themselves, to voluntarily agree to negotiate a stripping of contracts." The law would operate retroactively against recent contracts and unions engaged in contract negotiations. By penalizing workers without a collective agreement it would contravene the NDP government's own proudly heralded 1992 labour reforms.

Furthermore, OSSTF noted, "Bill 48 empowers the government to alter the bargaining rights held by public sector trade unions for the purposes of negotiating local sectoral agreements. Thus, the government could literally force the members to be represented by a different bargaining agent than the one they presently have, without any regard to the wishes of the membership."

"Can Premier Rae honestly say with a straight face that Bill 48 lives up to the spirit and letter of Article 3 of Convention 87, which requires that workers have the right to organize their activities free from government interference, and to bargain freely with employers with respect to wages and conditions of work?" the Federation asked. "Being blackmailed to come to the table, and forced to negotiate the stripping of contracts and the forced layoffs of one's members can hardly be characterized as free collective bargaining. That a so-called social democratic government should commit such breaches of international law is a disgrace to Canada's standing in the international community."[31]

A little later, the Federation of Women's Teachers Associations of Ontario challenged the constitutional validity of Bill 48 on issues of freedom of association, equality rights, and the right to life, liberty and security of the person. In its submission FWTAO was especially concerned to champion the civil rights of classroom teachers, the majority of whom are women.[32]

None of Ontario's teacher organizations had formal ties with the NDP. If they had, those ties would have been firmly broken at this moment.

The major organization that did have strong explicit connections with the Ontario NDP was the Ontario Federation of Labour, the organization which brings together both private- and public-sector unions in the province. The response of the OFL to Bill 48, after intervention of public-sector unions supported by the Canadian Auto Workers (CAW), was to put into place a fundamental separation between itself and the provincial party. The NDP, it said, in a resolution brought forward by the public-sector unions, "has betrayed an overall progressive agenda focusing on jobs and equality, and directly attacked workers, unions, and collective bargaining with their cynically named 'social contract'." The OFL then went on to deny support to candidates who supported the social contract, to minimize contributions to the Ontario NDP "to the level necessary for participating and influencing future party decisions and structures" and to channel its resources and energies to building coalitions among labour, the unemployed and other progressive allies.[33] For most of the people voting for these resolutions, the decision broke their hearts. For decades OFL activists had believed the NDP had been the party which spoke for them and for working people generally. Their loyalty had been unequivocal. Now it was clear someone else owned the party, and they had to face up to that reality.

That reality has not been clear to everyone. Bob Rae's Social Contract provoked a change so painful and so fundamental to Ontario politics, that even two years later a great many long-time union and community activists could not bring themselves to consider its implications. And the labour movement as a whole, once it put distance between itself and the province's NDP administration, was unwilling to translate its anger over Bill 48 into the kind of organizing that would do the government real damage.

A Teacher's Union In Politics

An Activist Federation

Nothing in the history of OSSTF had prepared it to face such a fundamental political struggle. When Bob Rae came to power, the Federation imagined for itself a continuation of the political success it had achieved in three decades prior to this NDP victory. As these teachers figured it, they would be dealing with the new government from a position far stronger than any they had achieved in the past. Not only would they be facing a more teacher-friendly administration, which many teachers had helped to elect, but they would also be able to call on the most politically conscious and active membership in the history of the Federation. However badly events may have turned out, OSSTF activists had every reason to think the way they did. And particularly to feel pride and strength in the political organization they had built, in the Federation itself, and in the role they had come to play in the political life of the province.

To understand something of this development, I want to

revisit an interview[34] I had with former OSSTF president Jim Head, who was the major architect of the Federation's 1990 political strategy and who led the attack on David Peterson's Liberals once the election was called.

In analyzing the growing politicization of OSSTF, Head argues that "conservative professionals" were clearly dominant up to the 1960s. These teacher leaders believed in a relatively strong teachers' federation, particularly in stressing its members' professional concerns. They were, however, very uneasy about what they understood as unnecessary union militancy. They felt far more comfortable in developing smooth personal relationships with the Ministry and with the administration of their local boards. Such relationships, they argued, would lead to more real influence in educational decision-making, particularly in curriculum policy and development. They also argued that such relationships resulted in a better shake on the wage front. Much of this leadership was Liberal or Tory.

Then came what Head calls "progressive professionals," who stressed the union side of OSSTF, and who didn't want to be "pushed around" by government. "This new emphasis," says Head, which emerged in the 1960s, should be linked with presidents like Ward MacAdam and Doug Dinsmore, "who paved the way," and with Jim Forster, Malcolm Buchanan and Rod Albert. Head adds himself to this group and his successor Liz Barkley. (It would also include, I should add here, the current OSSTF president who has just replaced Barkley, Earl Manners.) This new leadership was preponderantly NDP, stressing the social and labour policy thrust of the party while vigorously challenging its support for the extension of separate school funding.

Just as the "conservative professionals" could not neglect the collective bargaining side of the organization if they expected a political future for themselves, so the "progressive professionals" knew they had to take into account "professional issues." Head recounts that "one of the things Jim Forster had to do in order to get elected for a second time — the first time a second term had happened within OSSTF — was to show he wasn't 'rock-hard' union, but that he also had curriculum concerns. *At What Cost?*, a major curriculum document, was developed at that time, with Forster's support."

I think it's fair to say that, over the last decade or so, the publication of curriculum documents like *At What Cost?* took place in a context pretty much as Head describes it. The issues raised were clearly recognized as fundamental to both teachers and students. But in terms of the organizing emphasis within OSSTF itself, such issues remained peripheral, and the documents framing them have mostly gathered dust on the shelves of high school libraries. The Federation is only now beginning to come forward *actively* with its own long-term approach to curriculum and to the structure of education in which that curriculum should be taught. I stress the word "actively," because in the past the Federation has put forward, often with considerable eloquence, its own perspective on curriculum and governance for secondary schools. But, for all their eloquence, such documents did not serve to mobilize the membership into action on these perspectives or indeed to engage members seriously in their development in the first place. What emerged were simply some very good arguments on various "professional" subjects. But, as we shall see, the rootlessness of such arguments within the membership was a key factor in making OSSTF vulnerable to the attack they would face from the Rae government.

What mattered far more than curriculum to OSSTF militants was the long-term goal of strengthening the union side of the Federation and eventually shaping it so that it could take in large numbers of non-teaching school employees. This was the key issue the "progressive professional" leadership figured had to be won in 1990, when Jim Head was elected for his final term of office. Head's description of this emphasis is worth recounting. "My election," he says, "in my last term was determined by this issue. The final debate on the extension of organizing non-teaching personnel was at the 1990 assembly, and you saw the results. We won solidly. I was identified very clearly with that particular organizing drive.... If it had gone the other way, the presidential vote would have gone the other way also. We knew this so clearly. The agenda was organized to deal with it. To have that organizing vote first, I think, was really gutsy of us. We believed in it. If we lost it, it wasn't a bad way to lose. So in a fundamental way, we were given a real mandate on this extended organizing…."

"I came out of a union drive," Head concluded, "with strong stands in collective bargaining. My claim to fame at the time was stopping the erosion of gratuities. That background really counted."

While the lack of rooted policies on curriculum and restructuring ultimately weakened OSSTF in its struggle against Bob Rae's Social Contract, this tough pro-union stance and the Federation's long experience in collective bargaining clearly worked to strengthen it. As we shall see later, it allowed the Federation to recover a substantial amount of ground lost during the early days of the Social Contract struggle.

Jim Head understood that a tradition of "business unionism," with its emphasis on the material well-being of the membership, could not be the fundamental base on which the Federation built its future. "When I look back," he said, "I know … you have to look after the protective side of the organization. Working conditions, professional concerns, however, must drive collective bargaining." Head then went on to stress the importance of internal democracy within the Federation — emphasizing the significance of the often bitter battle for political control of OSSTF's excessively bureaucratic "secretariat" — and the larger implications for curriculum and for educational decision-making that have emerged with the organization's growing politicization, both within and without.

This politicization would make a big difference for the future, Head argued. "The Ministry's way of operating," he said, "has always been to lay things on us. We've always been consulted a bit, but we're rarely in on curriculum policy development from the ground up. This is not only true in our relationship with the Ministry, it is also true of the way local boards treat us. Teachers are supposed to be the experts in curriculum matters, but we're never really asked to deliver on our expertise on policy matters."

"Teachers," he continued, "feel very strongly about this. They are sick and tired of programs like the Robarts Plan and OSIS — and now restructuring — being laid on them. Over what has been almost 30 years of continual change, teachers haven't been engaged in any serious discussion of philosophy or implementation. They were just told to do it. One year, under one framework, they were told to do it one way. Another year, another framework, and they were told to do it another way. What teachers are increasingly telling us is that they aren't going to take this anymore. This means that we have to negotiate curriculum changes, not just consult. These matters have to be contracted, put down on paper, so when they get worked out they stay that way unless both sides agree to a change."

"It's the 'union' side of the organization, Head went on to stress, "who are used to dealing with governments in this fashion, who have to run with this new curriculum initiative. They are the only people who really can. They don't work with Ministry people on the mythical idea that honey gets you more than vinegar. That's never been true of government. The Ontario Teachers' Federation, our umbrella organization which doesn't do collective bargaining, has really tended to compromise with the government liaison committees and with Ministry officials. Real educational change in this province has always come through rough politics." Head's hope was that the recent internal restructuring of OSSTF's department of Professional Development to Educational Services would eventually provide the administrative structure "for a more effective organization for negotiating curriculum matters... to translate our various concerns in this area into the collective bargaining field."

For OSSTF, Jim Head's perspective here was clearly the way of the future, even if Head himself seems to have abandoned the tradition of OSSTF leadership with which he earlier identified.[35] It is a perspective strongly held by the current leadership of the Federation. What neither Head nor his successors understood at the time, however, was that somebody else's idea of the future would soon be upon them, before they got any chance to practise what they were now, slowly, beginning to preach.

Taking On The Liberals

When Jim Head was elected for his third term in March 1990, his view of the future looked especially bright. As he and his executive considered the failure of the Liberals under Peterson to take quality education or teacher power seriously, they figured the organization they led had now reached a level of political strength that would allow them to seriously challenge the government. OSSTF's Provincial Assembly agreed and gave them a mandate to work in direct opposition to the Liberals in the hope that they would be reduced to minority government status.

This push for minority government made a lot of strategic sense within the Federation, especially for leaders, who took their social democratic politics seriously. As a goal it seemed considerably more realistic than the defeat of the Liberal government. The Peterson regime still appeared very strong both in its organization and in the polls. Besides, minority government had some real attractions for OSSTF. They liked the open relationship they had developed with the government during the NDP-Liberal accord between 1985 and 1987. ("It was a time we got listened to" says OSSTF's Queen's Park lobbyist Larry French). A minority government strategy also meant OSSTF didn't have to choose one political party to back (which the strength of its "conservative professionals" would have made impossible). But at the same time the mandate allowed the Federation's support to flow in great measure to the NDP — a fact that was thoroughly understood by most of the delegates to the Assembly which had voted for it. Bob Rae's support for the teacher position on the pension dispute had been widely recognized and applauded. His appearance at the Hamilton pension rally had drawn even more support. In the dynamics of the pension dispute, a larger proportion of the delegates than might have been expected, as well as the general membership, moved towards the NDP. At the same time, the Tories were marked as increasingly hostile to teacher concerns.

Following up this mandate, a substantial majority of OSSTF workers and candidate funds at the local level ended up going to New Democrats. Most of these workers were also NDPers themselves. Colleagues who held other political affiliations, particularly Liberal partisans, were persuaded, in one way or another, to simply stand aside for the election. At the end of the campaign, OSSTF believed that "its most significant impact ... was to reduce the number of teachers who were active Liberal supporters."[36]

As a result of all their activity, OSSTF's leadership and

political activists came out of the 1990 election with a firm view that they had made a big difference in the NDP's eventual success.

And they had.

Most importantly, they had translated their members' intense anger over David Peterson's rip-off of teachers' pensions into a broadly-based and popular attack on the government's policy of funding Ontario schools. Facing new legislation that would make teachers pay more for their badly-managed pensions (while refusing them the power to help plan their pension fund investments), OSSTF successfully turned the issue into a reason to go after Peterson's underfunding of education generally. The Federation's campaign slogan, "Spending too little on public schools is child neglect," found its way into thousands of homes on brochures and canvasser buttons and, more dramatically, as part of a province-wide advertising campaign on prominent billboards and in the pages of the major dailies. OSSTF spent $100,000 on this media campaign and then another $150,000 for candidate donations and local organizing. By the end of the election, after having spent some $300,000, its members were working in virtually all of Ontario's 130 ridings. Nowhere, perhaps, were they more effective than in the three motor homes full of front-line Federation protesters directed by their president. Throughout the campaign these teachers criss-crossed the province attending all-candidates meetings and leaders' appearances, and winning the kind of media coverage that consistently damaged the government's credibility on educational issues.

All in all, it was a major escalation in political action for OSSTF's political activists, with results far beyond their wildest dreams. They had mobilized their own membership as never before. They had captured significant media attention and public support. A party sharing their goals had won handsomely. And they now had reason to believe their Federation had become a major player in the politics of the province. It was the logical outcome of the last 30 years of struggle.

Feeling proud and feisty, this OSSTF leadership expected both gratitude and respect from this new government. They figured they'd earned it.

The New Reality

OSSTF was not, however, naive about the situation in which they found themselves. The Federation had had a long history of hustling Queen's Park on behalf of their members. They knew how the political game worked there. They understood perfectly well that whatever they got from a Bob Rae government would be a compromise worked out with a number of contending forces and interests. They knew the business community would now make its weight felt, as it had not before in party policy. But they considered themselves hard-nosed on these matters and braced themselves for tough bargaining.

They also knew that the NDP was a deeply divided organization at an ideological level — as they were themselves. This was reflected in a thoroughly contradictory set of NDP policy statements. OSSTF couldn't be at all certain what might actually emerge at the level of practical policy. Thus when the 1990 election brought an NDP victory, the Federation figured they had to keep a lot of options and responses in play as left and right within the party struggled for influence.

OSSTF's leadership was particularly worried that the "idealistic left" of the NDP would somehow manage to impose policies like destreaming (the removal of "ability" groupings) on the backs of teachers, without proper preparation and a realistic assessment of how such a policy could go wrong at a school or classroom level. At the same time, the Federation leadership was concerned that the party's centre — including Bob Rae and most of his cabinet — would continue to neglect both education and the teachers' organizations, as they had usually done in the preceding decade of opposition. The Federation worried that their newly won political clout would turn out to be an illusion. It had happened before.

In the first few months of Rae's government, after Education Minister Marion Boyd's office had been captured — almost instantly — by her bureaucracy, it was the second concern that seemed more likely to make itself felt. The government, now under new management, was still paying no attention to its teachers, and OSSTF was very unhappy about it.

At this point, neither OSSTF's leadership nor its broader

membership had any inkling that there might be a powerful neo-conservative initiative waiting in the wings. The Federation did know, however, that there was a darker side to the NDP's long-term neglect of education and to its unwillingness to create a consistent set of education policies along with teachers, parents and community activists. OSSTF had no clear expression for their sense of unease about the internal workings of the party. They themselves had only recently taken up the issue of democracy in dealing with parents and weren't at all certain where these new politics were taking them or whether they would actually prefer a more democratically-restructured educational system. (The old school hierarchies were set deep in the bone.) But they were aware that there was an unusual amount of hostility to teachers and their opinions within the NDP, and that this didn't bode well for education.

This was not paranoia on OSSTF's part. I spent a number of years within the powerful NDP caucus at the Toronto board, as a trustee and later as its non-voting chairperson, and teachers were regularly scapegoated in the discussion around the table. Few of these trustees understood the position of teachers as workers in schools — as people who are obliged to respond defensively to aggressive management, including NDP management, unless it is proven in practice that such management is acting in good faith. Most of these trustees figured teachers should simply trust them to do the right thing and stop complaining about their lot. Indeed, they routinely judged that teachers were overpaid and underworked and ought to be a primary target in explaining the faults of the school system. Occasionally, NDP trustees found common cause with the elementary school federations on issues like class size, but mostly, when they found teachers behaving in what they figured was a reactionary fashion — on issues like destreaming or heritage language programs — they wrote them off as the enemy.

These trustees — like their party as a whole — largely took for granted the hierarchies of the educational system and the place of teachers within them. Few ever asked themselves what made teachers so untrusting of educational innovation from above. NDP trustees frequently seemed to be supporting an administration that was indifferent to classroom teachers and hostile to their unions, and they regularly imposed their most reactionary bureaucrats on teacher-board contract negotiations.

In spite of this kind of NDP response and the failure of their most recent attempts to reach Marion Boyd, OSSTF remained optimistic about the new NDP government. (Tories and Liberals were usually worse.) Surely, they said to themselves, their efforts in the last election would not be forgotten. Somebody would soon realize that a terrible mistake had been made in neglecting such an important and sympathetic organization. When Tony Silipo replaced Boyd as Minister of Education, the Federation thought perhaps its time had finally come, though they were deeply uneasy about Silipo and his allies. For OSSTF, the coming of this new minister meant that the left-wing "idealists" were back in the saddle. More worrisome, these new people seemed to have the capacity to actually get something done. Silipo, the son of an Italian construction worker, had been a strong chairperson of the Toronto board as well as an effective champion of heritage languages. Unlike Marion Boyd, he knew the school system. He was also understood as a big-time destreamer, who had taken the trouble to bring University of Toronto professor David Clandfield (another former Toronto board trustee) with him as one of his policy advisors. Clandfield had a tougher reputation than Silipo on issues like destreaming and, perhaps even more worrisome, on major curriculum reforms to go with it. Still, OSSTF was hopeful. While they felt grumpy about some of Silipo and Clandfield's policy perspectives, they saw them as relatively "good guys" who cared about kids and who made friendly noises in the Federation's direction. Maybe, OSSTF figured, a deal could be worked out that put destreaming and curriculum reform in a realistic framework that classroom teachers could support. And after that, who knows? Perhaps a serious long-term consultation process could be put into place.

These hopes did not last long.

With the new minister in charge, OSSTF found out two things quite rapidly. First, neither Silipo nor Clandfield could move their agenda. They were usually blocked by their own ministry's bureaucrats and could not persuade the premier's inner circle that education should be a major focus for reform.[37]

It became increasingly evident that the real policy decisions were going to be made elsewhere. As Deputy Minister Robert Mitton (a former Social Credit technocrat who had been kept on from the former Liberal regime) continued quietly on his established path, the premier's office increasingly put the brakes on new education policy, until it was ready to make its own move.

Bob Rae, it turned out, wanted to call all the major shots himself. And, as a result, the main lines of politician-to-bureaucrat communication in education were eventually established between Deputy Minister Mitton and the premier's office. Once a conversation had taken place at this level, it eventually emerged, the deputy was then free to interpret Rae's agenda in his own way. The education minister's office became largely irrelevant.

In addition, the Federation learned that Bob Rae was not about to replace the minister's office-to-teacher connection with one linked to his own office. (This connection, I might add, never amounted to much even at a personal level.[38]) The premier's office was determined that OSSTF would be out of the loop altogether.

So once again, the Federation hunkered down to face a largely hostile bureaucracy in dealing with education policy matters and to return to the same Queen's Park lobbying tactics they had mastered over years of Tory and Liberal administrations.

Then more changes.

After thoroughly undercutting what remained of Silipo's policy initiatives in destreaming and curriculum, Rae bumped him as minister in February 1993 and sent him over to run Community and Social Services.[39] Clandfield stayed on for four more months but, after an interview in which he voiced his opposition to indiscriminate government downsizing and the change in policy direction under the new minister, Dave Cooke, it was the premier's office that insisted that his offer to resign, as a result of the interview, be accepted. Clandfield thus joined a long line of progressive-minded Ministry employees who had been forced out in one way or another by Bob Rae and Robert Mitton's downsizing of the organization. Silipo, on the other hand, kept his mouth shut and knuckled under. In a few months he would reappear as the premier's chief hatchetman in a broad assault on social security and in the development of more intensified control over the welfare poor.

As part of a general reorganization of government, Rae had appointed Cooke to head up a new super-ministry of Education and Training, committed to standardized testing, a Royal Commission on education, and a special focus on creating "a well-trained and adaptable work force."[40] Dave Cooke, a former social worker and Windsor school trustee in the 1970s, was a slick and powerful member of the inner cabinet and a trusted Rae loyalist. With his arrival, Robert Mitton, who had by now made himself a number of enemies, could then be transferred comfortably to a deputy minister's post elsewhere. Charles Pascal, another bureaucrat with no school system background, was made deputy minister in his place. Pascal, not noted for his management skills, brought with him, however, the more fundamental qualification that got Cooke his job: he was a Rae loyalist. Indeed, one senior Ministry source describes him as "Rae's puppet … whose only concern is to implement what the premier wants."

Pascal's other virtue for the premier was that he knew how to get rid of undesirables. And this time there would be no resistance from the minister. Once he arrived on the job, "fresh," as David Clandfield writes, "from his house-cleaning in Community and Social Services," he began "removing all existing senior executives in the old Ministry of Education — the job Robert Mitton had begun — and replacing them largely with bureaucrats from other departments."[41] Pascal soon filled his assistant deputy minister posts with trustworthy right-wingers, while still managing to fly the NDP flag of affirmative action. He hired all women this time and even thought to include one woman of colour, who, alone among these senior bureaucrats, had the additional public relations benefit of having a background in curriculum.[42] The curriculum department itself, however, came increasingly under the control of noneducators committed to the kind of programming best suited to a framework of standardized tests. The department's old Liberal Arts advocates were by now largely back in local school boards.

A serious corporate agenda could now begin in Ontario education. The team was in place.

From the perspective of OSSTF, however, matters were not so clear. All the signs from Rae's office, of course, made them more nervous than ever. The premier's rhetoric on fighting the deficit (as opposed to his early emphasis on fighting the recession) had by this time become quite scary, as had his government's reversal of NDP policies on everything from public auto insurance to casino gambling. Still, OSSTF managed a certain degree of hope in their dealings with the new Ministry, even with the premier's office itself. They continued to believe that their contribution to the success of the NDP would somehow be belatedly recognized, and that the NDP swing to the right was some kind of limited aberration that would eventually be brought into line. The Social Contract hammer was more than a month away, though small rumours of its appearance were starting slowly to emerge. These rumours, however, were still easily dismissed. And while the Federation knew something was definitely afoot, Cooke's style at the Ministry was deeply distracting. A much more able politician than Silipo, and one without Silipo's old reformer instincts to trip him up, Cooke immediately began to woo the province's teacher federations systematically. There were more formal meetings now, and he was regularly at the end of the phone, charming and available, as Silipo had not been. He was also a lot more powerful than his predecessor. Maybe what OSSTF was sensing in the wind wouldn't be all bad for the school system. Maybe here was a guy who could get something done for them.

As it turned out, once the Social Contract agenda was put into place, Cooke became a far more formidable enemy than Tony Silipo could ever have become. In a startling reversal of his former left-wing politics, Silipo turned into a crude bully boy in defending the government's assault on the welfare poor. Cooke, on the other hand, maintained a much tighter grip on his slick public persona and developed a far craftier strategy in sticking the Social Contract to the province's teachers. He was particularly successful in setting up the local boards as the teachers' main enemy during the Social Contract implementation period while maintaining a surprisingly sympathetic public image. For many Ontario teachers Cooke continued to sound believable as he told them that government cuts in education hurt him just as much as they hurt the province's schools, but he was powerless to stand in their way. It was all out of his control, he would say: the cuts, the structure of local negotiations, the deficit, and the workings of global capitalism which have made this government's deficit fight so all important for securing Ontario's place in an increasingly competitive world economy.

But we're getting ahead of this story, which begins again in Chapter One.

What is clear at this stage, is that OSSTF, like its allies in the Public Services Coalition, was not ready to take on the government as it brought down its Social Contract agenda. By early spring of 1993, the Federation was still vacillating between hope and trepidation in its dealings with the Rae administration. It retained an early sense of its own power, both as a union and as an actor on the Ontario political stage, but it did not yet recognize the nature of the adversary it would now be called upon to face. The Federation had mastered the weapons of an old war, and it was about to deal with a whole new set of battle conditions which would make these weapons largely unusable.

In the two and a half years following Rae's election, what OSSTF now routinely called "the corporate agenda" had made some extraordinary advances. Its focus on reducing the deficit was now front and centre in the media and in public policy debate. And with that focus came a powerful new emphasis on public sector wage, service and job cuts. The agenda also involved a new set of arguments for more government centralization to link institutional markets to corporate suppliers, to provide a consistent corporate interpretation of society, to institute more effective social control over those who will suffer the consequences of that interpretation, and to promote a "lean and mean" restructuring of government, including such "local" techniques as "school-based management." In addition, there emerged a renewed stress on the need for increased corporate profitability. Extra profits, it was argued, would eventually trickle down to workers and to society as a whole but could only come, in these times of brutal global competition, from increased government assistance to business, lower corporate taxes, and a reduction in the bargaining power of labour.

Put together, this agenda, as we have seen, involved a massive assault on any democratic or socialist vision of public education. As OSSTF put it a couple of years later: "The public school system, which is the bedrock of our democratic system, [was now] being challenged on two fronts. In the first place the inadequacies of public education [took on] mythical dimensions. In the face of massive evidence to the contrary, public school bashing continued unabated in the 1980s and 1990s, seriously dampening public confidence. Secondly, as confidence waned, the recognition that education is a fundamental good was attacked with calls to throw schools open to the logic of the marketplace ... [which] would overcome a 'failed' public monopoly by unleashing the competitive spirit, thereby forcing educators to provide the quality programs which parents and students have been demanding...."[43]

For OSSTF it was a disastrous scenario for public schooling. But it was also a scenario against which the old slogans for better funding — the old politics of money — were increasingly no defence. As an issue, "child neglect" had pretty much disappeared from the public arena. It would take two years of government hammering before a concern for student welfare could once more be woven by the Federation into an effective defence of the public system as a whole.

We turn now to stage one of that hammering — Bob Rae's Social Contract — and to the resistance mobilized against it by OSSTF and its allies in the Public Services Coalition.

FOOTNOTES

1 Because of its ambiguity among a broader public, I have not used the word "neo-liberal," which might with equal accuracy be applied to NDP policy. This latter term, as I understand it, refers to neo-conservatives with a smidgen of compassion or an analysis that says the state must provide a min-

imal welfare net to prevent public unrest. That's pretty much the stance of current NDP policy and practice. On the other hand, neo-liberalism can also mean more of a hard-line Manchester-type liberalism, before someone like John Stuart Mill got hold of it. This latter sort of neo-liberalism is indistinguishable from neo-conservativism, and it was the position held by the most influential bureaucrats of the Rae government. A more common sense understanding of neo-liberalism (and the one furthest removed from its reality) links it to a more humane post-war liberalism, supposedly being brought up to date for the 21st century. In this light, it seems simpler to use the term "neo-conservative" for the new NDP, with the knowledge that this perspective is now at the core of the party's position. When compassion or realpolitik has resulted in a softening of the party's harder edges that will be noted.

2 See Walkom, Thomas, *Rae Days: The Rise and Follies of the NDP*, Key Porter Books, Toronto, 1994, p.4, 136-137. Walkom writes: "Of this $8 billion, $2 billion in cutbacks had already been announced [prior to Rae's social contract initiative] ... In the end ... a decision [was] made to apportion the [additional] $6 billion in three roughly equal lots — $1.8 billion from tax hikes and other revenues; $2.4 billion from more spending cuts; $2 billion from the social contract. [Treasurer Floyd] Laughren called this his 'three-legged stool' strategy." See also Walkom, Thomas, "Klein's real goal is dismantling of government," *Toronto Star*, January 31, 1995.

3 Walkom, Thomas, "Rae blowing smoke with recent talk about job creation," *Toronto Star*, November 10, 1993.

4 Walkom, Thomas, "Rae blowing smoke with recent talk about job creation," *Toronto Star*, November 10, 1993.

5 See Walker, William, "Employment outlook 'bleak' in NDP's budget forecast," *Toronto Star*, January 20, 1994.

6 Rusk, James, "Reality Check: NDP pitch ignores first year in office," *Globe and Mail*, January 7, 1995.

7 OSSTF, *Job Cuts Register* (As Of October 24, 1994), CBC #6 (iv)/94–95.

8 Rusk, James, "Reality Check: NDP pitch ignores first year in office," *Globe and Mail*, January 7, 1995.

9 See the analysis in the *Report of the Royal Commission on Learning*, Vol. 1, cited above, pp. 25–26 and below, Chapter 6, p. 249. In 1992 across Canada, 42 percent of workers were employed part-time, full-time on a temporary basis, or were unemployed for part of the year. Forty-six percent of those with full-time, full-year jobs, earned less than $30,000 per year.

10 Toughill, Kelly, "Rae's grand plan for welfare reform flops," *Toronto Star*, April 1, 1995.

11 Philip, Margaret, "Ontario hasn't always had the best rates," *Globe and Mail*, March 23, 1994.

12 *Report of the Royal Commission on Learning, Volume 1*, Queen's Printer for Ontario, Toronto, 1994, published February 1995, p. 26.

13 Ontario Ministry of Labour, Labour Management Services, Office of Collective Bargaining Information, "Collective Bargaining Ontario Highlights, February Report," 1995. Based on collective agreements in Ontario covering 200 or more employees, this figure comes from a composite of Ontario Ministry and Labour Canada settlement data. In the last five years settlement base rates in Ontario have risen by 16.2 percent and the CPI by 12.8 percent, which in real dollars makes a 3.4 percent rise in rates over this period.

14 See Baker, Tom, "Memo To Program Staff: Nominal minimum wages in Ontario," Social Planning Council of Metropolitan Toronto, April 12, 1995.

15 Ontario Ministry of Finance, Chart 1984 — Third Quarter 1994, "Ontario: Business Profits and Investment."

16 See OSSTF, "Fair Taxation for Responsible Education, Report of the Funding Initiatives and New Directions Committee," Submission to the Ontario Fair Tax Commission, September 22, 1992, p.7.

17 Ontario Federation of Labour, *Unfair Shares: Corporations and Taxation in Canada*, Toronto, 1995, pp. 1–2, Table 4, p. 48. The profit and tax information in this publication is from InfoGlobe's *Report on Business Corporate Database* as of December 19, 1994.

18 See OSSTF's Submission to the Ontario Fair Tax Commission, "Fair Taxation for Responsible Education, Report of the Funding Initiatives and New Directions Committee," September 22, 1992, pp. 6–7.

19 Ontario Federation of Labour, *Unfair Shares: Corporations and Taxation in Canada*, cited above, pp. 1–2.

20 See Chamberlain, Art, et al., "Uncertainty fuels politics of resentment," *Toronto Star*, Section F, June 3, 1995. "... the Bob Rae years have been a big come-down for Ontario residents. Average incomes stopped rising faster than inflation for the first time in years, while government spending, interest costs and taxes kept climbing. The money left for us to spend averaged $18,000 each last year, 8 percent or $1,586 less than in 1989, after discounting inflation."

21 Ironically enough, though, with the election of a Tory government ideologically committed to social spending cuts and more inequities in employees' rights and remuneration, there is evidence that corporate interests no longer feel that deficit-fighting has to have the same priority it had when the NDP was in power. Downward pressure on wages and lower taxes on the rich and the corporations are what really count. See Walkom, Thomas, "Read Harris' lips — it's taxes not the deficit that count," *The Toronto Star*, Section B, June 17, 1995.

22 The umbrella board for seven public school boards (six English and one French) in the Metropolitan Toronto area. It accounts for 75 percent of the school enrolment in Metro, the remainder being enrolled in publicly-funded Catholic schools operated by the Metropolitan Separate School Board.

23 Teachers paid for by an extra tax levy raised at the local (City of Toron-

to) level rather than through the Metropolitan Toronto School Board.

24 Green, Joan, Director of the Toronto Board of Education, *Report to the Chair and Members of the Education Finance Committee*, "Staff Proposals for 1995 Budget Reductions," March 23, 1995, Part 5, pp. 5–10. See also Duffy, Andrew and Daly, Rita, "School tax freeze will hit top staff, students," *Toronto Star*, January 27, 1994.

25 Duffy, Andrew, "Parents give school a D for decay," *Toronto Star*, October 31, 1993. and "Trustees cut back on school repair work," *Toronto Star*, December 11, 1993.

26 Duffy, Andrew, "Parents give school a D for decay," *Toronto Star*, October 31, 1993.

27 See Toughill, Kelly, "Rae's grand plan for welfare reform flops," *Toronto Star*, April 1, 1995 and Philip, Margaret, "Middle-class parents caught in day-care trap," *Globe and Mail*, April 3, 1995.

28 See Toughill, Kelly, "NDP stalled plan to feed kids, minister says," *Toronto Star*, December 31, 1993; Ferguson, Jock, "Dishing it out so teens will take it," *Globe and Mail*, April 7, 1994; Mittelstaedt, Martin, "Ontario to help feed school children," *Globe and Mail*, June 16, 1994; Cooke, Dave and Pascal, Charles, Memo to School Board Chairs and Directors, "Child Nutrition Initiative," June 16, 1994; Ministry of Community and Social Services, News Release, "Silipo Announces Province-Wide Nutrition Program," June 26, 1994; Toughill, Kelly, "Rae's grand plan for welfare reform flops," *Toronto Star*, April 1, 1995.

29 See *Inside Queen's Park: Government and Political Analysis*, July 14, 1993, v. 6, n.13; Canadian Press, "Crackdown on welfare cheats expected to save $50 million," *Globe and Mail*, March 28, 1994; Walker, William, "NDP set to root out welfare cheats," *Toronto Star*, March 29, 1994; McInnes, Craig, "Ontario takes tough stand against welfare cheats," Globe and Mail, March 29, 1994; Small, Peter, "Crackdown on welfare fraud called pre-election gimmick," *Toronto Star*, March 30, 1994; Philip, Margaret, "What are welfare boasts built on?" *Globe and Mail*, March 30, 1994; Yakabuski, Konrad, "How Ontario's 'welfare police' could work," *Toronto Star*, April 2, 1994; Swanson, Jean, "Cheating the Poor," *Canadian Forum*, April 1994, pp. 20-21; Vittala, Kalyani, "Welfare check on children's school records causes uproar," *Globe and Mail*, June 1, 1994; Philip, Margaret, "What are welfare boasts built on?" *Globe and Mail*, March 30, 1994.

30 Walkom, Thomas, "Rae's old law firm joins the outcry," *Toronto Star*, June 28, 1993. See Sack Goldblatt Mitchell, "Client Memorandum, Re: Social Contract Act, 1993 (Bill 48)," June 21, 1993.

31 OSSTF, "Draft Statement for Press Conference Concerning ILO Complaint," June 26, 1993. The ILO has yet to rule on this complaint.

32 Federation of Women Teachers' Associations of Ontario, "Press Release," July 22, 1993. The Supreme Court has yet to rule on this complaint.

33 Ontario Federation of Labour, Convention Resolutions, Toronto, November, 1993.

34 Head, Jim, Interview with George Martell, "High School Teacher Politics in Ontario, Part 1, What's Going On Inside OSSTF?" *Our Schools/Our Selves*, v.3, n.3 (#21), December 1991, pp. 138-156.

35 Jim Head supported the Liberals in the last provincial election and Earl Manners' opponent in the 1995 OSSTF presidential race. More importantly, he endorsed Metro Toronto's corporate-backed "Learning Paternership," and he accepted an appointment with the College of Teachers—an institution OSSTF's current leadership strongly opposes.

36 Gagnon, Georgette and Rath, Dan, *Not Without Cause: David Peterson's Fall From Grace*, Harper Collins, Toronto, 1991, p. 219.

37 It may have appeared, for example, that the government was willing to move on the issue of destreaming. A major effort to delay it had first been mounted by the bureaucrats who wanted to put it off until after the next election. This was reversed by Silipo's announcement in January 1992 of his intention to proceed with Grade 9 according to schedule (fall 1993) and to begin discussions about Grade 10. Then, a major offensive was launched at the Ontario NDP Convention of June 1992 to slow things down. Despite a strong lobby by OSSTF, the minister's office, with the blessing of Ross McClellan and the Premier's Office, successfully mobilized party opinion in favour of a motion to proceed to Grade 10 destreaming. But the government soon began to lose its nerve as right-wing opinion that had previously favoured destreaming turned against it. George Radwanski, whose commission report on drop-outs (*Ontario Study of the Relevance of Education, and the Issue of Drop-Outs, 1987*) had recommended destreaming, personally intervened with the minister to speak out against reforms that did not include his version of back-to-basics schooling. Andrew Nikiforuk's infamous columns in the *Globe and Mail* that had appeared to promote destreaming as a way to avoid featherbedding the education of the weak, turned against the NDP's version of it for its apparent failure (at the time!) to back it up with a lock-step curriculum and constant recourse to standardized testing.

38 Silipo persisted for much of his ministry in meeting OSSTF only in the framework of formal meetings with the Ontario Teachers' Federation as a whole, when all five Federations were present. The opportunity to discuss specific issues at any length was consequently rarely possible.

39 This was a major demotion for Silipo, since he was also bumped out of the Policy and Priorities Sub-Committee of Cabinet (the inner cabinet), and he was given a deputy Minister from the premier's inner circle who would keep a tight rein on him as he moved into two policy minefields dear to the heart of the premier's office: childcare reform (which eventually collapsed) and welfare reform (which ended in neo- conservative policies).

40 Mackie, Richard, "Rae to push 'equity agenda'," *Globe and Mail*, December 30, 1993.

41 Clandfield, David, "The NDP and the Corporate Agenda in Ontario," *Our Schools/Our Selves*, v.5, n. 1 (#31), October-November 1993, p. 17.

42 Ministry sources have told me that this appointment had already been recommended by Silipo before he left.

43 OSSTF Provincial Executive, *Public Education: Retracing our path, An examination of the goals of public education, its role in society and directions for reform, A brief to the Royal Commission on Learning*, December 1993, p. 2.

Part One

Fighting the Social Contract

Chapter One

Premier Bob's Coalition

March 30, 1993. From an NDP caucus retreat in Niagara-on-the-Lake, *The Toronto Star* announced that "Premier Bob Rae's government has suspended contract talks with its [public sector] unions pending the outcome of an unprecedented forum with union leaders aimed at dealing with Ontario's deficit crisis."

What is remarkable about this simple announcement is that its two fundamental, and quite contradictory, characteristics remained a constant in all major government pronouncements concerning the Social Contract process — from this early "unprecedented forum," through the height of centralized bargaining in the early summer of 1993, to the protracted and impossibly complex implementation procedures in the months that followed and which continue to the present day. First, there is the suggestion of an unprecedented discussion with labour, and then there is the reality of an unprecedented government assault on its unions in the fight against a growing provincial deficit. And, interestingly, the reality is not at all hidden by the rhetoric. It remains on the surface for everyone to see and it is meant to be seen. What Rae made clear in Niagara-on-the-Lake that day would be equally clear at the end of the process as his caucus prepared for a provincial election and likely defeat. Whatever the political cost, he intended to take hold of a new agenda for the province's public service — an agenda he defined as a "Social Contract" — and he wanted little backtalk from uppity unions, unduly sensitive to outmoded notions of collective bargaining. Vigorously supported by his finance minister, Floyd Laughren, Rae let Ontarians know that whatever discussions he had with his unions, their "cooperation" would now be required in the massive changes the provincial government intended to make in order to deal with its deficit. Wage and job cuts "would be combined with tax hikes, assets sales, program and service cuts" in a major restructuring of the public sector.[1] This was settled policy. Everyone should get that straight. The next day the premier was obliged to withdraw his suspension of negotiations. It was, it turned out, illegal. Really, he said, it was just a request to suspend negotiations voluntarily. But the signal was clear enough. This "unprecedented forum" wasn't simply concerned with a specific deficit problem. Another project was also on the table, and in the end it was far more important and unprecedented: public sector union-busting.

OSSTF had no trouble getting the message: "Dictatorial and arrogant," declared Federation president Liz Barkley at the time. She was "appalled that a so-called social democratic party — our so-called friends — would do this."[2] Her statements were echoed by the entire public sector union leadership.

Liz Barkley's outrage is understandable. What is harder to grasp is her surprise. Of course, an official kind of public relations surprise — an acting out of an institutional form of hurt and betrayal — is to be expected under such circumstances, and Barkley shared this reaction with her fellow public sector union leaders. But she also shared with them a genuine sense of shock and betrayal that on the surface did not seem warranted. It might be said that Barkley and her allies should have seen it coming. Certainly, OSSTF's leadership were not political neophytes, as we have seen. They knew a lot about provincial politics, and they had a shrewd appreciation of the inner workings of the NDP and its strained relationship with the province's teacher organizations. Surely, they should not have found themselves so deeply betrayed, in Barkley's words, by their "so-called friends," should they?

But this critique is far too easy. OSSTF and its allies had spent decades in shared struggle with NDP activists. As we have also seen, the personal and institutional ties that bound them were very strong, tying together hearts and minds over many years, not just bits of paper ideology. They retained a deep respect for the social activist traditions of the NDP. There was also much honest fear involved in considering such a break. The NDP was the only vehicle most OSSTF leaders understood as capable of mobilizing popular protest. Without it, future political action seemed impossible. Abandoning the NDP for an unknown model of political organization appeared unthinkable. Like a partner in a bad marriage, whose cracks are just beginning to show, OSSTF could not stop believing that it was just a matter of time and talk before the old relationship would be re-established. Only continued experience could tell them otherwise.

Being attacked by your friends ("so-called" or otherwise) is the most dangerous predicament in politics. If they have simply made a mistake, then things can be rectified. No potential ally should be written off quickly. But when the attack is systematic and persistent, and many attempts at reconciliation have been made, then it seems reasonable to begin considering such "friends" as enemies.

In this section I want to show the extent to which the behaviour of the Rae government in imposing its Social Contract was both long-term and systematic, moving directly against the interests of those who care about the well-being of the school system. At the same time I want to see if I can frame OSSTF's understanding of this reality as they experienced it, before moving on to a more detailed analysis of the Federation's pattern of resistance.

OSSTF, as is evident so far, did not think the actions of Bob Rae's government were arbitrary. They knew perfectly well there was a tough logic behind them. The Federation stressed — and rightly — that this process involved a corporate game plan; it was an expression of "the corporate agenda." The day after Bob Rae's suspension of negotiations, President Barkley not only decried its illegality, but she also went after his broader policies and their link to increasing pressures from business. Rae, she said, had been "rattled" by "international financiers." His government had "abandoned its social democratic principles in favour of a destructive neo-conservative agenda ... acceding to the blackmail of the international financial community."[3]

OSSTF remained uncertain, however, of how this NDP policy reversal actually happened and what that meant for the future. The Federation couldn't see at the time — or couldn't take in at a deep enough level to permit a sufficiently strong response — that this reversal had powerful political as well as economic forces behind it.

In the months prior to the Social Contract, OSSTF had nursed hopes that the government would eventually turn its way. But such hopes were no longer possible. The logic of this new government had now turned clearly against the teachers and their fellow public-sector unionists. And it wasn't just the logic of business lobbyists who had somehow found the right opening. The Social Contract didn't hinge on the decision of a few NDP leaders and spin doctors who had lost their bearings, had taken up with bad companions (corporate or bureaucratic) who could be set back on a proper track, given enough pressure or persuasion. What had emerged instead was much harder to acknowledge — the creation of a surprisingly tight and very powerful coalition of corporate leaders, government and party bureaucrats, and social democratic politicians.

Much of the infrastructure of this coalition was solidified through the two Premier's Councils. These were trilateral policy forums (made up of top government, business and labour leaders) that had been set up by the Peterson government in the late 1980s. The first (on Technology) had promoted an agenda of global competitiveness through an emphasis on the new high-tech economy and skills training as well as the new management strategies of just-in-time inventories, statistical process control, shallow management hierarchies, quality circles and frequent retraining/adjustment schemes. The second (on Health) had been less active under Peterson's government. After his election, Rae reactivated them both with new names.

Technology became Economic Renewal, and Health became Health, Well-Being and Social Justice. But the agenda, the structure and even the membership (from outside the government) remained remarkably similar: CEOs from financial, industrial and service sectors; union leaders, public agency leaders, and academics, all usually with a track record of government work, regardless of the party in power.

The Social Contract was the policy consensus of the new power-brokers fortified by this kind of coalition. Across its bargaining tables what OSSTF and its allies faced were a group of people who were unalterably opposed to public sector unionists like themselves. These people knew what they were doing, believed in what they were doing, and had, moreover, a long-term lock on NDP and government policy formation.[4]

In many ways it was simply too hard a reality to grasp, too big an enemy to consider. Especially at such short notice.

Such a coalition might be understood as a somewhat unexpected, and, until recently, unselfconscious fragment of the province's ruling class. But whatever name we give it, its cohesion and commitment to action were unmistakable. And the new NDP neo-conservatism in education (as elsewhere) followed accordingly.

The Meaning Of Bob Rae

In trying to understand the reversal of NDP policy, OSSTF, like almost everyone else in the public sector, tended initially to focus on Bob Rae.

They knew, of course, that the explanation for such a reversal had to be much bigger than the machinations and character of one person. But they also thought that if it hadn't been for Rae, a very different and far more productive arrangement might have been worked out. It was for this reason that they lay the oppression of the Social Contract at his doorstep. It was a moment, they judged, when an individual really counted for something. In a few short months, the premier seemed almost single-handedly to have changed the political culture of Ontario.

The change was particularly noticeable in the Social Contract discussions and negotiations around education. Here

OSSTF found themselves faced with what they soon grasped were Bob Rae clones, appointed by the premier in his own image: detached, right-wing technocrats, deeply ignorant of public education and of any previously shared assumptions between bureaucrats and teachers about how schools work and what was good for kids.[5] "These people could have been Ford bargainers from Oshawa," says Earl Manners, now president of the Federation, and a very active player in the Social Contract negotiations. "They didn't know anything but numbers. They were entirely time and motion guys, with a weird sort of language borrowed from construction sites. When they talked about hiring new people to fill the jobs of those fired, they called it 'backfilling,' for God's sake. Trying to get across to them what might actually start happening inside schools if the Social Contract cuts took place was just impossible. And what you have to remember is that these creatures were Rae's people. He was responsible for them." For Manners, and for the entire OSSTF leadership, Bob Rae's Social Contract had all the appearance of a destructively potent act of leadership.

The Federation had a good common-sense explanation for Rae's behaviour. It knew the premier had a deeply conservative streak in him. He wasn't just any politician on the left being prodded by powerful business interests. He was a politician especially sensitive to such prodding. Brought up as a senior diplomat's son and a private-school boy, he continued to maintain close family and friendship ties with Canada's corporate elite. Moreover he had consistently represented the right wing of social democracy — as a student activist at the University of Toronto, in a brief flirtation with Pierre Trudeau's brand of Liberalism, as the NDP's finance critic in Ottawa, and in his current role as the Ontario party leader and premier. In this context, Rae was widely understood, to borrow a decade-old phrase from *The Financial Post Magazine*, as "a class chameleon," an ideological floater, moving with the shifts in the power configurations around him. He was someone who could "adapt his colouring to fit in with bankers, academics and business types as well as trade-unionists." That was what made him so valuable to the NDP.[6] Insiders at the time of Rae's election as Ontario party leader — some OSSTF leaders among them — knew perfectly well what the party had ended up buying. It was a Faustian bargain of sorts. And nobody wanted to look too closely at what this potential short cut to power would cost them.

But there was also something else about Rae's character (and which also applied to some of his key advisors) that has made OSSTF keep coming back to the premier — this time much more uneasily — as the beginning of an explanation for these profound changes in their political world. Take Earl Manners' comments on negotiating with Rae's technological clones. Underneath Manners' description, caught perhaps more in his tone of voice than in his words, was a sense that there was something very disturbing here, something really wrong, about the situation he had experienced. Many of those I spoke to about Rae had the same feelings about the premier's approach to public life. Something was really wrong here, though they found it hard to put their finger on quite what it was. Part of it, certainly, involved a sense that behind Rae's boyish good looks and his platform charm lay quite a traditional capacity for political manipulation and personal hardball. At the same time, however, people noted a mechanical quality to Rae that did not seem at all out of place in a world of high-tech downsizing and the fantasies of William Gibson's brave new world. And that was much scarier. When OSSTF's current vice-president Jim McQueen reflects on the palpable change of atmosphere that came with Rae's personal administration, he says: "A whiff of modern fascism, maybe?" And he's dead serious. In *Rae Days*, Thomas Walkom describes the premier as a thoroughly "abstract" man, fascinated, in turn, by abstractions, who when he leaves Ontario politics will not only have abandoned "the political landscape ... of all those who fought for and believed in an alternative to [business] orthodoxy," he will have "sowed the ground with salt."[7] Underneath these abstractions, to put this in different language while remaining consistent with Walkom's analysis, there seems to be a deep rage at work in the premier and a strong thirst for personal power.

Such a pattern gets us directly into the psychology of capitalism that has emphasized the use of abstract citizen-proof mechanics to keep such rage and lust for power under control. Theoretically such control applies to all citizens. In practice its focus is on those who are to be governed. At an intimate level what is implied (but sometimes made explicit) is that citizens must leave their human feelings at home. Morals can have no place in the market or in a state system that must support the market. Citizens must trust a "hidden hand," in politics as in the economy. So, at another level, must their leaders. They too must leave their morals at home, keeping their personal and political lives separate, if they are to be effective on the job. In order to frame an efficient economy — in this case a global economy — they must remain detached from the concerns of "ordinary people." Indeed, such a separation is central to what former federal finance minister Donald Macdonald once described as the "royal jelly" of modern capitalist political leadership. It is a separation which must take place within the character or soul of such a leader; it can't be a public-relations cloak. While such a pattern may be catastrophic to the fabric of the society as a whole, it is an everyday event within our ruling class at an individual level. And, as I see it, this is what has happened to Bob Rae. The illusion was that he might prove the exception to this rule.

There are, of course, exceptions to such a "rule," though rarely among those who have experienced Rae's particular set of family relationships. While Rae did not, unlike most neo-conservative politicians, abandon the language of love (which stands at the core of democratic socialism) until he achieved power, there is nothing in his early background that could have prepared him to hold on to such language and what it implied once he entered government.

Thomas Walkom describes Rae as "an outsider with insider connections." He emphasizes this point in Rae's worklife, but it is easily transferred, as Walkom also implies, to the premier's boyhood. Rae grew up a privileged "dip kid," "the foreign-policy elite's version of 'army brat,'" distanced from friends, neighbourhood and family. His parents "know him least," says Rae's close friend Lenny Wise. "He's confided in them less than anybody alive."[8] His father, Saul, a desperately ambitious boy from a working-class family, succeeded in making a place for himself in the Canadian establishment and expected no less from his sons. Possibly he expected more, since his own rise in External Affairs ended a little distance from the top. In taking upon himself the "public service" ideology of Canadian Liberalism, with its high-minded sense of duty, Saul Rae was always clear that Liberalism was the ideology of the powerful, its language a means to frame the governing of others. His oldest son, John, got the message clearly, becoming executive vice-president of Power Corporation and a major player in the back rooms of Jean Chrétien's Liberal Party. Bob, as a second son, developed an intense rivalry with his older brother on a wide variety of fronts, with John clearly in the lead for his father's affections. Bob retained a closer, though still distant, tie to his mother, Lois, whom Walkom says provided him "with a strong and abiding interest in religion and ethics."[9] Lois had been educated at Cambridge and had worked at the CBC and the National Film Board while raising her three oldest children.[10] She is described by another family acquaintance as "the real social democrat of the bunch" — the person who honestly believed in medicare, in good public schools, and in a decent set of social services.

To some extent his mother's ideology — perhaps it is better to say her social conscience — stayed with Rae as he went through his university years in the late sixties and early seventies, even though he remained "fiercely ambitious" (as Michael Ignatieff describes him at the time) and thoroughly comfortable with those establishment figures he took on as a moderate student activist. It seems to have been a time of adolescent rebellion against his father's brand of "tweedy Liberalism" in which he embraced what Walkom calls his social democratic "scepticism." It also seems to have been a time of honest doubts and genuine pain, which ended in his failure to get a doctorate at Oxford — a humiliating failure given his father's and his brother's expectations — and in his attempt to touch the lives of the poor through social work in the east end of London. By the time Rae returned to Canada in 1974, however, Walkom argues that "his ambitions and his social conscience were at least partly resolved. He would do good, but as a social democrat rather than a Liberal. He would go to law school. And he would enter politics — but not in the easy way. He would not — as his brother John had done — operate through the governing Liberals. Rather, Bob Rae would take the harder route. He would join the NDP. It would be his crown of thorns, his expiation, his sacrifice."[11]

In many ways, this "resolution" of the tensions within Rae did not seriously change until he achieved office. Up to this point, he remained a fiercely ambitious "class chameleon" (his father's legacy) while putting forward (from his mother's perspective) an untested set of social democratic morals as his ticket to power or perhaps his "crown of thorns."

Rae's ethical rhetoric was, I think, honestly held at some level of his being. When I reread "What We Owe Each Other" — Rae's statement of political purpose created during his last months of opposition and which he reworked (giving it an educational focus) for the lead editorial of *Our Schools/Our Selves*[12] — I do not think he meant to lie to us. It especially makes sense given the moment in Rae's life in which the bulk of it was written. The NDP leader had recently lost his younger brother David to cancer and he thought he was coming to the end of his own political career. What emerged from this experience of loss and grief — briefly piercing his everyday defensive armour — was a powerful hope for decent human relationships, a hope his mother had kept alive when he was young. At this moment he wanted such hope writ large for others.

In his editorial he argues that "socialism … is not a 'system' … but a choice, based on values and emotions." He stresses the communal basis of freedom, and that "love and solidarity" are "political and economic duties … [not] private things best left to private moments." It is a position, he says, which stands in contrast to a "business civilization" that creates both economic inequality and the desire for power over others in its citizens' hearts. While the material basis of a society may be crucial to its well-being, what counts most are its "long-term" community values. "What we owe each other," he continues, "is love and the action that flows from that. We express that love … in laws, institutions and entitlements." In our schools, this means that "at the core of a common curriculum, our kids have to recognize that education is about all of their lives." This is what "a democratic school system" is all about. Our schools, said Rae, must be "based on the view that people have rights and responsibilities that flow purely and simply from being human, and that people express themselves in the world by working, by inventing, by being creative, by organizing their thoughts and actions, as they do in their social lives by growing up in a family, making friends, having sexual relationships, learning to love, and learning to care for others. At the same time, we know that this world we make as human beings is deeply and destructively divided: on the broad front of class and gender, race and nation, and on the more intimate ground of sexuality and friendship, family and neighbourhood. Kids have to learn to make sense of these divisions, and they have to be encouraged to join with others in a struggle to end them. Our school curriculum must bring our children into the broad human struggle for justice and for love." Nowhere was this struggle more important than in Canada itself. Rae called on his readers to re-establish the importance of "home" and to bring our children with us in "grasping anew ... what is precious about our country."

The editorial came out in late September 1990. By the time it hit the newsstands, Rae was premier of Ontario and had already tentatively embarked on an entirely new path: as a champion of global competition and of school reforms designed to fit children into their appropriate niche within an international corporate structure. Within a few days of the election he had severed all ties with a strong party-wide network of education leaders and activists he himself had helped build over his last three years in opposition. The network had been centred in his "Leader's Ad-Hoc Committee On Education," and it was far better prepared for a transition to power than most sections of the Ontario NDP. In cutting this network adrift, what the premier wanted to make perfectly clear was that senior Ministry of Education bureaucrats would have no internal opposition to their policy directions. It was a political message that would soon go out to all of his ministries.

This was, of course, a massive change in the premier's position, in his public character even. But it didn't take a long series of events to hammer it home, as you might expect. It required just one event: coming to power and having to deal with that reality.

At a personal level, what coming to power meant for Rae, more than anything else, was having to face his relationship with his father, still unresolved, and what it meant to become a man himself. He was now in power, taking up the role of the father as he had understood it from childhood. In this context, I think his only choice — his destiny, if you like — was to go the way he did. He was in no position to transcend his experience of patriarchy and social class.

Being "an outsider, with insider connections" was crucial to this destiny.

Rae's outsider status continued directly from his childhood and student experience into his relationships with the NDP and the labour movement. In both cases he was parachuted in from the top, and thus had no lived roots to hold him when the pressures of power hit, no everyday experience of struggle alongside others which would temper the demands of office. He had only a few close friendships, made in university or afterwards, and mostly within his own class. They could hardly help him face the choice he had to face from his first day as premier: Would he stay with social democracy (his mother's distant ideals) or would he join his father (represented by the demands of a corporate and bureaucratic elite) in a man's work of governing?

To put this question another way, if Rae could find a means to free his "fierce ambition," his thirst for power, that at the same time would let him come home to his father's love and respect, would he choose that route? I can't imagine any other answer but "yes." It is so common a pattern, routinely traced in the psychoanalytic literature on the transmission of patriarchy from one generation to another. The son comes to understand he must leave his mother's warmth to take on his father's honour and purpose in the world. This, he has learned, is the only path to manhood. The break, however painful, must come. Otherwise, he will be suffocated by femininity. But once the break does come, he can delight in his new freedom, in his new-found warrior status. And this, it seems to me, is what Rae experienced in the last few years, as he slowly but surely joined his father in this "man's work" of governing. We saw his delight grow in his new role as a neo-conservative warrior and in his ability to wield government power and to reshape his party in his own image. I don't think there was a commentator on the Ontario political scene who failed to note the premier's new-found confidence and energy as he embarked on the task of slashing public sector services and confronting his former trade union allies.

With these thoughts in mind, it is hard not to turn back to the afternoon of October 1990 and the new NDP government's swearing-in ceremony at the University of Toronto's Convocation Hall. There, Rae told his cheering audience that he was "very, very proud." "I am especially proud," he went on, "that so many members of my family are here. Especially of the fact that we are able to have this ceremony in this hall, which has such special meaning for my father and me."[13] In the emotion of the moment, it was his relationship with his father he singled out.

I don't mean to argue, of course, that the premier was without his contradictions. The childhood rage remained in private (I am told he still screamed at union leaders who abandoned him), and he must have felt the bite of loneliness, and perhaps an increase in the "paranoia" referred to by former advisor Lynn Spink, once he had so thoroughly separated his private and public worlds and began living out the everyday ruthlessness that entails. Outside a small circle of friends, Rae was never able to achieve any sort of comfortable human warmth, and as time wore on this small circle diminished. As Lenny Wise said of him, "Bob ain't got many friends left." Occasionally, I understand, Rae drew from personal sources, especially from his wife Arlene, to make more humane policy suggestions and to soften his government's image. It happened, I gather, less and less, and finally perhaps not at all. In the past, I am told, these personal suggestions were almost always wiped out in debate with his "alter-ego" David Agnew, his last Secretary of Cabinet and as complete a technocrat as Ontario has seen in such a senior post. In these discussions, Agnew was reported to have enormous power over Rae which mostly consisted in showing the premier how impractical and contradictory such "humane" proposals were, how silly they were given present realities, how little Ontarians really cared about such things, etc. And in no time at all the proposal was off the agenda, and Rae had been led on to the next item for his consideration.

Such contradictions in Rae himself were almost entirely hidden from public view. Partly this was because Rae had always been a fine actor, who enjoyed the creation of a strong public persona and the playing out of his role on the various stages his premiership offered. More importantly, as I've suggested, it was because the premier had succeeded in burying these contradictions in his own mind and had learned to move with the grain of his social class, his family relations, and — what I want to consider in a moment or two — had learned to work comfortably alongside the major players in the bureaucracy he inherited with office. These are men who continue in his father's tradition, cloaked in his father's authority.

In linking up with these bureaucrats, the language of "public service" Liberalism that Rae inherited from his father remained remarkably serviceable, particularly when integrated with the even more malleable language of modern technology and corporate restructuring. Rae didn't have to change the words he used; he just had to change what they meant to him. In this process, his "public service" language could revert to the meaning it has had for generations of Liberal and "Progressive" Conservative politicians: a screen for class warfare. The "public good" could now mean crushing "hostile" public sector unions and their "selfish" and "greedy" members, while stripping "unnecessary and wasteful" services. The public service could now be subject to the same kind of "quality control" as the private sector. As for the premier's language of love, which he saw expressed in our public institutions, this could now be safely set aside. It was a childish thing, and almost always a media embarrassment. No one would miss it.

The Premier's Spin

At the same time as the premier was mastering the traditional language of Canada's ruling Liberal elite, he was also becoming increasingly creative at putting his own spin on the events in which he participated.

What Rae says about the Social Contract is that in the spring of 1993 he faced a true emergency — a crisis of government on which he had to act. He didn't betray his principles; reality went beyond them. He didn't change; the world did. The extent of the global recession and the reach of the international corporation finally convinced him that the Ontario deficit had become "a ticking bomb" (the Tory phrase at the time), which, if not defused, would destroy the economy and the educational, health, and social services net supported by that economy. The province had to adapt and adapt fast. Massive cuts in public sector services, jobs and wages could no longer be avoided. Someone had to have the courage to act. The Social Contract was the result.

Here, for example, is how this history got reported by senior *Globe and Mail* reporter Richard Mackie, who interviewed the premier for many hours on the subject:

"The first public hint of what was in store," Mackie writes, "came on February 9 in a speech to a group of University of Toronto business administration students [when] Rae talked of the need to control the deficit and to make government more efficient." The premier had just come back from Davos, Switzerland, where he had attended meetings of the World Economic Forum. There, he told his student audience, he had heard international business leaders despair over government deficits and inefficiencies in Europe, and he had listened hard as they stressed "the worldwide trend to redesign organizations, downsizing wherever possible and trying to make their organizations more responsive." These discussions, he said, convinced him that major changes in the Ontario public service were needed — "changes of the kind long proposed," Mackie notes, "by more conservative politicians and business leaders in the province."

What Rae got across to Mackie, and to the press generally, was that Davos was a defining moment for him — a time when the neo-conservative penny finally dropped, a monetarist's Road to Damascus, from which the premier emerged as a born-again deficit fighter for the nineties.

"Indeed," says Mackie, "[Rae's] speech to the U. of T. students was so emphatic on the importance of making government more efficient and cutting spending that reporters, remembering the antagonism between Mr. Rae and business leader Conrad Black, joked that the Premier had gone from being 'Comrade Bob to Conrad Bob.'"[14]

As we would expect, Rae is solidly supported by his staff in this interpretation of the Social Contract history, even if "Conrad Bob" was not their label of choice. Simon Rosenblum, a former senior policy advisor and now chief of staff to treasurer Floyd Laughren, says of that time: "We saw a situation unfolding very, very rapidly where debt-interest payments were going to cannibalize dramatically other programs [and] we could be headed toward a situation where our ability to borrow would be radically compromised." Peter Warrian, who took over from Michael Decter as the government's chief Social Contract negotiator, adds that once the bad economic news broke in February 1993, with its promise of lower tax revenues and higher welfare payments, "we had to do something. Public sector wages — which cost the government $43 billion annually — were a natural target for spending cuts. We didn't have too many alternatives."[15]

The darker side of the official press story sees the Davos moment as more a product of pressure than insight. *Maclean's* reported that "a secret ultimatum" had been delivered to the premier "by Canadian and international bond dealers." If he didn't get the deficit under $10 billion, they "would demand junk-bond interest rates in order to finance Ontario's debt."[16]

Thomas Walkom offers a third, and closely related, explanation for Rae's abrupt reversal of policy and his plunge into the Social Contract: pure panic: "From the beginning," says Walkom, "this social contract was fatally flawed. It began with panic inside government — stark almost lunatic panic — about the size of the deficit and the spectre of public finances tumbling out of control. Most governments are concerned with these matters. But in Ontario it was as if the NDP cabinet had suddenly had a revelation. It was as if — having never thought about public finance before — ministers suddenly discovered the obvious: when people are out of work they pay fewer taxes; during recessions welfare costs rise; when governments borrow to cover failing revenues and rising costs, debt results. For this government, the fear of debt carried special significance. The charge against the NDP has always been that it could never manage the economy. Horrified ministers thought to themselves: What if the critics are right? What if, through sheer incompetence, we run the finances of this province into the ground? ... Like all recent converts, they were enthusiasts. The province, they figured, didn't just have a debt problem; it faced a crisis. And to meet that crisis, it had to undergo extreme measures — including slashing the government's projected deficit by the arbitrary figure of $6.4 billion."[17]

Insight or pressure or panic, or all three, it comes to the same story in the end. February 1993 was when it happened: the moment when the government knew the world — or at least the international corporations — had caught up to Ontario.

Once Rae had gone public with his Davos agenda, it was evident there would be no turning back. In this sense, the moment turned out to be a defining moment. By the time the premier returned to Davos a year later, he was in full gear as a pro-business head of government. In this second visit Rae approached the World Economic Forum as an unabashed champion of the international corporation working against the expansion of workers' wages and government services. While there he proposed to hand over a good chunk of Ontario's investment planning to international banking and securities firms. He met with such blue-chip financial companies as the Deutsche Bank of Germany, Goldman Sachs of New York and Normure Securities of Japan, all of whom sold Ontario bonds on the world market. But instead of asking them to sell more provincial bonds, Rae now wanted them "to sell Ontario through their global networks." He was looking to "plug into" these private-sector networks, he told the press, rather than spending government money developing publicly-controlled avenues to investment. And what, he was asked, would these international banking and securities institutions find to say that was attractive about Ontario for foreign investors? Why, lower unit labour costs, he said, "which are now lower than in the

United States, Japan and Europe — along with low health costs [for business] and even payroll taxes."[18]

Such visits — and such a frank corporate perspective — became commonplace for Rae: whether in Israel, as "the mascot" of a contingent of Ontario business leaders, or in European centres to meet with new investment banking firms and to reassure anonymous German and Swiss bond holders, or in China with Jean Chrétien, as a fierce exponent of Ontario free enterprise, Candu reactors, and the importance of separating trade from human rights.

Rae had now unquestionably become the business premier of Ontario, even though the business community largely continued to hold him in contempt.

But had Rae been a business premier much earlier than February 1993? And was the Social Contract, therefore, part of a much longer and larger government process at work? Is there policy evidence to show that this is the case? Does the record hold evidence of the premier's growing and consistent support of a corporate agenda from the beginning of his term? I think it does.

I noted previously the disbanding of the premier's education policy network within the first few days of government and his very early support of corporate education policies. By the fall of 1991, however, as Thomas Walkom reminds us in *Rae Days*, the government officially lost its nerve on a much broader policy front and dramatically switched its rhetoric.[19] "Rae and Laughren no longer talked of fighting recessions rather than deficits. Instead, like the federal Tory government in Ottawa, the NDP now talked of the need for fiscal responsibility, deficit control, and rebuilding the economy through the efforts of the private sector."[20] The abandonment of public auto insurance at this point symbolized this change of position.[21] So too did its retreat from official NDP policies of people-based training, an emphasis on local investment and, perhaps most important, an interventionist industrial strategy. By July 1992 the government produced a document entitled "An Industrial Policy Framework for Ontario," which proposed a far less aggressive strategy than David Peterson's proposals for state support of leading-edge, high-tech industries. The government was now reduced to providing only the right climate for business. As Walkom comments, it was a policy direction "far closer to the Mulroney Tories than to the old NDP."[22]

Not only were significant policy changes going on long before February 1993 (not the least of which was Rae's acquiescence in Mulroney's free trade policies), but the premier had already gone to bed with some of the world's major corporate players. The best evidence of this is provided by Walkom in his *Rae Days* chapter entitled "Taking Care of Business."[23] Only two months after the premier had achieved office, he allowed British Gas, in opposition to NDP policy, to swallow up Consumers Gas — increasing foreign ownership in the province and foreclosing any prospect of public ownership of natural gas distribution. By the time 1991 was over, the government had not only capitulated to the insurance industry over public auto insurance, it had also — in direct contradiction to strong provincial pension legislation — allowed the province's major auto manufacturers off the hook of pre-funding their workers' pension-benefits packages. By the fall of 1992, the NDP cabinet was working secretly in opposition to their federal NDP counterparts on the issue of drug patents and in support of the Mulroney government's proposed changes to the law in Bill C-91, which Ontario Health Minister Frances Lankin estimated would cost the province's drug plan some $1 billion over a ten-year period. The Rae government accepted Mulroney's elimination of compulsory licensing of the drug companies, which had allowed generic companies to copy brand-name drugs at a much lower cost, and it also agreed to further support the multinationals in its own bailiwick, through protected access to the official drug list used by the Ontario Drug Benefit Program.[24] These drug policies took place despite a Ministry of Health report which argued that the province could expect not only lower costs from Canadian-based generic companies but also an expansion of local research and development.

These early links to the corporate world were then solidified throughout the Social Contract period. Rae continued his support of the privatized health sector by permitting the sale of the province's largest non-profit health insurance company, Ontario Blue Cross, to U.S.-based Liberty International. Blue Cross had been developed by Ontario's publicly-funded hospitals, and its sale to private owners came at a time, as both CUPE and the OFL pointed out, "when the business of providing so-called supplementary health-care insurance can only become more lucrative as governments continue to whittle away at basic medicare." It is one more example, as Thomas Walkom comments in *The Toronto Star*, of private industry "cashing in" on public investment.[25] Rae was so concerned not to disturb corporate sensibilities that he even held back Agriculture Minister Elmer Buchanan's regulatory changes that would have banned the use of animals for cosmetic testing and, in particular, the Draize test in which potentially harmful chemicals are applied directly to the eyes of animals. The Canadian Cosmetic, Toiletry and Fragrance Association, it seems, had successfully lobbied an NDP retreat on this issue, even though "22 other companies that manufacture what they call 'cruelty-free products' wrote Rae in January to support the Buchanan amendments."[26] By March of 1995, shortly before announcing an election in early June, Rae moved dramatically to increase public support for the international computer industry. As part of his response to the Royal Commission on Learning, the premier promised to buy 40,000 computers a year for Ontario schools for the next five years at a cost of $500 million.[27] Aside from the usual cheerleading in the rush to be first in line on the information highway, these purchases appear to be entirely unplanned in terms of their specific classroom use. What planning there was seems to have been primarily the work of industry sales managers.

It is hard to know the extent to which deals like these were the tip of a much bigger iceberg of government-business collusion. We can only imagine what transpired, for example, in the arrangements that eventually turned over Windsor's casino complex to a Las Vegas consortium, including among its three principals Caesar's, a formerly mob-controlled casino enterprise. (As late as 1991 and 1993 Caesar's had been fined more than $1 million by the New Jersey Casino Control Commission after it "inappropriately paid cash rebates or incentive payments" to gamblers.[28]) Even bigger questions arise over Rae's new task force to tackle the economic and political problems of the Greater Toronto Area and his determination to impose two new lines onto the nearly bankrupt Metro Toronto subway system at considerable provincial expense.[29] To what extent were these activities guided by an agenda built in the boardrooms of the construction and development industries, their banks, and their publicists at the *The Toronto Star*?

After four years of corporate wheeling and dealing, Rae and party bureaucrats quietly arranged for the Ontario NDP to accept corporate funding in the next election. Even though it involved a fundamental change to the provincial party's constitution, the premier made certain it went through the party's 1994 convention with hardly any debate. Now, as party officials expected, the construction bosses, who had received contracts for building Highway 407 and had had their party donations turned back, could be welcomed into the fold. The big multinational drug firms, with whom Rae has continued to meet secretly, would also be able to show their appreciation.[30] It was not unreasonable for party officials to think that companies like British Gas, Liberty International, Caesar's, Trizec, Elizabeth Arden, and IBM would not be far behind.

The final stage in the process seems to have been a pathetic search for NDP corporate candidates as part of a pro-business thrust in the 1995 election. Sandra Gwyn wrote: "The business community [was] not only no longer angry [with Bob Rae], it [was] starting to purr." She quoted an executive saying "Those guys really like Rae.They won't endorse him publicly. But a lot of them will vote for him," and she noted that Rae had to improve his position in the polls if he was "to attract first-rate candidates." The search was on "for business types." "We don't need any more schoolteachers or social workers," said an advisor to the premier."[31]

At the same time as this corporate perspective on the economy was getting on track in the early days of Rae's government, the premier was also coming to grips with a business-oriented down-sizing agenda within the public service itself.

As early as November 1991, during the pre-budget planning process for 1992, Rae and Laughren set up a series of cabinet meetings at which cabinet ministers were to be lectured by Treasury officials on the "crisis" in government finance. At one key meeting, after a particularly dark scenario had been painted and there was general silence in the room, and people like Frances Lankin reportedly looked at their shoes, Rae broke in with a remarkably coherent ten-minute speech. His proposal was a wage freeze for all public sector workers. It was, of course, for the public good. If we cut education or health or social services, he pointed out, we'll hurt people. That's unfair. We don't want to do that. What is fair, he said, was that everyone should take a cut. And he went on to say that the government should just announce that this is our policy. It's Draconian, sure, but isn't it fair? he asked. After this speech there was an even deeper silence in the room as cabinet members contemplated the firestorm such an announcement would produce.

Later, Rae was talked out of this position. But it was not something he forgot. A little less than a year later, in October 1992, Rae assembled his cabinet for another pre-budget meeting. In the previous year, grants to transfer partners — municipalities, universities, schools, hospitals — had been cut, leading to reductions in local services and mounting pressure on local jobs and property taxes. Provincial taxes paid by individuals, including senior citizens, had gone up. Public sector wages, however, had stayed pretty much the same. As cabinet members assembled, many of the same Treasury charts and slides from 1991 went up on the wall. Treasury officials went on to predict an even greater disaster for up-coming government revenues. When they had finished, there was another long silence, after which Rae is reported to have made almost the same ten-minute speech he made in 1991. My source is convinced it had almost a word-for-word similarity, though maybe, he thinks, there was a bit more about "fairness." After all the province's transfer partners had taken a big cut the year before and individual taxes had gone up while the economy had continued to go further downhill with harsh consequences for private sector workers. Surely, the premier argued once more, it was the moment for public sector workers to take their fair share of the pain.

The big difference this time, however, was that the cabinet was listening. They were now starting to take in what Rae and his officials were trying to get across to them and were beginning to move in his direction. In a few months, they would be ready to follow the premier's leadership in going after the province's public sector unions. Indeed, once they got on to this union-busting bandwagon, their enthusiasm for it would match his own. At this stage, however, cabinet members were still mighty wary of Rae's message. The political consequences seemed to promise overwhelming defeat in the next election. These ministers would have to be subjected to much more internal pressure before such a massive turnaround could be achieved. A really dramatic crisis would have to emerge or be manufactured. Such a prospect, needless to say, lifted the hearts of the province's Treasury officials, who were clearly prepared to find such a crisis. By February 93, they had revised their deficit projections from $4.6 billion to $17 billion,[32] and the Ontario cabinet faced its worst nightmare: the "debt wall" that had allegedly doomed New Zealand was now snaking across the Pacific on its way to Toronto.[33]

The Bureaucratic Alliance

Whatever we may think of Rae's personal evolution as business premier of Ontario or the process whereby he and his inner circle worked out their Social Contract strategy, one thing is certain: the movers and shakers in the Ontario bureaucracy were on to public-sector downsizing and union busting long before the Rae government got into the act. As David Clandfield has put it: the government's "multi-billion-dollar deficit reduction program [involving both the Expenditure Control Program and the Social Contract Act] is not a new initiative; it is the culmination of a well-prepared, neo-conservative program of a civil service imbued with this thinking in its highest echelons, and which clearly has the support of the Premier now (1993), and may always have had that support. What is new is that it finally found the rationale and the rhetoric of deficit-cutting to enable it to go public, and for most of the Premier's cabinet ministers to feel that they have no alternative."[34]

In the context of this long-term bureaucratic initiative, the slow but sure shift we have been examining in Rae's policy perspective, which led him to the Social Contract, can be seen as a process whereby the premier eventually built up (or was brought into) a close alliance with the neo-conservative leaders of this bureaucracy. It was an alliance confirmed as Rae claimed the Social Contract initiative as his own. It is hard to tell how rough and ready the process was. But at the end of the day, it is this alliance, more than anything else, which gave Rae the extraordinary power he had among his ministers and within his caucus. It also provided the base from which such an enormous project as the Social Contract could be made practical.

This alliance must have taken some time to build. It required considerable research on individuals and a good deal of political caution, given grass-roots NDP attitudes towards bureaucratic power. The Ontario NDP, however, did not have much more than attitudes going for it on this front and had very limited capacity to resist the premier's initiatives.

On coming to power the party had given little thought to how senior civil servants at Queen's Park actually worked, though when NDP officials did think about them, they showed a surprisingly low level of distrust or scepticism. Stephen Lewis, the former head of the provincial party and the new government's transition-team leader, offers a good example of the party's understanding of provincial administration. Coming out to meet the press, after his first meeting with cabinet secretary Peter Barnes, Lewis declared that he had "learned more in two hours about the process and functioning of government bureaucracy than in all his years in the legislature."[35] Lewis wasn't alone in his ignorance. George Ehring and Wayne Roberts report that in the early days of the Rae government, "the New Democrats were so unaware of the inner workings of the state that [the party's research chief Chuck] Rachlis went off to the legislative library to get an organizational chart of the government. Later, key New Democrats studied the chart, occasionally wondering out loud, 'What do you suppose *these* guys do?'" (Rachlis, it appears, eventually figured it out and went into private business as a lobbyist.) New Democratic Party historian Des Morton goes so far as to argue that this situation reflected a "wilful ignorance of public administration," part of the NDP's strategy of trying "to sneak up to power."

"Few New Democrats," Morton writes, "thought about government, and few of those few entered the circle of power in 1990."[36]

After nearly five years of government, only a charmed "few" of Ontario New Democrats had made their way into the bureaucratic circle of power. Bob Rae, however, was first among them.

Rae was not anxious to stress his cosy relationship to officialdom. What Rae preferred to do was to talk tough to the press about intervening when faced with bureaucratic inertia and about short-circuiting the institutional system when necessary. "If you ever want to get something done," he confided to one reporter, "and you ever actually want to turn the aircraft carrier [known as the bureaucracy] half a millimetre to the left or to the right, you sometimes have to drive it."

What the premier was referring to in practice, however, was not so much bureaucratic inertia, but rather ministerial misdirection. The people Rae was most concerned to short-circuit during his administration were those cabinet colleagues who were developing policies that didn't please him, and especially those who were resisting his corporatization of the Ontario state system. (There were, of course, old-fashioned bureaucrats who got in the way as well, but they were far less worrisome and much more easily disposed of.) "I think it's fair to say," the premier commented at one point, "that sometimes I get a bit far out ahead of the pack," but this was the price, he insisted, that had to be paid by those "who are prepared to lead." His ministers had to learn the hard truth of Ontario legislative politics: what mattered was going to be decided in the premier's office. As one senior official noted in more diplomatic language, "Rae has never learned the institutional restrictions on governing. He pre-empts his ministers, often without warning, by speaking directly to middle-level civil servants or by comments in speeches or to reporters...." In the same news report, other government sources "tell stories of Mr. Rae making decisions without consulting the minister responsible, or reversing decisions already made. However, they say, he usually goes to great pains to sell these decisions to cabinet and the caucus."[37]

At one point, Rae's direct dealings with Treasury officials

became so extreme that Floyd Laughren, the premier's clone as a deficit-obsessed finance minister, eventually rebelled. *Eye* magazine reported that senior bureaucrats at the Ministry of Finance were "in shock over a recent screaming match" between Laughren and Rae. The magazine's Queen's Park correspondent commented on the premier's "well-known habit of calling officials in ministries directly, rather than going through his minister," and wrote that "Floyd told Rae not to call people in his ministry. When he discovered that the premier was still talking to his officials behind his back, Floyd told Rae in a very heated way that if it happened once more he would resign and Rae could become his own Finance Minister."[38]

Whether or not Rae eventually gave Laughren a longer leash to deal with his department, it is clear that the kind of direct relationship he had with Laughren's officials was central to his style of government. And nowhere were such contacts more important than in developing the Social Contract strategy. Peter Warrian, who followed Michael Decter as the government's chief negotiator and was a key player in the Social Contract process, made a point of stressing that it was "hardliners" from Finance who had their game plan ready in early cabinet meetings for the push to "a legislated solution."[39]

What's crucial to emphasize here, however, is that Rae hadn't just been cosying up to bureaucracy in general even if he sometimes sounded that way. In one of his first speeches after the election the premier declared, for example, that as the son of a public servant, "I understand well their sense of professionalism and their sense of public service, and it's that sense of professionalism and public service that, as premier, I want to draw on." To make himself perfectly clear, he approved the contracts of nine deputy ministers from the previous Liberal government whose contracts had just run out.[40] No socialists need apply.

For Rae that was an important message, but as he took up the reins of power, he started looking for something a good deal more precise in his senior civil servants than their sense of professionalism and public service. As the editors of the Queen's Park *Go Report* (an insiders' news sheet for those who have to deal with the provincial government) put it in February 1993,

Rae's government had not only been "slotting its own people into the bureaucracy with more determination, and evidently with less subtlety, than its predecessors ... transforming [in the process] the top ranks of the Ontario public service ..." but it was doing so from a perspective that had little to do with traditional party politics: "Of the twenty line ministries represented around the cabinet table," these editors report, "eleven are now headed by deputy ministers appointed to that rank by the NDP. (Five were first appointed by the Liberals, and the remaining four were first promoted by the Tories.) In addition, the current government has attracted to the OPS [Ontario Public Service] or promoted within it a number of the DMs [deputy ministers] managing non-ministerial operations. This is not to suggest that DMs necessarily reflect the partisan stripe of the government which hires them. Most of the eleven deputies appointed since 1990 came from the senior ranks of Ontario's civil service or from other levels of government. While a few of these are known to be members or supporters of the NDP, most have no such ties. Moreover, the known NDPers come with substantial managerial experience — such as Jeff Rose, who ran CUPE before joining Intergovernmental Affairs, and Dan Burns who headed the Toronto housing department before moving to that provincial ministry. And it would be a mistake to stress the NDP ties of someone like Michael Decter, whose strong attachment to the traditional, non-partisan model of the OPS has emerged since he was appointed DM at Health. And some critically important bureaucratic posts have been assigned to those who have no partisan taint at all — e.g. Peter Barnes, former Secretary of Cabinet who is being relied on to manage the key economic ministry [Economic Development and Trade]. Others given key roles were initially recruited by, and seen as, backers of the Liberals — e.g. Dr. Charles Pascal, at the newly consolidated Ministry of All-Education. Indeed, there are some indications that zeal to cut costs, and energetic efforts to do more with less, have counted for more with the NDP than party slant."[41]

My impression of these appointments is that there is little evidence to suggest that Rae had chosen anyone other than the energetic downsizers referred to in this report.

It is, of course, very difficult to assess just how much this bureaucratic alliance came at Bob Rae's initiative and how much of it involved a "capturing" of government by its administration. But even if we want to place the emphasis on bureaucratic capture, it had to be a process Rae quite consciously allowed. It wasn't something that just happened, in former Research Director Chuck Rachlis' words, "because they were too busy getting themselves organized to really think about how to run a government." It also wasn't the result of an especially sly and aggressive group of bureaucrats, who held all the cards of information and implementation, and against which the NDP cabinet and caucus were powerless. There were remedies available, which Rae firmly resisted. Ehring and Roberts write, for example, that "Stephen Lewis and others, including former Saskatchewan premier Allan Blakeney, proposed that the cabinet office be structured following a model used in Saskatchewan, employing a so-called 'Red Secretariat.'" The Red Secretariat would have put in place "an umbrella group of senior advisors responsible for reviewing broad policy initiatives from all the ministries" and would have served "as a check on the bureaucratic administrators, helping provide overall policy direction and insuring that the government plans get priority." It seems like such an obvious structure for a new socialist government, and yet the premier turned it down flat. (In one of the funnier quotes of this administration, Rachlis says the idea was turned down because Rae's team "didn't like the *optics* of a big costly cabinet office." [my italics]) At the same time, Rae turned down the suggestion that the premier's office build in a relationship with the province's social movements by appointing a liaison officer to keep in touch with Ontario's political coalitions and the knowledge they brought to bear on public issues.[42]

There was to be no serious internal opposition, holding either information or power, to stand against an already entrenched administration.

It is also worth noting that with the appointment of "alter ego" David Agnew as Cabinet Secretary (the head of the province's civil service) in the fall of 1992, Rae's capacity to reach out to and support neo-conservatives in the bureaucracy was greatly strengthened through a more official and powerful institutional structure. Agnew was not expected to function as a traditional Cabinet Secretary, offering his deputy ministers advice on the smooth management of their ministries. He could hardly do that. He had not a shred of background in running a large administration. The role he was expected to fill, however, and for which he was eminently suited, involved quite different functions: a conduit between the premier and these new bureaucratic allies; a hatchet man to cut down senior officials regarded by Rae and his new allies as soft on downsizing; and finally, a centralizer of the government apparatus at the service of his boss and those senior officials with a neoconservative agenda who had very clear ideas on how to run (or dismantle) a department. The old Cabinet Secretary, Peter Barnes, it was generally agreed, no longer had the stomach for the job and had lost touch with the real levers of power among his underlings. In his final months as the province's chief civil servant, Barnes' own distaste for the administrative style of the Rae government had become glaringly obvious.

When the government introduced its major ministry restructuring in February 1993, Agnew was offered a perfect opportunity to show the world what he was hired for. Not only did he help engineer a very significant centralization of the entire provincial administration, he also managed to force the retirement of five unwanted long-time deputies, giving them only a few hours' notice, while he fired another three, two of whom had been at that level for less than a year.[43] He replaced them all with "energetic downsizers."

And long before this restructuring, Agnew was dealing forcefully with the control of ministry bureaucrats who were still not buying the premier's new agenda but who had managed to remain at their posts. Soon after he took up his job as Cabinet Secretary, he established an Information Liaison Section which examined all correspondence coming out of each minister's office to ensure that it followed the government line. Such correspondence was normally handled by ministry officials, with a passing nod from the minister or his aides.[44] With this move, oppositional bureaucrats (both progressives and traditionalists) got the message clearly: keep your head down or get out. Later Rae would berate them as people who resisted the demands of the modern world, retreating with their "quill pens" to the dark recesses of Queen's Park, wasting good time and energy as well as taxpayers' money. They needed a dusting off. As they currently functioned, they were irrelevant to the new world order of the Ontario government.

In his analysis of Agnew's appointment as the province's top civil servant, Thomas Walkom does not emphasize the neo-conservative character of the decision-making structure that emerged, but it is there in his description, nevertheless. It is particularly evident in the network of "bureaucrats and subordinates" he identifies.

"Bureaucrats," wrote Walkom, "worried that Agnew's appointment was the ultimate attempt to politicize the civil service. In fact, it was the opposite. It was the bureaucratization of politics. By placing his most trusted aide in charge of the civil service, Rae had given deputy ministers — the top bureaucrats — direct access to his ear. Political aides soon noticed that the lines of power no longer went through the ministers to Agnew and the premier's office and finally to Rae. Instead, they went from the bureaucracy to the deputies such as Jay Kaufman and Michael Mendelson, to Agnew and McClellan, and thence to Rae, effectively bypassing the politicians. Melody Morrison, who replaced Agnew as Rae's principal secretary, instituted the practice of having the premier meet with the most senior ministers — Floyd Laughren, Frances Lankin and Dave Cooke. But even this was not enough. In the end," Walkom writes, "… centralization [meant a focus] on one person — Rae — … coordinated by those who had his trust. With few exceptions, these were not members of his cabinet. They were bureaucrats and subordinates — Decter, Kaufman, Mendelson, McClellan, and in his role as cabinet secretary, Agnew."

With the exception of McClellan, who was reported to entertain the occasional (former) politician's hesitation over the ruthlessness of Rae's new policies, the remainder of these administrators — the "coordinators" of Rae's policies — can easily be accommodated within the neo-conservative camp. It was a camp, as I have argued earlier, that had been up and running from the beginning of this government. Agnew's appointment was simply following the logic of this bureaucratic organizing, as was the new emphasis he brought to by-passing ministers and building more direct links between the premier's office and senior ministry officials. Such direct links, as we have also noted, were established early in Rae's premiership.

At the same time that Rae was forging links with right-wing bureaucrats, he also made certain that the small but powerful "political" bureaucracy of ministerial aides was controlled as much as possible from his office. On coming to office, he appointed Janet Solberg, Ontario NDP president and a member of the Lewis family, to find key staff members for each minister's office — an executive assistant, a legislative assistant, and a number of policy assistants. "These roles," Ehring and Roberts remind us, "are crucial in helping ministers understand issues and avoid political quagmires...." Solberg's job was to ensure a trustworthy "cadre of yesmen and yeswomen in key jobs" — people who "were well aware that they had been recruited and hired by the Premier's Office and were primarily responsible to it, not to the minister with whom they were eventually placed. Many of these executive assistants in turn hired other staff and so the chain of obligation was extended." Rae was so concerned to maintain his line of internal political authority that he "insisted on reviewing [these] hiring decisions personally." Combined with Solberg's difficulty in finding the right people, Rae's interference, Ehring and Roberts write, made for "an agonizingly slow process" in filling ministers' staff positions. As a result, many ministers, after they had been sworn-in, "had to function either without their key staff, or with bureaucrats in the political jobs, because the process was taking so long." Thus, while "some of the more powerful ministers went ahead and hired people they knew and trusted," most were stuck with advisors not of their own choosing and dependent on either the premier's office or their deputy minister for their posts.[45]

Before we conclude this section, it is worthwhile recalling the position of the neo-conservative leaders in Ontario's bureaucracy as Rae and his New Democrats took power. At this point, of course, these bureaucrats were officials in the Liberal government.

By the end of David Peterson's second term these officials

had worked out the basis of a firm neo-conservative agenda for government restructuring and were getting anxious to implement it. Only the necessary election formalities were required. As the most recent, and best informed, chroniclers of David Peterson's "fall from grace" tell us, cabinet secretary Peter Barnes and deputy secretary Bernard Shapiro were proceeding apace on what was called "the Tomorrow Project." This was "an enormous reorganization of the government that promised to slash the fat in the interface between ministries, potentially eliminating thousands of public service jobs and cutting hundreds of millions in annual cash requirements from the province's treasury.... The overhaul had been pushed by Peterson's first cabinet secretary Bob Carman. Although only in its infancy, the Tomorrow Project helped clear the decks for an early election. A clean break was needed, the Liberals believed, before they could plunge into a massive and politically dangerous undertaking that would get to the very heart of the Ontario government's structural inefficiencies. The likelihood of giving the Tomorrow Project a green light after the election reinforced the need for a platform that would demonstrate a political commitment by the Liberals to cut programs and stop making costly promises. A conservatively priced, fiscally responsible platform, the Liberals thought, would earn them precious credibility as they attempted to justify the project's painful cuts and dislocations in the years ahead."[46]

These officials had three surprises coming. Their current political masters lost the ensuing election, their new ones eventually gave them the "green light" for such a project, and what's more, they gave it enthusiastically.

As the administrators left over from the Peterson regime moved into the new government apparatus, David Clandfield writes, not only did their boss, Peter Barnes, stay on at his old job as Cabinet Secretary for two more years, but "a branch or department devoted to downsizing was located within another ministry, the Management Board Secretariat, and it continued to operate." Education, too, was thoroughly integrated into the process. "The Deputy Minister of Education [Robert Mitton] was apparently spending a lot of time in something called the 'Billion Dollar Club' (a group of deputy ministers who controlled budgets sufficiently large that they could create huge reductions in their own ministries). When outsiders asked how he spent his time, his answer was that most of it was given over to what he called 'structure.'"[47] Once these bureaucrats were in place, Clandfield argues, a new NDP/corporate "vision" of government began to get off the ground, moving forward at different times, in different circumstances, and at different speeds within different government departments. By 1992, "ministers were being briefed on the process of a three-year program called the Multi-Year Expenditure Reduction Plan (MYERP is the acronym), the new name given to massive downsizing. The February 1993 cabinet shuffle and the subsequent restructuring of the civil service into superministries added to this process and, with the 1993 spring budget, the announcement of the Expenditure Control Program and the summer efforts to cut the public payroll by $2 billion through the Social Contract act, now completes the process."[48]

The Social Contract juggernaut had begun its headlong journey.

FOOTNOTES

1 Ferguson, Derek and Papp, Leslie, "Rae halts pay talks in battle on deficit," *Toronto Star*, March 31, 1993

2 Ferguson, Derek and Papp, Leslie, "Rae halts pay talks in battle on deficit," *Toronto Star*, March 31, 1993.

3 Barkley, Liz, OSSTF Press Release, March 31, 1993.

4 The public side of this coalition can be found in what Maude Barlow and Heather-Jane Robertson call "the conservative alliance," which includes, of course, the more explicit political and religious expressions of the right — from Reform Party activists to the leaders of "quality control" parent organizations" to fundamentalist Christians seeking to root out a satanic liberal humanism from the public schools. See their *Class Warfare: The Assault on Canadian Schools*, Key Porter Books, Toronto, 1994, pp. 112–137.

5 It was, in fact, writes Patrick Monahan, "an essential precondition that both the lead negotiator and the deputy lead negotiator be from *outside* the sector in which they would be negotiating." As a senior government advisor explained this precondition to Monahan, it was necessary because of the fundamental "restructuring" of government involved. Sector-based officials would be "tainted" by being too close to the actual services now under the gun; they wouldn't have the necessary distance to apply the new brand of

rationalization as ruthlessly as the government required. See his *Storming the Pink Palace: The NDP in Power: A Cautionary Tale*, Lester Publishing, Toronto, 1995, pp. 196–199.

6 Ehring, George and Roberts, Wayne, *Giving Away a Miracle: Lost Dreams, Broken Promises & The Ontario NDP*, Mosaic Press, Oakville, 1993, p. 90.

7 Walkom, Thomas, *Rae Days: The Rise and Follies of the NDP*, Key Porter Books, Toronto, 1994, p. 269. See particularly Chapter 2 on Rae's early years.

8 Ehring, George and Roberts, Wayne, *Giving Away a Miracle*, cited above, pp.74–75.

9 Walkom, Thomas, *Rae Days*, cited above, p. 14.

10 Ehring, George and Roberts, Wayne, *Giving Away A Miracle*, cited above, p. 74.

11 Walkom, Thomas, *Rae Days*, cited above, p. 26.

12 Rae, Bob, "What We Owe Each Other," *Our Schools/Our Selves*, vol. 2, no. 3 (September, 1990) pp. 5–15.

13 Walkom, Thomas, *Rae Days*, cited above, p. 50.

14 Mackie, Richard, "Rae says social contract a prelude," *Globe and Mail*, December 29, 1993.

15 Canadian Press Report, *Globe and Mail*, April 2, 1994.

16 Laver, Ross and Kaiha, Paul, "So Long, Solidarity," *Maclean's*, July 12, 1993, p. 17.

17 Walkom, Thomas, "Rae got his deal, but at what cost?" *Toronto Star*, August 3, 1993.

18 Crane, David, "Rae targets global advisors to help boost Ontario abroad," *Toronto Star*, February 1, 1994.

19 It is worth noting here that not all NDP flip-flops were directly caused by corporate pressure. For example, the party's collapse on its same-sex rights bill — particularly Rae's refusal to use the party whip to support even a watered down version of it — seems to have been a product of simple political opportunism. For a good short summary of the issue see, The Park, "Same-sex issue haunts Rae," *eye*, March 30, 1995. Political opportunism also seems to have been the main reason the Ontario NDP pulled back from its support of Ottawa's recent gun-control legislation. See "Ontario and guns," Editorial, *Toronto Star*, May 28, 1995.

20 Walkom, Thomas, *Rae Days*, cited above, p. 104.

21 In 1994 Ontario auto insurance rates jumped 11.5 percent — "six times faster than consumer prices in general." And early in 1995, the Ontario Insurance Commission, which monitors and approves auto insurance rates, indicated "a new round of increases which [would] average 9.8%." See Daw, James, "Auto insurance rates roar ahead," *Toronto Star*, Section B, February

2, 1995.

22 Walkom, Thomas, *Rae Days*, cited above, p. 107

23 Walkom, Thomas, *Rae Days*, cited above, pp. 147–178.

24 One of the small benefits of this reversal of NDP drug policy was that Eli Lilly promised to add 150 new jobs at its manufacturing plant in Scarborough. *Eye* magazine, however, reports that "the new jobs never materialized … [and at the same time, another] 200 jobs at the Eli Lilly plant in Scarborough will disappear. Senior management at Eli Lilly's head office in Indianapolis has decided to move all drug manufacturing jobs from Scarborough to Indiana or Puerto Rico. But the official announcement will not be made for six or eight months, which will end up being after the next provincial election and thus save Bob Rae more embarrassment over his flip-flop on drug patent protection." The Park Column, "Drug company hoses Bob Rae," *eye*, February 23, 1995.

25 Walkom, Thomas, "Inquiry would answer concerns over Blue Cross sale," *Toronto Star*, January 10, 1995. See also "Halting sale of Blue Cross not in works," *Globe and Mail*, January 19, 1995; Walkom, Thomas, "Province could block sale of Blue Cross if it wanted," *Toronto Star*, January 19, 1995; and "Blue Cross sale can — and should — be put on hold," *Toronto Star*, January 24, 1995.

26 Walkom, Thomas, "NDP in no rush to ban animal testing for cosmetics," *Toronto Star*, February 28, 1995.

27 See Duffy, Andrew, "Schools to get 200,000 computers," *Toronto Star*, March 3, 1995, and Lewington, Jennifer, "Rae promises more computers in every school," *Globe and Mail*, March 3, 1995.

28 Walkom, Thomas, Rae Days, p. 276. See Donna Laframboise, "Windsor Casino partner fined twice in the U.S.," *Toronto Star*, December 10, 1993.

29 See Papp, Leslie, "Province to proceed on transit lines," *Toronto Star*, March 2, 1995; Campbell, Murray, "Rae keeps new transit lines on the rails," *Globe and Mail*, March 2, 1995; and Barber, John, "Rae's sweet seduction of Metro," *Globe and Mail*, March 2, 1995. John Sewell writes: "Rae now insists that Toronto can be saved by new subway lines running where there are two few riders for regular bus service…. Can't Rae and his colleagues see that transit is in desperate shape in Metro and doesn't need this kind of help? For 50 years — from 1921 to 1970 — Toronto's transit system paid for itself out of the fare box, without a public subsidy. In the last 25 years, the TTC has grown into an abject beggar, with deficits hitting $250 million a year, or about 50 cents a rider. GO Transit, that provincial system that sucks the life out of Toronto, operates at a deficit of more than $5 a rider. It's madness to pile more routes and extensions — each of which will incur even more deficits — onto a transit system that can't meet its payroll now. For Rae to suggest that Metro must take two more subway lines is lunacy…. Lurking is the background is the relentless suburbanization of our cities. Think of the money being sunk into the encouragement of sprawl —

the construction of highway 407 at the fringe of the Greater Toronto Area, proposals to build the Red Hill Creek Expressway through Hamilton's last natural ravine, the widening of highway 401 to Kitchener, an inability to stand up to the superstores. And now a few more subways lines." [And all of this in the interest of the construction and development industries.] "Subway primes suburbanism," *Now*, March 2–8, 1995

30 See Walkom, Thomas, "New Democrats taking donations from big business," *Toronto Star*, December 22, 1994 and Walker, William, "Rae meets drug firm bosses at secret dinner," *Toronto Star*, December 15, 1994.

31 Gwyn, Sandra, "Heart and soul," *Toronto Life*, vol. 29, no. 2 (February 1995) p. 41.

32 According to most observers at the time, this figure was way out of line. However, given the pounding of the province's revenue base — with government-sponsored unemployment and wage cutbacks — it turned out to be a fairly accurate in the end.

33 New Zealand never faced a debt wall. What triggered its disastrous set of neo-conservative policies over the last decade was a short-term currency crisis, which was solved through devaluation and required no further new-right gutting of its high-employment economy and its strong social service sector. As Linda McQuaig writes, "[New Zealand's] international credit rating by Moody's, one of the big New York credit rating agencies, never dropped below Aa3 — the rough equivalent of an A minus — making it one of only twenty-four countries to receive a ranking in the 'low risk' range." See her *Shooting the Hippo: Death by Deficit and Other Canadian Myths*, Viking, Toronto, 1995, especially pp. 22, 43-46. See also Dobbin, Murray, Transcript, "The Remaking of New Zealand," *Ideas*, CBC Radio Works, P.O. Box 500, Station A, Toronto, broadcast October 12, 19, 1994.

34 Clandfield, David, "The NDP and the Corporate Agenda in Ontario," *Our Schools/Our Selves*, vol. 5, no. 1 (#31) (Oct.–Nov. 1993) p. 13.

35 Ehring, George and Roberts, Wayne, *Giving Away a Miracle*, cited above, p. 293.

36 Ehring, George and Roberts, Wayne, *Giving Away a Miracle*, cited above, pp. 293–294.

37 Mackie, Richard, "Meddling with the ministers," *Globe and Mail*, December 31, 1993.

38 The Park Column, "Hire the best — if they're NDPers," *eye*, February 12–18, 1994.

39 Canadian Press Report, "Paper anniversary a bitter one," *Globe and Mail*, April 2, 1994.

40 Ehring, George and Roberts, Wayne, *Giving Away a Miracle*, cited above, p. 294.

41 See two issues of *The Go Report*, vol. 5, no. 19 (October 28, 1992), "Paranoia at the Centre", and vol. 6, no. 3 (February 24, 1993), "Mandarins

and New Democrats".

42 Ehring, George and Roberts, Wayne, *Giving Away a Miracle*, cited above, pp. 294–295.

43 See *Queen's Park Update*, "Fallout from Shuffle Continues," February 19, 1994.

44 *Queen's Park Update*, October 23, 1992.

45 Ehring, George, and Roberts, Wayne, *Giving Away A Miracle*, cited above, p. 295.

46 Gagnon, Georgette and Rath, Dan, *Not Without Cause: David Peterson's Fall from Grace*, Harper Collins, Toronto, 1991, p. 163. Gagnon and Rath served as advisors to top members of the Liberal cabinet.

47 The official name for the Billion Dollar Club was the Expenditure Review Committee. It was co-chaired by Jay Kaufman, secretary to the Treasury Board, and Michael Mendelson, deputy secretary to the cabinet. In addition to Robert Mitton, it included such deputies as Michael Decter from Health and Val Gibbons from Community and Social Services. Its original mandate was "to find $1 billion worth of savings in time for the spring 1992 budget and keep [the 1993] deficit below $10 billion." Its targets grew as the government's deficit focus intensified. See Monahan, Patrick, *Storming the Pink Palace: The NDP in Power: A Cautionary Tale*, Lester Publishing, Toronto, 1995, pp, 143–146, 152–153.

48 Clandfield, David, "The NDP and the Corporate Agenda," *Our Schools/Our Selves*, vol 5, no. 1 (#31) (Oct.–Nov. 1993), pp. 12–13.

Chapter Two

The Social Contract Juggernaut

Any uncertainty we might have about the clarity of purpose and commitment of this coalition of NDP leadership and neo-conservative bureaucrats disappears once we see it in the process of bringing the Social Contract into being. Action within government speaks a lot louder than words. Only the most extraordinary long-term internal planning and toughness of collective will could have pulled off such a massive project in so short a time. Nothing of this scale had ever been tried in Canada. Somewhat similar efforts in British Columbia, where hospital employees accepted a 10 percent cut in exchange for more decision-making power and a shorter work week, affected twenty times fewer workers than those within the proposed framework of the Social Contract.[1] The B.C. agreement (a model of good public sector labour relations[2]) took six weeks of formal negotiation "in the context," as Graham Murray points out, "of a royal commission and much other activity extending over nearly eighteen months."[3] In Ontario, according to *The Globe and Mail*, 14 unions, 250 players, seven different bargaining tables, over 8,000 collective agreements, and more than 900,000 employees were expected to be involved,[4] and it was all supposed to happen within three or four months, starting from scratch.

It would happen all right, as we shall see, but not according to any principles of collective bargaining.

Consider the government's line of attack from the moment they announced that a Social Contract was on their agenda. Never once did they back off their original position, although on occasion they fudged some peripheral details. Never once did they significantly retreat from their operating schedule, though near the end they made some minor shifts in time-lines to accommodate the needs of opponents who had already suffered major defeats. For a while, the structure of negotiations was not to their liking, as they were obliged to deal with the Public Services Coalition at a central table longer than they would have wished. But by the time detailed negotiations were underway, Rae's negotiators had imposed a thoroughly divisive structure of different negotiating "tables" for different sectors of the public service. In all of this, the government was facing a coalition representing some 950,000 public sector unionists which had enormous organizing potential. At the same time, and with no exaggeration, Rae and his advisors were looking directly at the destruction of both the union and activist base of the NDP. But such prospects did not deter them. The government had made up its mind, collected its forces; it was ready to act and to act ruthlessly.

The NDP was in an especially favourable situation to take on the Public Services Coalition in this fashion. Rae's inner circle had good communication lines into the union movement, knew its strategies, and could play on its vulnerabilities. It had an informed judgement on how weak the various union responses would be to the government's assault on collective bargaining. There were also, of course, rough patches in the delivery of the Social Contract and sporadic failures of nerve among certain politicians. But none of this really detracts from a picture of clear and ruthless mobilization of a policy initiative.

Everyone involved in developing the Social Contract knew they had a very tough fight ahead of them. Government leaders could realistically have expected the Public Services Coalition (once it got off the ground) to engage in massive public demonstrations of the kind teachers' organizations had used so successfully in 1973 against the Conservative government of William Davis when it tried to impose compulsory arbitration on school board bargaining. The point is that they no longer cared what the impact of such resistance would be. The people in control of government policy had stopped worrying about their policy's political implications for a party of the left. Most of them had never given it much thought in the first place. They were marching to a different drummer. Rae and his allies, I believe, would have stood firm even with 100,000 people yelling at them on Queen's Park lawn or through a general strike held right across the public sector. It may be that such tactics would have peeled away enough NDP support in the legislature to have brought down the government — as few as two additional votes against Bill 48 might have doomed it, had both the Tories and the Liberals remained in opposition to it (not a sure thing, of course).[5] But whatever happened within the NDP caucus, I think Rae himself would have maintained his position and gone over the heads of the protesters and the strikers to "the people of Ontario" and to the "public good" he was representing.

Rae's coalition had faced up to the prospects of electoral defeat. Grateful corporations and sympathetic bureaucrats would be there to ease the transition to private life for those politicians who had proved helpful to them. For the coalition's administrative members, on the other hand, whatever happened at the polls could only bring a continuation of what they had been fighting for these past ten years or more. With Rae gone, most would remain to press the implementation of neoconservative policies now held as a matter of course among the leadership of all three major political parties in the province. As these officials looked into the future, their way seemed clear. Party preference and personal chemistry might doom some individuals among them as a new premier put his stamp on government, but they need fear no ideological shift of the ground on which they stood.[6]

Getting Down To Business

I do not exaggerate the clarity and ruthlessness of the government's Social Contract initiative. Consider the pattern of its responses to opposition throughout the Social Contract process. For weeks before the March 30 announcement of his "unprecedented forum" with public sector unions and his attempted cancellation of bargaining with his provincial employees, Rae had a number of private meetings with senior union leaders from both the private and public sectors. They begged the premier to open up what they understood as a real social contract process — along the lines of what had been attempted in Scandinavia, in Germany, in Great Britain, in Australia — which would (at a minimum) include all public sector employees and unions in the discussion and would insist on as collective and consensual a model as possible. The unions were quite prepared, they assured him, to deal honestly with saving the money necessary for significant deficit reduction. They would face up to getting rid of waste and inefficiencies on the service side of their work — what they judged "restructuring" was all about — and they were open to large-scale personnel cuts through such means as attrition and early retirements. The core of their argument was that the savings the government required could mostly, if not entirely, be achieved within the current framework of collective bargaining and without layoffs, provided they all dealt with this problem collectively. But it needed a year or so to be worked out. In the meantime, something could be negotiated on the issue of costs. Not said, but largely understood, was the acceptance of an immediate wage freeze, even a small rollback. And over a four- or five-year period, the unions could see offering the government "some security on wages," if similar provisions for job security were included. It was a saw-off other social democratic governments had seen as reasonable. Give us a chance, they said, to show you what can be done.

Despite substantial differences that persisted throughout the Social Contract process, this early approach to broad public sector bargaining was shared by all the major union leaders involved. These included Judy Darcy and Syd Ryan of the Canadian Union of Public Employees (CUPE), Fred Upshaw of the Ontario Public Services Employees Union (OPSEU), Gord Wilson and Julie Davis of the Ontario Federation of Labour (OFL), Leo Gerrard of the Steelworkers and Buzz Hargrove of the Canadian Auto Workers (CAW). During this round the province's teachers remained outside the consultation process.

On March 30, Rae answered this plea for a real Social Contract as if these union leaders had never spoken a word to him. By this time he was talking to the entire public sector, including Ontario's teachers. Cease collective bargaining in the public sector, he told them all. Accept a $7 billion cut from a projected $17 billion deficit, a figure they understood at the time was $4 billion in excess of any previous deficit projection. Reflect carefully on the recent Ontario Hydro decision to lay off 4,500 workers — a move the premier called "courageous" — and consider the prospect of 18,000 civil service jobs on the block over the next five years if this $7 billion cut is not made. And be back in front of me and my officials in six days ready to deal with *how* we are going to make the cut. I don't want to hear anything about reducing its size. I don't want your analysis of my current deficit or my long-term economic strategy for wealth creation. I also don't want your suggestions for new revenue sources. Just be there, ready to be creative, about how you're going to take the hit we demand. The next day, he called his remarks "a dialogue."

At the same time as the government was putting its public agenda on the table, it was also opening up private negotiations with different unions in order to play off one against the other. Rae's negotiators were especially interested in separating the relatively low-paid public sector unions from the more "professional" organizations within the public service. Very early on in the process, Syd Ryan, president of the Ontario Division of CUPE, recalls that he sat down with three of Rae's representatives, who assured him that they weren't after unions like CUPE or OPSEU or the SEIU (the Service Employees International Union). It was the teachers they said they wanted, and the professors and the doctors. These were the people with big salaries, Ryan was told, and with fat pension plans to be bled. "Play along with us," they said, "and you and your members will hardly be touched."[7] At the same time, "inside sources" were being quoted in the press as saying "the little guy" in the public sector would be looked after. It was "people who have had a good ride for a long time, like doctors, pharmacists, university professors and teachers" who would be hammered.[8] As it turned out, of course, it was the more powerful professional organizations which managed a better deal in the final days of individual bargaining. But at this stage of the game Rae's offer was credible, and it is to the credit of organizations like CUPE that they didn't buy into it, and turned instead, alongside their professional allies, to coalition building.

By April 4, the Public Services Coalition had emerged, shaky but functioning, and along with the various public service employers (representatives of school boards, hospitals, etc.) it showed up at Rae's April 5 meeting. What, its leaders asked, was the premier's game plan? How did he see these cuts being taken from government workers? It was all open for discussion, replied Michael Decter, the government's new chief negotiator, leaving the situation deliberately vague. But how was it possible, union leaders wondered, to open with such a framework, with no specifics, and expect any conclusion in less than two months? Even with specifics, it seemed impossible. The budget had to come down in May, when everything would be decided. Surely this was a setup. What most of them figured, Geoffrey Scotton reports, was that the talks were "a public relations exercise designed to portray the government as trying to negotiate the impossible. When the talks fail, participants suggest, Queen's Park can then act unilaterally to cut payroll costs by slashing jobs and rolling back wages, telling the public they had no choice." OSSTF was certainly among such sceptics. Rae's "edicts, vague references to social contracts which go counter to the laws of the land, and lack of respect for the invitees," the organization judged, "do not foster a climate of cooperation." Faced with "a mere six days to respond to [this] vague proposal for a new social contract," OSSTF wondered "... if there is a hidden agenda which is driving the haste."[9]

At the same meeting, Decter "refused to deny persistent rumours that Queen's Park [was] developing legislation that would allow the government to act unilaterally should the talks ... fail. 'I have no comment on any alternative. I don't intend these talks to do anything else but succeed,'" he said.[10] *The Go Report*'s Graham Murray reported sources saying "that a management law firm has already been commissioned by the government to prepare draft legislation."[11]

At the end of the process many months later, the union leaders who turned up on April 5 had no reason to change their minds on the "public relations" quality of their talks with the premier's negotiators. The threat of massive layoffs and wage cuts, however, was enough to have them eventually sign what the government was pleased to call "an agreement."

In the days and weeks following April 5, Rae and his government felt the flak. The unions were hopping mad and insisted everything be on the table: deficit analysis, economic strategy, new revenue sources. "We will not choose between cyanide and the chopping block," declared OPSEU's Fred Upshaw. He called the discussions "a deliberate ploy by this government to whip up media hysteria and terrorize our members."[12] CUPE's Syd Ryan focused on the government's lack of honesty and realism in setting out its bargaining scenario. "If Rae had been sincere about negotiating cost-saving, job-saving sectoral 'social contracts,'" Ryan argued, "he would have begun a process months ago and sought the input of unions on how to salvage services and jobs.... This is where there is a parting of the ways with the government and Bob Rae. We would have expected a partnership, instead he's thrown us into the whole mess with employers and anybody else who's shown up."[13] And OSSTF's Liz Barkley, having earlier called on the NDP government "not to abandon its social democratic principles in favour of a destructive neo-conservative agenda," now "declared war" on the province's budget cuts.[14] Ontario teachers, with Barkley providing their most dynamic leadership, vowed to end their isolation from the union movement and plunge into the struggle to help create a broader public sector union coalition — a 950,000 member "united front" against a government seemingly determined to gut Ontario's public services. Barkley went on to remind Rae that she was now facing pressure from those who "wanted to shut the system down" rather than agree to wage rollbacks and imposed concessions. And she went after the premier on his "divide and rule" tactics. "It was very uncreative in there," she said of this first meeting. "They're saying to the country: 'Somebody's overpaid, so let's kill them.' That's not a solution."

This kind of pressure kept up — indeed it increased — during the weeks leading up to the May 19 budget, when the issue had to be resolved.

But Rae and his inner circle didn't budge, though they did expand their rhetoric supporting a government-union "partnership" and "fair share" taxation policies for the corporations. Individual taxes, however, were going up, as Rae's April 13 Throne Speech made clear, and major wage and service cuts were still on the agenda. Public sector unions would be obliged to take the hits he'd promised them. It was all in the aid of new investment for Ontario and the jobs that would follow. The unions were dead wrong, Rae continued to argue, in saying that current unemployment can only increase if the government takes more money out of the economy through increased taxes and fewer services.

The government also engaged in political tactics. When the premier and his advisors reached out to union leaders it was to see what issues and deals could divide them and weaken their capacity to resist. With this in mind, the government brought forward items on which no immediate resolution was possible: for more democracy in the workplace; more open administration and accounting; more labour involvement in such matters as government investment policy, "delayering," and the review of waste and inefficiency; more effective bargaining structures; the development of province-wide seniority lists; a shared examination of different ways to "reskill" workers or to deal with those new jobs that emerged with new technology. In the discussions surrounding such issues, Rae and his people looked for the soft items to offer labour that would appeal to union members through vague hopes for the future, but which advanced nothing concrete in the present. At the same time, of course, they also searched out those more specific items that might effectively pull one or two unions away from the rest. But they were certainly not about to consider, for example, the sort of broad reform of school governance, through confederated boards, that OSSTF proposed as one way of dealing with the money crunch.[15]

More importantly, Rae's negotiators were operating beneath their populist rhetoric of "reskilling" and "restructuring" to achieve a much tougher union-busting scenario. It was a position that Michael Decter did little to hide. The Social Contract process was to be no exercise in democracy. As Decter told *The Globe and Mail*, he liked the Inco experience in Sudbury as a model for avoiding "mass dismissals." Over the last decade, Inco had gotten rid of 30 percent of its workforce, while increasing nickel output by 42 percent. Such a pattern, he said, had been "going on in every big organization: IBM, Ontario Hydro, General Motors." Restructuring blue-collar work had come first and then given way "to an effort to raise output of office workers." It was time for the Province of Ontario to come to grips with "the white collar productivity issue."[16] As a Peat Marwick associate and a former chairman of the board at Shawinigan Energy,[17] Decter understood such patterns on a first-hand basis.

Rae had to budge briefly on the structure of negotiations when the Public Services Coalition insisted that they stay at a central table when they met for formal negotiations on April 19. The premier had planned on dividing them into six or seven negotiating groups, but the unions managed to hang in at the central table for a month, while waiting for budget day. As Liz Barkley explained, "there was no point going in and talking about what cuts are going to be made when you don't know what's coming down in the budget." Barkley and other leaders figured the longer they held out together, the more they might reduce the government's bottom line. With the budget in place, that bottom line would be immovable.

For Rae, the wait was inconvenient, but irrelevant as he made clear in the "mini-budget" he presented on April 23, a few days after negotiations began. There he announced the same level of cuts he had previously promised. A three-year wage and benefit freeze was demanded from provincial employees as well as 12 unpaid days leave per year.[18] That meant a $2 billion saving for the province, which included $635 million to be slashed from that year's total education budget of $9 billion. At the same time, Floyd Laughren announced an additional $4 billion in program cuts, which would remove between 9,000 and 11,000 jobs from the public service.[19] Once again the unions cried foul and threatened major reprisals. From OSSTF, President Barkley warned that an already "wounded" school system would suffer "much larger classes" as well as significant reductions in classroom and individual services for children. Once again the government paid virtually no attention to these voices. At a press conference held three days later, Michael Decter "expressed little worry over the unions' early militancy toward the government's proposals, saying: 'I don't take great concern from initial reaction.'" He then warned the unions that they "could face as many as 40,000 more jobs lost if they refuse[d] the government proposals,"[20] thus bringing the government's estimate of possible layoffs to 51,000. Decter then demanded that the unions be back at the table in three days time ready to deal with these cuts. If they failed to show up, things could get a lot tougher.

With each moment of resistance, the government seemed to harden its resolve.

Facing these hard numbers and even harder negotiating conditions, the unions figured they'd better stall and play for time. They didn't want to show up to talk if that implied that they had caved in to government's demands. At the same time they were genuinely worried about what Decter and his boss had in mind for them if they didn't show up. The teachers' solution was to schedule a meeting of their joint board of governors for May 3. Before returning to the table, they argued, they had to wait for this meeting; their various positions had to be clarified. Other unions made similar excuses. Then, on April 27, the day before Decter's deadline, the Public Services Coalition met for a five-hour meeting. Afterwards, their leaders emerged to say that they all remained committed to the fight. The elementary women teachers' federation (FWTAO)[21] president, Margaret Dempsey, acting as spokesperson, declared that the Coalition was "redefining 'social contract' and ... we are not meeting the government's agenda." The Coalition, she added, would "reconvene next Tuesday to consider a set of counterproposals."[22]

When Rae heard the news he smiled and assured the press that negotiations would be underway at the appointed time, whatever the unions planned. He and his people, the premier indicated, had lots to say to the "employer" groups in the public service. All sorts of ground could be covered. Besides, he didn't find the Coalition's need for time to develop counterproposals "a completely negative thing." Why, it could be seen as "a very welcome development." "If there are other [options] to be put forward," he said, "that's fine. But the fact that people are responding, that there are going to be counterproposals ... I call that negotiation." He wanted them all to know, however, that he was "absolutely" firm in his present focus on deficit reduction and in his plan to cut $2 billion from the public payroll.[23] With his budget cuts safely out in the open and with the threat of legislation in his back pocket, Rae could now afford to wait his opponents out. Whatever they contained, the unions' counterproposals could make no difference one way or the other to the final outcome. The government's confidence remained unshaken. Two days later, Michael Decter was reported to be "encouraged that 95 groups, primarily employer organizations, attended [the first] all-day [negotiating] session aimed a finding ways to cut $2 billion from the pay cheques of 900,000 employees."[24]

Rae's new-found determination was particularly evident in facing the anger of the powerful Canadian Auto Workers union, a key supporter of the Ontario NDP, with the most politically effective organization of all the private sector unions. As the 1993 CAW convention opened on May 4, its president Buzz Hargrove declared that his union would "stand side by side with the Public Sector Unions against any attacks on their rights by the Province of Ontario." There was no conflict of interest, Hargrove argued, between private and public sector unions. "Public sector layoffs will give no comfort to the 3,000 CAW members who will lose their jobs this week when General Motors of Canada shuts down its van plant in Scarborough." On the contrary, his members saw public sector layoffs "as a threat to their ability to find new employment." When Rae came to speak at the convention later that day, Hargrove promised him he would find CAW members forcefully telling him he was "headed in the wrong direction." No employer, he said, even if that employer was an NDP government, "will succeed in driving a wedge" between the CAW and its public sector allies. It was a promise Hargrove kept, and his determination to do so was evident from the very beginning of the Social Contract struggle. For Rae, however, such determination proved simply a spur to raise the ante in his public face-off with the unions. "If you think all the rhetoric in the world is going to blow me off course, brothers and sisters," he declared later that day to the 500 CAW delegates, "you've got another think coming. I have not fought my entire political life to see us achieve political success in this province to see that success thrown away because we do not have the internal discipline, the guts, and the fortitude to say there's a limit to how much we can spend."[25]

On the same day that Rae spoke to the CAW, Michael Decter asked the government to extend the Social Contract bargaining deadline to June 4. In a sense it was a concession to the unions' continuing need to see the government's bottom line before they could get down to any kind of bargaining. But it was also a gesture that came from a clear and strongly held position. Decter and Rae knew that nothing would change in the government's position. But what they finally seem to have grasped was that the unions required an iron fist — in the form of the budget — to be put directly in front of them before they would talk turkey. It was something the government was quite prepared to offer. The rhetoric of worker "involvement" and "empowerment" was always irrelevant — a see-through velvet glove — and the government knew that everyone, including the public and the press, understood this. After the budget bottom line was presented, the government would be happy to stuff its proposals down union throats in little more than two weeks.

The government got its chance right on cue — sooner, in fact. In the week prior to budget day, the Ontario Nurses Association and the Service Employees International Union caved in and turned up at the sectoral bargaining table of Rae's choice. On the day before budget day, the Ontario Public Services Employees Union decided it too would break ranks with

Coalition policy to collectively review the budget before taking action, and turned up at its allotted table. OPSEU was then joined by the Law Officers of the Crown, the Association of Ontario Physicians and Dentists and the Federation of Women Teachers' Associations of Ontario as they formally let the government's chief negotiator know that they too were planning to join his version of negotiations before the budget was brought down.

What would the remainder of the Coalition do now?

The government had held firm: the big spending cuts were still in place. Finance Minister Laughren not only kept his $2 billion cut in wages for Ontario public servants along with $2.8 billion in spending cuts, he also increased individual taxes and fees by $1.84 billion ("the largest tax grab in Ontario history") and sold about $800 million worth of provincial assets. It was everything the unions asked him not to do, although they were pleased that if individual taxes had to be raised, the province had at least hit those in higher income brackets harder than it had the poor. What was particularly disturbing to the Coalition was that in the midst of these cuts and higher taxes, the big corporations had gotten off practically scot free, in spite of the introduction of a "minimum corporate tax." As a *Globe and Mail* business reporter put it, "Mr. Laughren left the business community almost unscathed. The new measures actually reduce the corporate tax bill this fiscal year, and even when the changes are fully implemented, business will be paying only about 5 per cent of the new taxes levied."[26] When Laughren's new "minimum" tax went into operation later in December, William Walker of *The Toronto Star* described it as "a tiny sliver in Bay Street's thumb, not the giant hammer [Rae] promised to bring down in the name of 'tax fairness'.... Some 90 per cent of Ontario's 172,000 corporations will not be affected."[27]

With the corporations off the hook, the government was left with no new money for public works and its attendant job creation. Laughren argued that the unions should be pleased he hadn't cut back on public works. They should be grateful he'd spent as much as $3.9 billion in this area. But as Thomas Walkom commented at the time: "The previous Liberal government [had] spent about $3.4 billion on public works in 1988-89, at the height of the boom. Laughren [was] spending only about $500 million more — not much when compared to a total government budget of about $45 billion."[28] Using the treasurer's own calculations, Walkom estimated that this budget would cost the Ontario economy about 90,000 jobs. With "575,000 Ontarians ... already out of work," Walkom concluded, Laughren's cuts and taxes were "surely the wrong thing to do." The public sector unions couldn't have agreed more, but the pressing question was, What to do with a government hell-bent and determined to do exactly the wrong thing?

What the Coalition decided, finally, was that they did not have the power to face the government down. And, in a few days, all its members turned up at their separate bargaining tables. OSSTF did not go quietly. Liz Barkley promised the premier "the fight of his life."[29] She stressed just how destructive these cuts would prove inside the school system for both teachers and kids, and she declared it "indefensible" that the corporate share of total tax revenue in the province should remain at 7 percent, while personal income tax contributed as much as 33 percent.[30] But Liz Barkley knew, just as the premier knew, that the unions and their teacher allies would have a much tougher time than the government holding their own in this struggle.

Indeed, as the situation stood in reality, it was the teacher federations who were in for the fight of their lives. Not only did they have to deal with a provincial administration looking for blood, but they also had to fend off the trustee representatives of Ontario's local school boards — their "employers" from public, separate and francophone boards who had joined the teachers and the government at the school system's sectoral bargaining table and who couldn't wait to present their own slash and burn agenda. What the trustee representatives immediately proposed was a 22-page package that included "leave without pay, reduced benefits, increases in pupil-teacher ratio, a longer school day to permit more flexible scheduling of classes, fewer days for exams, a reduction in the number of secondary school teachers in positions of paid extra responsibility, and a phasing out of payments at retirement for unused sick leave." They also asked the Ministry to "suspend current class-size limits for special education and Grades 1 and 2, as well as review a number of so-called regulatory inefficiencies, such as using teachers for school administrative duties that could be handled by lower-paid staff." Gene Lewis, the president of the elementary men's federation (OPSTF)[31], called the package "a compilation of every contract strip" his organization had ever seen.[32] It was a made-to-measure situation for Rae's negotiators, who could then present trivial reductions in their demands (like increased flexibility in negotiating unpaid leaves) as quite reasonable in the face of what such mad-dog Reform-minded trustees would be likely to impose. The whole experience, as the current OSSTF president Earl Manners puts it, was "an unmitigated sham" as a negotiation process.

During this period, however, the province began serious manoeuvres designed to provide alternative ways to meet their current demands and to help frame future cost-cutting exercises. Rae's negotiators opened up proposals — surprisingly contentious as it turned out — to use pension plan savings as one way to absorb the cuts in education. At the same time, the government closed down its earlier rhetoric concerning waste reduction as a key avenue to reducing its target cuts. "Only one-third of any savings found through the elimination of waste," Michael Decter now declared, "would be credited to the $2 billion cost-cutting goal."[33]

While the province was engaged in these manoeuvres, the Public Services Coalition was still attempting to stall discussions at the sectoral tables and was pressing hard for more central table negotiations. At this level, the unions wanted "'realistic' incentives for early retirement and enhanced severance packages, along with extended leave-of-absence policies." They wanted "joint worker/employee committees on the elimination of wasteful spending and a guarantee that workers facing layoffs will get an alternative job offer 'within a reasonable geographic area' and be ensured previous wages and benefits would be maintained without interruption." They pushed for "training programs to assist workers who must move to a new job requiring different skills and for province-wide benefit plans for all public-sector workers with dental, group life insurance, extended health care and long term disability." And they asked for legislation "to ensure they get access to all government financial records, accounting journals and contract tender bids" and "to protect the jobs of whistle-blowers who identify wasteful government spending."[34] These points, the Coalition figured, made up only a minimum package, considering the hits they all were about to take.

For the province, however, there was to be no consideration of a central package whatsoever. Now that it had its own structure of sectoral tables on the go — with its capacity to fragment union initiatives and to pit one union against another — it did not intend to move from it. And as the government approached its new deadline of June 4, it turned the screws again. It posted notices saying it was preparing to lay off up to 3,794 employees at the end of the year. Laughren had announced the cuts in April, but said then that "most of the jobs would be lost through attrition or early retirement." The notices got the real message across. OPSEU president Fred Upshaw called the posting "a gun to our heads" in the Social Contract talks. The government called it a "flexibility" move, allowing them to cut staff "should other cost-cutting measures fail."[35] Then on May 31 Rae announced he would not extend the negotiating deadline beyond 6 p.m. on June 4, and he repeated his assertion that he would not scale back his plan to slash the province's payroll costs. And for the first time, he began to hint that the legislation card he always held was soon be be played.[36] If the talks were not concluded by June 4, the premier promised, he'd "take action before the Legislature rises for the summer on June 24."[37]

By this point, the government judged it had taken the measure of the Public Services Coalition. The wedge it had continued to drive between the coalition's poorer-paid members and those from better-off professional associations was still in place, and it had managed to keep coalition leaders thoroughly off balance and asking "Should we give in now or wait for something worse?" — with "something worse" appearing to loom larger and larger. As June 4 came into view, the government figured, as most people did, that the Coalition was about to fold, and another small turn of the screw was in order. On

June 1 "government sources" were reporting the existence of legislation to implement the Social Contract cuts through straight expenditure reduction. There would be no enforced rollbacks, they predicted, just the strong possibility of "widespread layoffs,"[38] the unions' worst case scenario.

On June 2 came the sweetener. Michael Decter announced he had found an extra $500 million from projected pension plan savings from the Social Contract, which could be subtracted from its $2 billion in payroll cuts. This extra money would also help finance a $100 million a year "job security fund," which would be used to "top up unemployment insurance benefits for laid-off workers for one year or to pay for extensions to the notice periods given to workers who are going to be laid off." As it turned out, the fund proved mostly a paper promise as did an additional guarantee to offer full-time laid-off workers other jobs "where suitable vacancies exist." But at the time it appeared to be a genuine last-minute sweetener, made sweeter by the government's hard-nosed attitude to negotiations before offering it. Only the teachers, who were most affected by the proposal — it appeared to "hijack" about two-thirds of their pension savings for non-educational reductions[39] — spoke out immediately against it. They were outraged by this "intrusion" into their "pension-partnership fund," said Horst Schweinbenz, president of the Ontario Teachers Federation. It would "not be tolerated." But who else among their allies shared this view? The government calculated they would be few and far between. It had, after all, taken this moment to underline its earlier commitment to limit wage rollbacks to those earning more than $30,000 (which turned out to be less than reliable[40]) as well as its promise to allow other public sector unions to share in the teachers' privilege of becoming joint-trustees for their own pension plans.[41]

On June 3, Finance Minister Floyd Laughren turned up the heat again. He tabled his budget estimates, formally committing the government to a $2 billion reduction from the public sector, and thereby letting the unions know the government was still "playing hardball" with 24 hours to go to its imposed deadline. Without an agreement, the government could get a lot meaner.[42]

It was at this point that the government got its first genuine surprise in its Social Contract manoeuvring.

Rae's negotiators had badly miscalculated when they made their decision to target pension plan surpluses. Once Coalition members had a moment to think about this proposal, they responded angrily. They saw that this was a path fraught with danger. God knows, they thought, what the next move would be. Besides, as a Hydro activist reminded the Coalition, pension-partnerships were precious institutions for the future; Ontario's teachers had to be supported in maintaining theirs.[43] Even OPSEU's Fred Upshaw, the most sympathetic of the major union leaders to the Rae government, declared that he, too, "could not tolerate the government's raiding members' pension plans."[44] (It would eventually mean, his accountants had told him, higher individual pension contributions.[45]) Later that night, the Public Services Coalition finally found the courage to say No in a way that seemed to suggest their members meant it. They rejected Decter's sweetener and walked out of negotiations en masse. The government was now faced with what appeared to be an unequivocal act of defiance. Rae was reported to be "furious."[46]

It was, unfortunately, simply a short moment of defiance with little long-term strategy attached.

The walkout really began almost unnoticed a few days earlier when the Service Employees International Union joined the Amalgamated Transit Union and the Ontario Coalition for Better Day Care in a refusal to return to the talks. The cuts were so extreme, they said, they couldn't even consider taking them back to their membership. Within a couple of days, they were joined by three more unions, including the Ontario Confederation of University Faculty Associations, which claimed that "the plan being put forward would produce massive losses in the quality of post-secondary educational services at a time when such services are needed more than ever."[47] But it was the highly charged Coalition meeting on June 3 that really turned the tables. The government's demands were simply impossible to meet. A mass walkout was a very hard decision to make — a lot of very complex and difficult manoeuvring was required in an organization which had seen little serious planning for large-scale resistance and a good deal of distrust from previous contacts — but it was the only decision possible at the time. Though they had no other strategy to put forward, union leaders could not be seen to knuckle under at this point. Because of their vulnerability on the key issue of job security, they had to keep this struggle going. The June 3 walkout made that clear to the Rae government, as it had not been clear before.

Thomas Walkom reports that the cabinet was divided in its reaction and unsure of its strategy. Rae and Laughren, he says, were leaning towards a soft solution: letting the cuts happen through attrition, early retirement, voluntary leaves and short-term layoffs. (It was a solution they knew was possible in financial terms, but it would certainly have undercut any larger-scale "restructuring" initiatives). Lankin, it seems, was "for some kind of wage freeze in exchange for job security." A third position, with even less support, was pushed by Evelyn Gigantes. She said the government had "to legislate controls." The main enemy, as she saw it, was the unions' "vested interests." Walkom's story is that the NDP caucus, having been led by the nose for almost three years, finally decided the issue. At its June 10 meeting, it seems, the caucus turned into "a dance of scorpions," as one source reported it. Its members called loudly for union blood and ended up making Gigantes' minority view a strong majority position. They insisted, says Walkom, on a very tough bill, which included the infamous "fail safe" provision allowing "the government to open up and roll back public sector union contracts."[48]

Given the history of the Social Contract we have seen so far, I am somewhat sceptical of this story. Or at least about its implications. It may be that this was, indeed, a moment in which Rae and Laughren lost their nerve, and their bureaucratic allies had to rely on the caucus members they had been priming over the last few months. But I think it is just as probable that Rae and Laughren knew what would happen when cabinet split on their response to this new-found union militancy. Aided by Treasury officials, these two had been hammering the caucus on the twinned issues of an uncontrolled deficit and a "fair-share" public service wage hit for a long time. They ought to have been able to take its pulse on these questions. It made a good deal of strategic sense for them to now come on as doves, somewhat above the fray, forced by popular demand to carry out their original position. When some of their remaining union friends continued to complain about the harshness of the Social Contract, they could wring their hands in private about "these caucus crazies." Having the decision come from caucus also made life easier for Rae and Laughren inside the party and among the more progressive organizations in Ontario. The decision seemed so much more democratic, however long the Social Contract legislation had waited in Rae's back pocket.

Hammering Home "A Deal"

Whatever was actually going on beneath this "dance of scorpions", one thing is clear: Rae and Laughren's dove-like demeanour did not last long, and they were soon spearheading the legislative assault on collective bargaining in the Ontario public service. Moderates like Frances Lankin, Bud Wildman and Howard Hampton, who wanted to soften the legislation's "fail safe" provisions,[49] were simply rolled over. Four days after the fateful caucus meeting, on June 14, Rae and Laughren introduced Bill 48 to the legislature. It was law by July 7.

At the same time, Rae continued to try to make "a deal" with the unions — a move that was just as important to long-term government strategy as the ruthless imposition of Bill 48. The day after the coalition walkout, he mused to the press that "these things are never over," and promptly went back to his office to work on enticing coalition members to meet privately with himself and his advisors. Within days he had opened up a series of one-on-one meetings with the major players in the Coalition.[50] At the same time his ministers "worked the phones [as did the premier himself] explaining the merits of the deal and the more painful alternatives." Boasting of rank-and-file union support, Rae took special pains to "sound out his caucus to ensure their backing" for tough action (not the approach one would expect of a passive premier among the "scorpions") while "working through the media to get his message out" to public sector unionists, over the heads of their leaders. The contract was "a good deal," he told them. It had been "foolishly rejected.... It should be reconsidered."[51]

As Rae's June 14 deadline for legislation approached, however, these leaders remained unconvinced. His private meetings had gotten him nowhere. OK, said Rae, with time running out, I'll do you a favour: I won't hit you any harder than our final offer prior to your walkout. I'll include the sweeteners, but nothing else, mind you. The $2 billion target will stand. And I'll give you one more chance to negotiate the details on how we do it, with a deadline of August 1. So here's the choice you've got: if you don't sign by August 1, "fail safe" will stand. (Fail safe was a big stick: it imposed an automatic wage freeze for three years; no COLA (cost of living allowance), merit increments or upgrading increases were allowed; employers would be permitted to reopen collective agreements to lay off their workers "for up to 12 days a year, require them to take unpaid leave or refuse to pay them for vacations or statutory holidays;" and if they were still short of their target, they could fire their workers.) If you do sign, however, the premier said, you'll be getting a bonus of 20 per cent reduction in the cuts we've demanded so far (mostly achieved through savings from worker and teacher pension funds — Decter's sweetener), which Tom Walkom calculated at $420 a head.[52] It meant, for example, "$110 million less cut from schools and $120 million less from the health sector."[53] This was a pretty big carrot for a government that said it was desperate for ready cash and that every nickel counted.

At this point, you may well ask "What is going on here?"

On the surface, Rae's intense desire for more "negotiations" didn't make much sense. Why, if he so clearly intended to impose Bill 48 (which really only frames local bargaining for most of the public sector) was he so intent on getting a negotiated deal of sorts at the provincial level? Why not let local public employers handle all the problems of implementation? Such negotiations wouldn't change the bill's content in any fundamental way, and they involved public relations hassles the premier didn't need. Most of the press corps were not with him on these manoeuvres; even the most jaded among them smelled far too much hypocrisy. It also wouldn't make the unions less mad at him, if somehow he manipulated them into signing on the dotted line — perhaps with an additional sweetener or two. It had the possibility, in fact, of making them a lot madder by rubbing salt in their wounds, and that's largely, it seems, how it turned out. Yet, as Thomas Walkom pointed out, the government wanted an "agreement so badly that it changed the definition of the word," allowing the Finance Minister (through Bill 48) "to declare an agreement even if no one else agreed."[54] Why go to all this trouble?

My answer comes from what we saw of Rae's earlier behaviour. This particular push for "negotiation," it seems to me, sprang from the fact that Rae's inner circle was marching to a very different drummer than any of us had expected. As I argued earlier, this was a thoroughly "neo-conservative" drummer, for whom there could be no real "negotiation" with labour. The premier's actions involved a far more brutal understanding of government than we normally associate with social democrats. What Rae and company were looking for in their "negotiated settlement" was a way to break public service unionism at a much deeper level than the imposition of legislation would involve. It was the exact opposite of what the words meant to ordinary listeners. The government wanted unionists' complicity in their own oppression. Nothing is more demoralizing for labour than such complicity, not only for future organizing but also for the daily defence of the contract they already hold. There isn't a management negotiator alive who doesn't know this.

But perhaps equally important for this government, there was also a language of agreement they wanted nailed down for the future. If the unions could be persuaded to formally accept a bargaining framework and legislation which undercut their right to struggle for better wages and power on the job, such an agreement could turn out to be a very effective government weapon in years to come. Right now, it would be understood as just words on paper, hypocritically forced on the unions by a hostile government under circumstances beyond union control. In the future, however, these circumstances could be expected to blur, while the written words would remain — to be writ large in the legislature, the media and in the public mind. "What are the unions complaining about?" it will be said when another version of the Social Contract comes down the track. "They've already agreed to this sort of arrangement. They have no right to ask us to turn back to an older and less efficient form of collective bargaining. It's not fair." And, in this way, the label "bad-faith bargainers" can then be added by future governments to the "selfish" and "greedy" labels they already apply to their union opponents. It will be a powerful label, not only among the general public but also among the union rank-and-file. It is hard to argue against the written word, as Education Minister Dave Cooke grasped in dealing with the province's teachers. A year after the Social Contract's imposition, Cooke wrote to OSSTF member David Bowers, who had complained of the difficulty teachers faced in negotiating increments with their local boards: "This element of the Framework Agreement was negotiated on your behalf by members of the teachers' Federation. I encourage you to discuss the rationale for their position on this issue with members of your bargaining unit."[55]

From the beginning of the Social Contract process, Rae and his negotiators were especially careful to use the language of "consultation," "involvement," "negotiation" and "agreement," even though it was always evident to onlookers that such language was never appropriate. Indeed, its inappropriateness is perhaps one of the key reasons individual members of the press stayed largely sympathetic to the unions, despite what their bosses might be saying on the editorial page. To anyone who listened, the government appeared to be stating the most extraordinary bald-faced lies. The "Social Contract" itself had no relationship whatsoever to "social contracts" worked out in other industrial countries, nor did it connect to any older notion of what that term might mean (say, for Rousseau). Until Bob Rae started using the term, a social contract always implied some genuine agreement among the parties concerned. His version had it entirely imposed, even though he continued to say that "this was co-operation not confrontation."[56] The premier's use of the language of democracy and empowerment became so incongruous that someone like OSSTF's Earl Manners found he routinely equated it with its opposite — the lack of freedom and power associated throughout the world "with corporate downsizing, rationalization and restructuring."[57] He consciously acted as if it were some form of Orwellian "newspeak." Manners' approach turned out to be sound practice for Bill 48, where, as we noted above, "an agreement" was defined to be what Floyd Laughren said it was. Union signatures would not even be required for an agreement, however much the government may have pushed for them.[58]

For someone trying to get a grasp of government policy, the experience of Rae's public statements on the Social Contract often seemed surrealistic. Here's a routine example of the premier's rhetoric: "I want to emphasize at the outset that a social contract is both a process and a product. It is a dialogue. It is not unilateral. It is a negotiated process that respects collective bargaining and recognizes the diversity of workplaces and the needs of workers."[59] What was one to make of such a statement, when every word of it was so obviously untrue? Where, asked the unions, were these words coming from? They seemed to make no sense and were contrary to common sense. How was such a person to be reached by reason or even through experience? How was it possible to change his mind?

The answer, obviously, was that such a person could not be reached. Nobody could change his mind. And with that answer comes despair for many people and a deeper sense of their own powerlessness. This is how this language functions. It is about what in the past we have often called "the big lie" — a mass fantasy created by the powerful, which cuts people off from any kind of public truth and isolates those who would oppose the government. In this society, we tend to associate such a lie with entertainment and advertising — "coke is the real thing" — while we are not so ready for its use by politicians. At a government level, big lies are still mostly reserved for German fascists and Soviet dictators who made their deceptions live through fear and violence. They are not for decent Canadians. We always knew, for example, that Brian Mulroney lied through his teeth to us, but somehow we also knew he didn't really expect us to believe him. He was only a huckster doing his job for Corporate Canada, he seemed to say to us, and we shouldn't take him too seriously, however destructive his policies. Would we buy a used car from him? Of course not, as Mulroney himself seemed to understand perfectly well, though he may have wished it otherwise. Rae, on the other hand, appeared as a much more committed believer in such lies and in the necessity of telling them. It made him potentially a far more dangerous politician than "Lyin' Brian." As CUPE's Syd Ryan put it, the premier's eventual success in breaking the unions was "a triumph of fear."[60]

With the approach of the provincial election, Rae's claims for the Social Contract became even more extravagant. It must be seen as a triumph, he told us, that would be communicated to Ontarians not only in the language of financial responsibility and worker democracy, but also (returning to his original mandate) in the old language of love. This time it would be associated with the "caring" corporation. As 1994 came to a close, the premier took two *Globe and Mail* reporters into his confidence to share his deeper feelings on the meaning of his government's Social Contract and expenditure reduction program. It was, he said, "an extension" of his "sense of compassion," which now had to be made clear to the people. "At the beginning [of my government]," he continued, "... I had to give speeches on the deficit. I had to give speeches reminding people of some of these basics in getting the economy back to work. Now what I feel the need to do is to express as clearly as I possibly can how we combine this respect for having an economy that works well ... with the question of how we can find these resources within ourselves to look beyond our immediate self-interest as human beings and as a society. That is what the next mandate is going to be about."[61] There is no irony available to match such integrated falsehood. All that was left for his opponents was a simple decision to fight or to surrender.

In mid-June of 1993, such a choice was not quite so clear, as the Ontario NDP gathered at Gananoque, a small tourist town in eastern Ontario, for its Provincial Council meeting. Perhaps, thought the Public Services Coalition (hoping against hope), the NDP rank-and-file would finally send a serious message to cabinet attacking the Social Contract and insisting that the party get back to its old ideals. There wasn't a chance. Rae's organizers correctly judged that the coalition didn't have the energy to effectively lobby delegates or to mobilize a serious demonstration so far from a major population centre. (No more than 2,000 people showed up, most of them local teachers and OPSEU members.) Inside the convention hall, an alliance between the conservative wing of the private sector unions and the premier's party machine wiped the floor with his opponents. It stifled any possibility of a leadership review and persuaded the Ontario Federation of Labour to back a motion which demanded only generalities of the government — to respect free collective bargaining and signed collective agreements and to emphasize jobs and job security — and avoided all specifics, like withdrawing Bill 48.

Now Rae had all the room he needed to manoeuvre rhetorically. He'd always defended the Social Contract, however falsely, in terms of jobs saved and the preservation of collective bargaining. When the motion passed almost unanimously and the premier approached the podium to give his scheduled address, he was treated to a wild standing ovation by most of the 200-plus delegates attending the convention. Don't worry about that motion, they were telling him, it's just public relations. When he had finished his speech attacking "the luxury of holding to positions of abstract principle" and offering a tough defence of deficit reduction and wage rollbacks as the political wave of the future, his standing ovation was even longer and wilder than before. He had also been interrupted seventeen times by applause and by four additional standing ovations.[62] The party had spoken, as its soon-to-resign president Julie Davis put it. It was Rae's to do with as he wished.

After Gananoque, the public sector unions — with CUPE as a major exception[63] — drifted back to their various bargaining tables, as Rae knew they would. The walkout was over. OPSEU had already given notice that it would be back and was just waiting — in deference to its coalition allies — for the NDP's Provincial Council formalities to be wound up.[64] The others would have to follow once Bill 48 officially became law on July 7. On July 15, Ontario's six health-care unions became the first big group to sign an agreement,[65] and this put increasing pressure on organizations like OSSTF to get into the process to save what they could. A few days later, two big CUPE locals broke ranks with their parent organization to make a deal[66] and, even more important for OSSTF, the 34,000-member English Catholic Teachers' Association decided to go back to the table.

"We're a bit shocked, to be truthful," said Liz Barkley, when informed of the Catholic teachers' decision. "It puts us in a difficulty we hadn't anticipated, no question." The rest of the teacher organizations, she added, would now have to decide by the end of the week if they too would return to the table. But she knew then it was all over. "I'll tell you, if we do [return]," she declared with as much defiance as she could muster, "it will be yelling and screaming."[67] A day later, government negotiators were telling the press there was a "new optimism in the air" and that they already "had in hand agreements and tentative deals for about 600,000 of the 950,000 Ontarians employed in public sector jobs."[68] And on the day that followed all five of Ontario's teacher unions met for a five-hour closed-door meeting and emerged with the announcement that they, too, would be returning to the Social Contract talks.[69]

For OSSTF, this return was not only to salvage what they could for teachers, but also to make certain that the non-teaching employees OSSTF had organized pushed for a better deal than some of their allies were about to accept.[70] Relatively speaking, this salvaging exercise for both teachers and non-teaching employees went better than OSSTF could have expected. Some especially damaging employer demands were pushed back. On the whole, however, OSSTF's losses were dramatic (as were those of the Public Services Coalition as a whole), and no number of small victories in later fights should obscure this.

OSSTF and its allies had lost and lost badly. Why?

There are many threads to such an explanation. I want to focus on two of them: the collapse of the Ontario NDP, which should have been supporting the province's public sector unions, and the policy failure within OSSTF (and other teacher unions) which prevented an effective campaign against the Rae government

What Happened To The NDP?

At the conclusion of the NDP Provincial Council meeting at Gananoque, Liz Barkley declared that its meetings had been "stacked" with Rae loyalists and "did not reflect the feelings of rank-and-file New Democrats."[71] This should not come as any surprise. The feelings of NDP members have been largely unrepresented in the vast majority of party forums and policy formulations for some time now. Party conventions are routinely stacked, and rank-and-file views are rarely given credence within them. What active party members actually think and feel about most political issues is largely to be found in the policy statements of fragmented single-issue movements and organizations. There is no broad-based organization to speak for them, either inside or outside the party. By the time of its 1990 election victory, the Ontario NDP had become a party representing almost no one but those who ran it.

Consider the 1990 NDP platform on which its victory was crafted. As the campaign was initially conceived, there was to be no platform at all. As David Reville, a key NDP strategist, has laid it out, the campaign was to focus entirely on the image of "fat cat" Liberals who didn't listen to regular folks like the NDP did. "The strategy didn't visit the platform part, really," said Reville. "Ultimately, we did not decide on an issue campaign."[72] Reville and David Agnew had been listening to the psychographic analysis of Peter Donegan, a Toronto market researcher who taught his corporate clients how to peddle their products by exploiting consumers' subconscious thoughts. Donegan was reported to be "fascinated by the challenge of applying [his] principles to a political product."[73] For two weeks, the campaign followed his advice to the letter: attack Peterson and "his rich developer cronies" as greedy and power-hungry. "Do not present options."

Then, as Gagnon and Rath describe it, on the third week, "NDP pollster David Gotthilf found the party's support was 'flat-lining' at about 32 percent of decided voters." It was four days before the leaders' debate, with NDP strategists now feeling the heat. Finally, they decided "they could no longer get away with adhering strictly to their attack strategy. Rae would have to reveal a platform or risk being clobbered in the debate for failing to take a constructive stand on any issues.... The challenge became how to get a $4.4 billion platform out, far larger than the Liberal's $200 million promises, without taking away from the main message [that the Liberals were bad guys]." They decided "'to do it all at once in a friendly crowd on a Sunday,' as David Reville explained. That would prevent careful scrutiny of the platform by either the Liberals or the media before the debate. Rae could refer to the platform without being questioned on it in detail. 'There was no story there, because how are you going to cover anything that big?' said Reville. 'But it allowed us to say, "Hey, you want to know what the platform is, here it is..."' The NDP plan succeeded so well that the policies in [its] *Agenda for People* would not be thoroughly analyzed by the media for most of the campaign."[74] Even at the end of the campaign, when the NDP was coming on as a serious contender, such analysis was sporadic.

(It was an election strategy the NDP repeated in 1995. This time, as *The Globe and Mail* reported, the party platform was released on a Saturday, "rather than announcing it with great fanfare on a weekday as the other parties have done, when they would have received more extensive news coverage." Bob Rae explained his avoidance of specific promises in the campaign by saying that "voters are more interested in the values and priorities of political parties than in detailed policy announcements." He stressed his party's "compassion" for those who need "assistance and partnership and solidarity with the rest of our society."[75])

Alongside this cynical and manipulative approach to elections (mirrored in the development of riding associations as nothing more than election machines), we have also seen a remarkable growth in the power of neo-conservative/neo-liberal thought within the NDP, and particularly in its upper echelons. It is an ideology deeply hostile to what elections are supposed to be about: pressing governments to take charge of the public good. Patricia Best of *The Globe and Mail* calls its advocates "neo-socialists," and among the most important she includes the two men Bob Rae brought in to negotiate his Social Contract: Michael Decter and Peter Warrian.

Caught up with the demands of a global economy and hostile to Canadian nationalism, Best's neo-socialists have focused on taking care of business, reducing the deficit, downsizing government services (particularly those intended for welfare recipients) and undercutting an "unrealistic" union mentality within the NDP. These views are then combined with the kind of "compassionate" rhetoric we have just heard from Bob Rae. As the chief executive of the C.D. Howe Institute put it in describing John Richards, the NDP's leading neo-socialist theoretician: "his is market economics with a heart."[76] How much "heart," of course, remains the question. It was Richards, Best reminds us, who convinced Saskatchewan premier Roy Romanow that his "finance-department officials — perceived as Tories — were not going far enough in tackling the deficit. Since then, the Saskatchewan [NDP] has blazed a trail of fiscal renovation, culminating in a budget last February [1993] that brought the province's deficit to the lowest level per capita in the country." Michael Decter, certainly, is impressed with Richards' hard-nosed approach to government finance. This is a man, Decter says, who hasn't stopped thinking, "unlike too many other Canadians on the left who've been trapped in denial for 15 years or so." Thankfully, he adds, others "have gone a shorter way. Look at Bob Rae in the last 36 months. There's someone who's come to terms with globalization and some of the things Canada has to face." When the federal NDP followed its debacle in the last election with a national conference on policy renewal, John Richards and his neo-socialist colleagues were given a central place in the debate.

Within the NDP, it had now become respectable to suggest an end to universal social programs, a federal sales tax on food, deep cuts in government spending and a severing of the link between the NDP and the labour movement.[77] It hardly seems possible that not more than a few years ago, such views were regarded in the NDP as the preserve of the right, even the far right, however many "compassionate" qualifiers might be added.

This shift to the right within the NDP did not, however, come overnight. In many ways, it was there in embryo from the very beginnings of the party, as it was within all social democratic parties of the West. Built on the sand of capitalist social relations, particularly on the right to private control of production, the "human face" of these parties crumbled as capitalism found a way to further mechanize and rationalize production on a global scale. In the wake of such change, social democratic leaders felt obliged to follow the logic of their most basic assumption: that capitalism was here to stay and that while its forms may shift from one historical moment to another, capitalism itself was inviolable. Workers, communities, minorities, women, native people, the poor — all those who pay the price for capitalist profit — would thus have to bite the bullet a little harder now. And it was the job of social democrats to persuade them to do so.

In Ontario, the NDP shift to the right has been especially evident over the last twenty years or so, and it comes within two broad categories: the crushing of democratic process within the party (particularly when this process has been tied to policy dissent) and the gradual ideological move to the right (meaning a more full-blown acceptance of capitalist relationships at the core of the society).

Let's take the decline of party democracy first.

Rae's control over the party, reflected in his Gananoque triumph, did not come out of thin air. It was built on the efforts of other party leaders for a similar level of control, and particularly on the efforts of Stephen Lewis, the leader of the provincial party from 1970 to 1981. It was Lewis' job — pressed by the leaders of Ontario's international unions — to deal with the most serious democratic push the provincial NDP had experienced in decades. This came from the Waffle movement, a network of NDP activists centred in Ontario, who insisted on a locally developed industrial strategy for the province and for the country as a whole. Lewis saw to it that the Wafflers — among them the most dynamic of the party's intellectuals — were finally expelled from the provincial organization in 1972. With their expulsion, the NDP leader ushered in a long period of passionate do-good speeches, in which social work banalities passed for hard thinking about the economy and its impact on society. Fourteen years later, his successors crushed a much weaker "Campaign for an Activist Party," which emphasized the need for a more democratic and community-based process within the NDP. By 1990, George Ehring and Wayne Roberts write, this kind of suppression "had led to the virtual extinction of organized dissent within the NDP and the self-imposed exile of many of its left-wing members out of the party and into the social movements..."[78]

Purging dissidents, however, made up only one side of the control agenda. It was equally important for NDP leaders to control the machinery of the party, particularly its executive. As Ehring and Roberts describe the process, "the [Ontario NDP] executive is made up of people hand-picked by the party establishment and put on a 'slate,' which is then offered to convention delegates for election. Rarely does someone not on the slate get elected; even running 'against the slate' is frowned upon as a defiance of the delicate equilibrium worked out by the party brass. Members of the executive thus owe their election and their loyalty to the party leadership and feel accountable to it, not to the people they are supposed to represent." Ehring and Roberts also note that within the party machinery itself, work is centralized in the hands of a few "trusted people," who are pushed "to the limit to get things done. They get so buried in detail they lose their [own] critical capacity," as well as their ability to stay open to the perspective of others. A genuine self-evaluation of their performance becomes next to impossible to carry out. "Like its intolerance of dissent, the party engages in continuing rounds of self-congratulation even in the face of major setbacks."[79] Once in government, as we have seen, this propensity for centralization and bureaucratization grew exponentially.

The democratic functioning of the Ontario NDP has also been deeply weakened, Ehring and Roberts argue, by the party leadership's insistence on keeping the province's social movements at arm's length. When it first emerged, the CCF was quite explicitly a coalition of farmers, workers and socialists. But in the period after World War II, the influence of the Communist Party in building coalitions turned social democrats away from this form of political organizing. With the anti-war movement in the late sixties, however, coalitions gained "a new legitimacy," and the Ontario NDP (particularly in contending with the New Left policies of the Waffle) had to learn to deal with them. But the distrust of coalition radicalism remained. By the 1980s, as Ehring and Roberts describe it, the political coalitions then emerging were left "chant[ing] outside the Ontario legislature, [while] the NDP played its own tune inside. The NDP in the House was rarely a home for the coalitions, though their politics were often brother and sister…." As a result, the coalitions learned, in turn, to distrust the NDP. To these activists, the party seemed prepared only "to scavenge them for photo opportunities … [while] dumping them when party leaders [thought] an issue [had become] a political liability." Trying to develop "a special relationship" with the NDP no longer seemed worth the effort. With the party's victory of 1990, that position seemed entirely borne out. On coming to office, Rae made certain, as we have noted, that Ontario's social movements would be cut off from any serious influence on government policy.

A final note on party democracy: the Ontario NDP has also abandoned all programs to educate its general membership or its youth in the knowledge necessary to play a activist role within the organization or in society. Such knowledge now has to be won outside the framework of the NDP. The only thing the party teaches is the mechanics of electioneering.

The other side of its move to the right — through the party's basic ideology and program — is more evident in contradiction than in a series of clear moves over time towards a pro-business position. The NDP had to come to power first before such a perspective could come to light. Prior to 1990, beyond the Keynesian consensus on a little more money going into workers' pockets from corporate profits and into government coffers through corporate taxes, a careful reader of the policies of the Ontario NDP would not know whether the party stood for centralization or democratization in government and whether it believed in controlling its citizens through state services or freeing them and enriching their lives. All these positions were represented. Out of power the party seemed prepared to be many things to many people. It would take a year or so of Bob Rae's government before its future became evident: centralization and control would be the order of the day. But it is also important to note, as Ehring and Roberts make clear, that the party was slowly moving away from its Keynesian perspectives as well.

As early as the 1975 election, Stephen Lewis was supporting the idea of reduced government expenditures — "Even I say they have gone too far." — and his party platform promised cuts. "The effect of this," say Ehring and Roberts, "was to lessen pressure on the government to maintain or expand programs; it also helped to bolster the Conservatives' image as effective managers." Lewis had been softened up for such a perspective by the Ontario Tory government's commission to review government spending, co-chaired by Maxwell Henderson and Darcy McKeough. It called for $1.3 billion in cuts for 1976 and $2.1 billion for 1977. McKeough, who was Ontario Treasurer at the time, then announced he would "freeze government programs, cut back on grants to municipalities, charge user fees for some government programs, and reject future shared-cost programs with Ottawa. Direct government employment was cut by 5,000 people over the next five years.... These changes," say Ehring and Roberts, "spelled the end of Ontario government programs to promote social equality, and prepared people to expect less and less from government. They were the blueprint for the next decade of government cutbacks and marked the beginnings of neo-conservatism." Lewis didn't raise a finger to stop them.[80]

Lewis was also unconcerned with the bureaucratic restructuring necessary to achieve such widespread cutbacks. This restructuring had been carried out by the province's Committee on Government Productivity (COGP) from 1969 to 1971, and it went very deep. McKeough judged it was "probably the most revolutionary reorganization of any government anywhere in Canada at any period of history." Ehring and Roberts comment that "the COGP put the stamp of the corporate managerial elite on the bureaucracy, modelling its labour relations after the private sector, filling it with professional technocrats, and sustaining it with an elaborate system of boards and commissions. With its emphasis on 'productivity,' the COGP ended a decade of enormous government expansion in the 1960s — not just in regard to services provided by government, but also by the establishment of the community college system, additional hospitals, educational television, the Ontario Science Centre and other government programs." When the time came for legislation to implement the recommendations of the COGP, the NDP voted for it. "Th[is] bill," said Stephen Lewis, "doesn't carry with it a sufficient relevance in public terms to get excited enough to oppose it."[81] As is evident, history has not been kind to Lewis' judgement. In many respects, the job Bob Rae finally found for himself has been to fine-tune Darcy McKeough's achievement for the 1990s.

When we combine the growth of centralized power within the NDP, Rae's centralizing alliance with neo-conservative bureaucrats within government, and the substantial ideological drift to the right we have seen in the party's public relations, the premier's capacity to divorce government policy from party policy (even when clearly stated) is no mystery. By the time he came to office, it had become a "leader's decision" (in consultation with his inner circle) to become "everybody's premier" and to represent "all Ontarians" — the code for supporting a business agenda. It was in his hands to reverse such old NDP standbys as its opposition to casinos and Sunday shopping or its support of public auto insurance and the right to collective bargaining. There were no avenues left for serious grass-roots resistance to such moves or even for serious discussion. As a real policy-making body, the party had died. Thus Rae's dismissal of well-established party policies — "that was then, this is now" — went directly to the media. There was no one else he had to talk to first.

He did discuss such questions, of course, with party insiders, with his cabinet and, to a lesser extent, his caucus. But the point is, he didn't have to, and everyone in these circles eventually understood this. With his bureaucratic/inner-circle alliance, Rae did not, in any fundamental way, need party help in getting things done or in determining what should be done in the first place. If the party's leaders or its elected politicians contributed to the alliance's agenda, they would be praised and supported, if they did not, they would be gone, banished to the back benches or out on the street. He wanted their allegiance, of course — Rae never liked the "optics" of dissent — and he took considerable time and effort to hold their allegiance, to persuade the party hierarchy and NDP MPPs of the soundness of his policies. But this was almost entirely an effort in public relations, not in genuine policy development. In this effort,

Rae was overwhelmingly successful because of the power he possessed. The choices facing his party opponents were stark: Rae's way or the highway. To this should be added that his ministers and backbenchers were inexperienced in government and, more importantly, were caught up in the mindless rightward drift of the party, coming to office with only the vaguest sense of what practical socialism might actually be about. They were ripe for a neo-conservative hammering. They were ready to see their social democratic programs as "unrealistic," and their purposes as "utopian," and to accept the powerlessness they faced vis-à-vis their leader and the international corporations he had come to represent.

It is in this context that we have to understand the acquiescence of NDP MPPs in the Social Contract. The caucus' "dance of scorpions," which gave a final stamp of approval to a hard-nosed attack on collective bargaining, had been programmed years in advance. It was, in reality, not much more than a dance of the powerless, an expression of child-like rage directed at the scapegoat its leaders had staked to the horizon. The welfare poor would soon be next.

A year later, with a provincial election in the offing, rumours surfaced that caucus and certain cabinet ministers had panicked over what seemed to be a real possibility that the 1994 budget would contain even higher taxes and more rollbacks to welfare, heath care for seniors and local transfer payments. As a consequence, said the reports, NDP MPPs finally showed some collective muscle and successfully pushed for a more moderate budget: tax increases and rollbacks were stopped, and the status quo maintained.[82]

Again, I'm sceptical of the story's implication of even this level of incipient caucus power. I'd be much more inclined to credit such "moderation" to David Agnew's influence in stressing what he called the "negative fallout from shelved policy promises" in preparing for the election. The "critical challenge," he wrote in a memo leaked to *The Toronto Star*, "will be managing expectations relating to initiatives which we will be unable to pursue.... We will be developing a communications strategy for the exercise as a whole."[83] Another budget assault coming so close to an election would hardly fit such a strategy. It is, besides, quite common for governments to run up the flag of increased austerity prior to a budget, so that its actual content — in this case, a reaffirmation and extension of its first Social Contract budget — would be greeted more with relief than anger from those it targeted. Rae's inner circle would certainly have had no compunction in scaring the caucus for public relations purposes. Finally, Rae's concluding presentation of himself as a born (once) again leader of a "compassionate" corporate society — his "next mandate" — was unlikely to have been the product of a caucus rebellion. It seems much more probable that it was part of what the premier and his allies had long understood to be the rhythm of parliamentary government, with its elections every four or five years. At the end of the 1994 pre-budget process, it is worth noting, those old softies in Finance miraculously found internal solutions to cover most of their projected deficit shortfall. The new cuts and taxes weren't needed after all. On hearing this extraordinary news, it was later reported, without a trace of irony, that the Ontario's NDP "breathed a sigh of relief."[84]

Whatever the machinations that produced it, this was also a sigh of relief that extended far into the ranks of the Public Services Coalition, already preparing themselves to accept an even harsher set of cutbacks than they had experienced the year before.

It is this level of acquiescence, that I want now to consider, in looking more carefully at OSSTF's response to the provincial assault on the public sector and particularly on the school system in which its members worked.

Pulling Their Punches

What is immediately clear is that the Public Services Coalition did not take on the Rae government in any serious way. On occasion, it talked a good fight, but it delivered next to nothing on the ground.

Consider what didn't happen. There was no media blitz systematically putting forward the Coalition's position, only a few scattered ads. Local resistance — in which OPSEU, CUPE, and teacher activists engaged in some very spirited actions — was not brought together in any concerted provincial campaign. Even though the Coalition kept in touch with the Ontario Coalition for Social Justice, there was no real effort made to bring community organizations on board as part of a widespread organizing effort. "Mass" demonstrations were non-existent. The biggest demonstration was at Queen's Park, and it was reported as no more 3,500 out of a total membership of 950,000. The meetings held by regional coalitions across the province to put "a human face" on the cutbacks had much smaller turnouts and next to no resonance among the local membership or in the communities at large. And there was no effort to go after the NDP at the constituency level, where concerted organizing could have made an enormous impact. Nowhere, in fact, was any serious focus to be found.

Somehow it was grasped by almost everyone involved in the process that the Coalition was only going through the motions of resistance. As far as I know there was no formal agreement to pull its punches. Reluctance to fight was rarely made explicit, either, except in the occasional cynical shrug of someone's shoulders or in a small shaking of heads. It was simply understood by Coalition members that their rhetoric of solidarity was all they would be left with at the end of the day, given who they were and the reality they faced. Maybe there'd be another day, a great many Coalition activists continued to hope, OSSTF among them. Maybe there would be a future when this rhetoric would show its value. As things are now turning out, I think that judgement is proving accurate. As Mike Harris's Conservatives step into government, the need for strong Coalition politics grows more evident, particularly among the rank-and-file of the public sector unions.

An adequate description or explanation of this collapse during the crucial months of the Social Contract is beyond the scope of this book. But its dynamics, were straightforward enough: the politics, the structures, the traditions, the operative ideologies and conflicting goals of this extraordinarily wide spectrum of Ontario public unions and associations ended in a mix that contained too much conservatism, too much organizational complexity and lack of leadership, and too many close ties to the Rae administration to mount an effective struggle. There were too many weak links in the chain, in other words, which then broke at different times and in different circumstances. And in the end, the chain couldn't be mended in time for this particular battle.

Of all the big unions, OSSTF was clearly the most willing and able to fight. But even here there was a deep level of reserve. If CUPE and OPSEU had been prepared to join them, the Federation might well have thrown down the gauntlet. But not even OSSTF's leadership can actually tell us for certain, if only because neither they nor the membership had really considered it in the bright light of day. A real fight was never a serious option. A senior OSSTF administrator put it this way: "There was never a concerted strategy to let the chips fall where they may, to say, as we have in the past, this is Armageddon, and we'll mobilize everyone we can lay our hands on. Instead, we all seemed to accept a kind of paralysis." A no-holds-barred battle was, of course, part of various "war-game" scenarios carried out by the OSSTF executive and its staff. But reality, they understood in their bones, was different. As Jim Ross, OSSTF's chief negotiator, describes the situation: "From day one, it was clear that the government was not going to negotiate the $6 billion. That was gone. So the issue was not could we push them back — they weren't pushable here — but could we defeat them on the whole issue of the cuts? And it was just as clear, given the fragility of the Coalition, that we couldn't."

There is no doubt that OSSTF wanted to fight, and would have done so if there had been some real chance of success. They may not have wanted to topple the Rae government — even to shake it hard — but they certainly wanted to change its mind. If the organization had been able to find a way to mount the kind of pressure Ontario teacher organizations had directed against against Bill Davis' imposition of compulsory arbitration in 1973, it would unquestionably have taken it. OSSTF had not forgotten December 18, 1973, when it had helped bring together the largest protest rally in Ontario history, over 30,000 teachers at Queen's Park, while participating in smaller rallies right across the province. And no one would have been more pleased with such a rally than OSSTF's then president, Liz Barkley, who had been chief marshal at the 1973 event and who remained a firm believer in such pressure tactics. But the base wasn't there, either in the Coalition, among the teachers' organizations within the Coalition, or in the membership of OSSTF itself.

As I've already noted in Chapter 1, the corporate assault on the Canadian state system and its schools, particularly in Ontario, had moved to centre stage between 1990 and 1993. The rallying cry of insufficient school funding, so helpful in defeating David Peterson, seemed to have been thoroughly undercut in the public debate on the future of schooling. Teachers were deeply shaken by this new corporate attack, particularly as it focused on the schools in which they taught. Not only were they being hammered by the press (alongside an increasingly vocal business elite) on the lavishness of Ontario's school funding and on the high salaries of its teachers, but they were also taking a beating on the question of what that money was being spent on in the first place. A right-wing back-to-basics movement was in full swing by 1993, focused on a corporate vision of "skill development" and on students' acceptance of and acquiescence in a corporate view of society and their place within it. The language of business had increasingly become the language of school policy-making: downsizing, value-added, productivity, return on investment, total quality management.[85]

By the time the Social Contract approached in the spring of 1993, the Ontario NDP government had joined this chorus, finding its way over the objections of all its educational constituents to support a growing national and local board system of standardized tests, with a special emphasis on the development of "workplace skills." In line with these new policies, the government gutted the Education Ministry of its liberal-progressive curriculum specialists and replaced them with people who were suspicious of the learner-centred rhetoric of their predecessors. These people wanted, instead, a system measured in mechanical test scores and devoted to preparing Ontario's children for global competitiveness. And so, according to a relentless media campaign, did the public, even though most people supporting such tests had no idea what such an emphasis would actually mean for the "quality" they hoped would result.

As teachers saw public opinion mounting against them, they

felt increasingly powerless to meet this new hostility with an effective response. They knew that many of the recent criticisms of the schools were a bum rap.[86] They felt they could hardly be expected to stem a broad social collapse all by themselves. There was a lot that was right with the school system, they argued, that could be built on. At the same time they recognized that there was a lot wrong with it, too, and that parents and students had legitimate concerns about education. Most teachers wouldn't hesitate to say that there was far too much disorder in the schools and not enough learning going on. But while much of what was wrong was not their fault, teachers recognized that neither they nor their federations had really focussed attention on the kind of changes that were needed. The danger, they felt, was that this would simply put even more weapons into the hands of the forces now arrayed against public education. As a consequence, their federations hadn't worked out among their members or among themselves a coherent plan of school reform — a more adequate and equitable funding system, a more democratic decision-making structure, a more purposeful and higher-quality curriculum. There was no shortage of individual opinions and positions about what was wrong and what ought to be done. They were often passionately and eloquently expressed, and they naturally reflected some very deep divisions among rank-and-file teachers and their federations. But the teacher organizations were unable to put together a solid majority position and a campaign to carry it forward.[87]

Without a strong position on reform, no serious alliance could be built to protect the public schools and the teachers who work in them. While support for a public school system in Ontario (indeed in Canada generally) remains strong, hopes for mobilization in its support require a much clearer answer to the question "What for?" And that's true for both working-class and middle-class parents, despite differences in the experience and reaction of each class. The experience of failure among working-class students has done much to arouse powerful hostility to schooling in working-class communities. But many middle-class parents experience considerable anxiety about school "quality" and this has resulted in a growing (though not yet major) movement towards private education. In a surprisingly short space of time, a major offensive had been mounted against the public school system, and teacher organizations like OSSTF would have to find a way to come to its defence.

But as the Social Contract came down on them, OSSTF had yet to find such a way.

Both internally and externally, the Federation thus remained very vulnerable to attack, half knowing that a right-wing juggernaut was coming at them with its policies of public sector cutbacks and central control, and half hoping (against hope) that an NDP government would never actually nail them with such an agenda. A hidden inevitability lay at the heart of OSSTF's paralysis, and it is hardly surprising.

It had been quite clear for several years that the forces of global capitalism were alive and well in Ontario and in the country as a whole. The Federation was especially conscious of the rising panic among provincial governments, who had been watching their deficits soar as the recession deepened and the federal government held back on its transfer payments. In 1989-90, for example, aggregate provincial deficits had stood at only $4.7 billion, but by 1992-93 these deficits had jumped to a total just under $25 billion. As the numbers grew, credit-rating agencies and bond dealers began making loud rumblings in the press. An extraordinary array of corporate heavies toured the country, from conference to conference, in an appeal for "fiscally responsible" government. In no time at all, governments in New Brunswick, Quebec, Manitoba, Saskatchewan and Alberta were on the run. By 1993, these governments had committed themselves to a policy of complete deficit reduction within the next four years.[88]

Could Ontario, OSSTF wondered, be far behind?

In the 1989-90 fiscal year the Ontario government had been looking at a cosy $90 million surplus. As the NDP was about to take office, they learned they were to inherit a $700 million deficit. Then, within months and without having made any future spending decisions, the government saw its deficit climb to $2.5 billion, and its new premier slipped into his now familiar role as a downsizer of public expectations. Ontarians, he declared, would have to face up to "the new realities of the '90s" and learn to live with "cod-liver oil and cough syrup" rather than "strawberries and cream or crème caramel." By the time the April 1992 budget arrived, the deficit had skyrocketed to $9.7 billion.[89] Then, in mid-1992, it looked as if there might be a bit of a respite as treasury officials predicted that the 1995-96 budget deficit would decline to $4.1 billion. However, by early 1993, these officials had reversed themselves and were predicting instead that the provincial deficit would rise to $18.6 billion.[90]

Under these circumstances, it would have been hard for OSSTF to imagine any Ontario government moving in a direction opposite to that of her sister administrations. Indeed, when Federation leaders looked at their press reports a month prior to the imposition of the Social Contract, they found their premier getting some special support for such deficit-slashing policies from his two fellow NDP premiers, Mike Harcourt of British Columbia and Roy Romanow of Saskatchewan. At a meeting on March 1, Richard Mackie reported, "Rae got needed political legitimacy for his anti-deficit fight.... Romanow was especially helpful, stressing 'the need to reorganize the delivery of services in order to make sure that they're there for the year 2000 and beyond.'" Covering the same meeting, Thomas Walkom wrote that Rae and Harcourt "were especially unnerved when Romanow reminded them that the number of institutions willing to handle Saskatchewan bonds had dropped from 150 to 25 over the past decade."[91] Mackie's story noted it was these comments by Romanow that "Rae frequently cited ... to justify his cuts in spending." But he goes on to say that we ought not to take this broader NDP influence too seriously. His "Saskatchewan sources" had told him "that Mr. Rae was making too big a deal of a routine comment by Mr. Romanow," with the implication, as we have seen a number of times, that the premier was using this occasion to support a predetermined policy direction.

When that direction eventually came into being on March 30, the world changed for OSSTF and its public sector allies. A hostile government-bureaucratic-corporate juggernaut was now upon them, and that meant something very different had to take place within the practical politics of their organizations.

What did that mean for the Federation?

In the first few months of the Social Contract experience, it meant, as I've argued here, pulling punches in many key battles. In the long run, as we shall see in Part 2, it has also meant a fundamental rethinking of its policies and its own role. But during the period in which the Social Contract became law and its implementation began, this new reality has involved something else again: the discovery of a remarkable new determination within OSSTF to take on the struggle wherever it could find a place to dig in its heels. It found some of these places alongside its coalition partners, as they worked under enormous difficulties to form a political organization that would eventually survive to fight another day. Other places were found among the members of the Federation itself, standing shoulder to shoulder against new assaults by their local boards. It is to both these avenues of day-to-day resistance that we now turn.

FOOTNOTES

1 Mittelstaedt, Martin, "Rae taking a gamble on getting agreement in public-sector talks," *Globe and Mail*, April 6, 1993.

2 In the B.C. health agreement, CUPE accepted reductions of up to 10 percent in the acute-care sector. These reductions would take place, however, only through attrition, early retirement and a province-wide framework agreement in which workers let go from the acute-care sector would be placed in local community health-care facilities. The new jobs had to be offered *before* these workers were released from their old jobs; it was serious job security. At the same time, a union member's work week went from 37.5 to 36 hours, and they gained an effective voice in the restructuring of health care through participation in a newly-created joint labour adjustment agency. While there remains significant union resistance to the general direction of B.C. health care restructuring, the labour adjustment process connected with it has worked reasonably well and has broad union support. Bob Rae could have learned a lot from this process.

3 Murray, Graham, "Social Contract — or set up?" *The Go Report*, April 10, 1993.

4 Mittelstaedt, Martin, "Rae taking a gamble on getting agreement in public-sector talks," *Globe and Mail*, April 6, 1993.

5 At the time, the House had 130 members, 71 in the NDP government and

59 among the opposition Liberals and Tories. Four NDPers (Drainville, Haslam, Kormos, Morrow) were determined to vote against it, and 1 (Akande) to abstain. That made 66 votes for the government and 63 for the opposition. With a shift in two government votes, the bill might have failed, 64 to 65.

6 In the early days of Mike Harris' administration, this judgement seems to be holding up. Some of Rae's personal cronies are gone, but the Conservative transition team seems determined, as Thomas Walkom puts it, "to soothe the insiders and quiet their fears." "Senior civil servants," Walkom continues, "can now enthusiastically busy themselves working out how to eliminate the jobs of their colleagues and underlings." Walkom, Thomas, "Harris' revolution looking more like a restoration," *Toronto Star*, June 15, 1995.

7 Interview with Syd Ryan, February 15, 1994.

8 Fergusson, Derek, "Rae targets higher-paid in big cutback," *Toronto Star*, April 3, 1993.

9 OSSTF, Press Release, April 7, 1993.

10 Scotton, Geoffrey, "Unions demand specifics from Rae," *Financial Post*, April 10, 1993.

11 Murray, Graham, "Social Contract — or set up?" *The Go Report*, April 10, 1993.

12 Papp, Leslie, "We won't discuss layoffs, union warns Rae," *Toronto Star*, April 6, 1993.

13 Ferguson, Derek, "Contract unlikely, union boss says," *Toronto Star*, April 7, 1993.

14 Mittelstaedt, Martin, "Unions form common front against cutbacks," *Globe and Mail*, April 5, 1993.

15 Manners, Earl, Interview with George Martell, January 11, 1994.

16 See Mackie, Richard and Mittelstaedt, Martin, "Workers to be offered input on spending," *Globe and Mail*, April 17, 1993, and Mackie, Richard and Mittelstaedt, Martin, "NDP's top negotiator '40 going on 80'," *Globe and Mail*, April 19, 1993.

17 Steed, Judy, "Man with a mission impossible," *Toronto Star*, April 25, 1993.

18 Casella, Emilia, "It's war, vow angry unions," *Hamilton Spectator*, April 24, 1993.

19 "More cuts," *Toronto Sun*, April 24, 1993.

20 Scotton, Geoffrey, "Ontario to use taxes, cuts to slash deficit," *Financial Post*, April 26, 1993.

21 Federation of Women Teachers' Assocations of Ontario, which represents only women elementary teachers in the province.

22 Galt, Virginia and Mackie, Richard, "Union leaders reject deadline for

negotiation," *Globe and Mail*, April 28,1993.

23 See Galt, Virginia and Mackie, Richard, "Union leaders reject deadline for negotiation," *Globe and Mail*, April 28, 1993, and Papp, Leslie and Ferguson, Derek, "Defiant unions set to boycott talks with NDP," *Toronto Star*, April 28, 1993.

24 Canadian Press Report, *Hamilton Spectator*, April 30, 1993.

25 Casella, Emilia, "Unions won't stop cuts: Rae," *Hamilton Spectator*, May 6, 1993.

26 Little, Bruce, "Business gets off easy," *Globe and Mail*, May 20, 1993. See also Ferguson, Derek, "Big firms hit with new tax on profits," *Toronto Star*, December 9, 1993.

27 Walker, William, "'Minimum' tax another muffed promise," *Toronto Star*, December 9, 1993.

28 Walkom, Thomas, "Fatally flawed document has nothing for jobless," *Toronto Star*, May 20, 1993.

29 Duffy, Andrew, "Teachers vow to fight pay cuts," *Toronto Star*, May 20, 1993.

30 Barkley, Liz, "A response to Budget 93," *OSSTF News Release*, May 10, 1993.

31 Ontario Public School Teachers' Federation, which represents men elementary teachers in the province, but would also like to represent women elementary teachers. Hence the inclusive title.

32 Lewington, Jennifer, "School boards table cuts," *Globe and Mail*, May 22, 1993.

33 Toughhill, Kelly, "NDP eases its proposal for days off without pay," *Toronto Star*, May 27, 1993.

34 Walker, William, "Rae unveils talks strategy," *Toronto Star*, June 2, 1993.

35 Canadian Press Report, *The Hamilton Spectator*, May 28, 1993.

36 Editorial, "Unions choice: Cut pay or jobs," *Toronto Star*, June 1, 1993.

37 Walker, William, "Settle or else, Rae tells unions," *Toronto Star*, June 1, 1993.

38 See Walker, William, "Rae unveils talks strategy," *Toronto Star*, June 2, 1993, and Galt, Virginia and Mackie, Richard, "Ontario battles to save talks," *Globe and Mail*, June 2, 1993.

39 Barkley, Liz and Ross, Jim, "OSSTF Memo," June 2, 1993.

40 Ferguson, Derek, "NDP ax to hit low-paid, too," *Toronto Star*, July 21, 1993.

41 Mackie, Richard, Galt, Virginia and McInnes, Craig, "Ontario sweetens offer to unions," *Globe and Mail*, June 3, 1993.

42 Walker, William, "NDP sending tough message at last minute," *Toronto*

Star, June 3, 1993.

43 From an interview with Earl Manners, January 1, 1994.

44 Mittelstaedt, Martin and Mackie, Richard, "Unions to abandon talks," *Globe and Mail*, June 4, 1993.

45 Papp, Leslie, "Pension changes were key to unions quitting talks," *Toronto Star*, June 5, 1993.

46 Walker, William, "Rae fights to lure unions back to talks," *Toronto Star*, June 5, 1993.

47 Mackie, Richard, Galt, Virginia and McInnes, Craig, "Ontario sweetens offer to unions," *Globe and Mail*, June 3, 1993.

48 Walkom, Thomas, "Lankin's near-defection put NDP on thin ice," *Toronto Star*, July 10, 1993.

49 Walkom, Thomas, "Lankin's near-defection put NDP on thin ice," *Toronto Star*, July 10, 1993. See also Walker, William and Ferguson, Derek, "Social contract law delayed by NDP split," *Toronto Star*, June 30, 1993.

50 Walker, William, Rae takes it on himself to get a deal," *Toronto Star*, June 12, 1993.

51 Walker, William, "Rae fights to lure unions back to talks," *Toronto Star*, June 5, 1993.

52 Walkom, Thomas, "Some contract! Some NDP government!" *Toronto Star*, June 15, 1993.

53 Papp, Leslie, "Pension cut is vital to NDP's proposal," *Toronto Star*, June 18, 1993.

54 Walkom, Thomas, 'Some contract! Some NDP government!" *Toronto Star*, June 15, 1993. See also Mittelstaedt, Martin, "Union signatures not needed on social contracts, Rae says," *Globe and Mail*, July 15, 1993.

55 Cooke, David, quoted in Barkley, Liz, "Memo to OSSTF Representatives re: Lobby of Policy and Priorities Board of Cabinet," May 30, 1994.

56 Ferguson, Derek and Walker, William, "Rae promises protection for lowest paid," *Toronto Star*, April 6, 1993.

57 Manners, Earl, Interview January 11, 1993.

58 Mittelstaedt, Martin, "Union signatures not needed on social contracts, Rae says," *Globe and Mail*, July 15, 1993. See also Casella, Emilia, "NDP spins image of real negotiations," *Hamilton Spectator*, July 24, 1993.

59 Rae, Bob, "News Release, Premier's Office," April 5, 1993.

60 Papp, Leslie, "A triumph of fear, not of true negotiation," *Toronto Star*, July 21, 1993.

61 Valpy, Michael, "The kind of capitalism that Bob Rae wants," and Mittelstaedt, Martin, "Compassion a must, Rae says," *Globe and Mail*, December 20, 1994.

62 Mackie, Richard, "NDP backs Rae on payroll cut," *Globe and Mail*, June

21, 1993.

63 Canadian Press Report, "CUPE says: No way Bob Rae," *Hamilton Spectator*, June 23, 1993. See also Van Alphen, Tony, "NDP-bashing union leader claims 'smear,'" *Toronto Star*, December 26, 1994.

64 See Walkom, Thomas, "Why unions blinked first," *Toronto Star*, June 20, 1993, and Ferguson, Derek and Papp, Leslie, "Rae may bend on deadline to freeze pay," *Toronto Star*, June 22, 1993.

65 Mackie, Richard, "Ontario health unions sign agreement," *Globe and Mail*, July 16, 1993, and "Health institutions offered $50 million signing bonus," *Globe and Mail*, July 17, 1993.

66 Canadian Press Report, "2 CUPE locals join social contract camp," *Toronto Star*, July 20, 1993.

67 Daly, Rita, "Catholic teachers' union back at talks," *Toronto Star*, July 20, 1993.

68 Papp, Leslie, "A triumph of fear, not of true negotiation," *Toronto Star*, July 21, 1993.

69 Papp, Leslie and Ferguson, Derek, "Teachers' unions end boycott of key talks," *Toronto Star*, July 22, 1993.

70 To head off a sell-out at the education worker table, where OPSEU was threatening to cut a deal, OSSTF rejoined negotiations at this table before the official announcement. See Papp, Leslie, "'Solidarity' easier to sing than practise," *Toronto Star*, July 26, 1993. CUPE, on a matter of principle, was not at the table, preferring to tough it out under "fail-safe."

71 Mackie, Richard, "NDP backs Rae on payroll cut," *Globe and Mail*, June 21, 1993.

72 Gagnon, Georgette and Rath, Dan, *Not Without Cause: David Peterson's Fall from Grace*, cited above, p. 146.

73 Gagnon, Georgette and Rath, Dan, *Not Without Cause: David Peterson's Fall from Grace*, cited above, p. 148.

74 Gagnon, Georgette and Rath, Dan, *Not Without Cause: David Peterson's Fall from Grace*, cited above, p. 313.

75 Mittelshaft, Martin, "Reject 'mean-spirited' rivals, Rae urges, *Globe and Mail*, May 15, 1995.

76 Best, Patricia, "The chastened socialists," *Globe and Mail*, April 30, 1994.

77 See Carol Goar, "NDP glimpses a future at the end of a dark tunnel," *Toronto Star*, September 1, 1994.

78 Ehring, George and Roberts, Wayne, *Giving Away a Miracle*, cited above, p. 12.

79 Ehring, George and Roberts, Wayne, *Giving Away a Miracle*, cited above, pp. 13–14

80 Ehring, George and Roberts, Wayne, *Giving Away a Miracle*, cited above, pp. 57–58.

81 Ehring, George and Roberts, Wayne, *Giving Away a Miracle*, cited above, p. 51.

82 See Walkom, Thomas, *Toronto Star*, "Can Ontario's NDP save itself?" March 26, 1994, "The reasons Bob Rae may risk all on a fall election," April 2, 1994, "For this budget, we should all be thankful," May 6, 1994; and Walker, William, *Toronto Star*, "Rae moves warily as election looms," March 24, 1994; "NDP puts election over new policies," March 30, 1994. This budget was also, as Fred Upshaw put it, "a lollipop for business." See Galt, Virginia, "Business, labour disappointed," *Globe and Mail*, May 6, 1994. OSSTF called it "a be-nice-to-business budget," with the government abandoning its "fair tax" reforms and offering an employer health tax holiday. See OSSTF publication, *Queen's Park*, "Ontario Budget: 1994."

83 Walker, William, "NDP puts election over new policies," *Toronto Star*, March 30, 1994.

84 Walkom, Thomas, "Can Ontario's NDP save itself?" *Toronto Star*, March 26, 1994.

85 See Barlow, Maude and Robertson, Heather-Jane, *Class Warfare: The Assault on Canada's Schools*, Key Porter Books, Toronto, 1994, p. 15

86 See, for example, Barlow, Maude and Robertson, Heather-Jane, *Class Warfare*, cited above: "Part of schools' vulnerability ... comes from doing anti-chaos work [preventing social collapse] under rules that prohibit naming the true problems. While schools have been struggling haphazardly with their new role as social, emotional and intellectual food banks for ever-increasing numbers of damaged children, parents — such as those who described their children as 'marketable commodities" before Ontario's Royal Commission on Learning — began to worry. The best educated, most articulate and prosperous parents have come to believe that the academic achievements of their less needy children are being sacrificed to the classroom's non-academic goals. Those who have 'struggled to the top' worry that their children's strategic advantages are being eroded. Some blame those 'struggling to the bottom': single parents, recent immigrants and those lacking middle class values." (p. 9.)

87 Maude Barlow and Heather-Jane Robertson note that this lack of direction in curriculum policy is part of a broader set of contradictions among the membership of teacher federations: "During the 1980s, teacher associations began to be visible advocates of 'progressive' social policy. This received the grudging support of fee-paying teachers as long as bread-and-butter union issues were proceeding reasonably well. However, as cutbacks created job insecurity, as wage increases were replaced by rollbacks, and as teachers were routinely bashed by the press and politicians, teachers began to have doubts. Some blamed their new vulnerability on their unions' concentration on issues such as global education, violence against women, NAFTA and the

constitutional accord. Some teachers saw their union leadership as having escaped the trenches of the classroom to the expense account. When these same union leaders protested that the key decisions affecting teachers and schools were being shaped by forces well beyond negotiations with local school boards, and often beyond ministries of education and provincial governments, it sounded like excuse making to many activist teachers. Unions had taken the credit in good times and shouldn't duck responsibility when things turned sour. What would constitute doing a good job in the eyes of their members is by no means clear. Some teachers are embarrassed by an unseemly militancy advanced by union leaders; equal numbers believe their unions are too cosy with those who like to be described as partners: trustees, the government, and, increasingly, business. The swift and often critical initiatives of these partners have left teacher unions feeling outflanked." See *Class Warfare*, cited above, pp. 16–17.

88 See Contenta, Sandro, "Deficit reduction continues across Canada," *Toronto Star*, December 24, 1993.

89 Ehring, George and Roberts, Wayne, *Giving Away A Miracle*, cited above, p. 339.

90 Walkom, Thomas, "Labour, NDP on course for collision," *Toronto Star*, April 7, 1993.

91 Walkom, Thomas, "Labour, NDP on course for collision," *Toronto Star*, April 7, 1993.

Chapter Three

Digging In For Battle

Organizing Solidarity

OSSTF knew that this neo-conservative/NDP policy wave would soon be upon them but they were unwilling to grasp what that implied for the NDP as a negotiating partner. This put OSSTF (as it did the entire labour movement) into an almost schizophrenic frame of mind when dealing with the government. As we have seen, this frame of mind led to serious paralysis during the Social Contract negotiations.

But this schizophrenia did not extend to the inner workings of OSSTF.

At the same time that its public strategy was stalled, the Federation's leadership was moving in the one direction that could eventually allow the organization to achieve a broad level of political success: this was the effort to help organize solidarity between teachers and the labour movement as a whole. Such a move, of course, was made partly to prevent further isolation of the province's teachers from their public sector allies during the Social Contract struggle. But it was made equally with a view to resurrecting an alliance, composed of both working-class and middle-class Ontarians, in support of public services and, especially, in support of the province's public schools.

It began with the attempt to help unite Ontario's public sector unions against the Social Contract's cutbacks and its attack on collective bargaining. In the short run that attempt largely failed. At the same time, there is no question that the very existence of the Public Services Coalition prevented a much harsher program being implemented.

OSSTF understood the vital importance of such a strategy for the future. And so it insisted that the efforts to forge an effective coalition between public sector unions must be maintained, whatever the difficulties. In a September 1993 memo, OSSTF's Queen's Park lobbyist Larry French put this focus into clear context for his Provincial Executive: "If the Coalition ceases to function, it will be a tacit admission on our part that the real battle was over jobs and wages, and that the government has won. Our attempt to mobilize against the 'social contract' and its dismemberment of public services will be greeted with understandable cynicism. An immense vacuum will be created that other groups with agendas opposed to the Coalition will be eager to fill. The voice of clear opposition to the government's irresponsible attack on public services will be blurred, and the government will have less inducement to both terminate the 'social contract' and to cease promoting it as a model for other provinces.... It is all too apparent that the Ontario Public Services Coalition is the only determined defender of public services on this continent against the assault waged by the multi-national neo-conservative forces that have captured even the Ontario government. The battle we are fighting has enormous implications for our province and our country. The Coalition can join with enlightened private sector unions to maximize our chances of surviving this neo-conservative blight."[1]

Throughout this process, OSSTF has played a pivotal role in building a base from which such alliances could flourish. Its eventual success is no sure thing, but the effort that OSSTF put into making the Public Services Coalition happen will go a long way in convincing more sceptical labour and community activists that the Federation is finally getting serious about such issues.

Central to this work was OSSTF president at the time, Liz Barkley. Barkley was extraordinarily effective in helping keep the Coalition united and focused on its enemies in the government rather than on its own internal difficulties. Alongside executive members like Earl Manners and Jim McQueen and

OSSTF staff, like Malcolm Buchanan and Larry French, Barkley worked non-stop for months to help shape the Coalition into an effective vehicle for protest. At one Coalition meeting, after watching two hours of Chairperson Barkley pouring oil on one patch of troubled water after another — in a remarkable mix of shrewd diplomacy, down-home charm, intense practicality, and a very clear-minded determination to offer OSSTF's bureaucracy as the Coalition's administrative infrastructure — a seasoned CUPE activist sitting next to me said: "You know, for all my disagreements with Liz in the past, I think she was born for this moment. There's not many people who can hold a room like this together — half of us anxious to be at each other's throats and the other half pleased to watch. It's good to have her here with us. Today, anyway."

The Coalition's success meant a lot to Barkley, and it is worth listening to her description of the Coalition's beginnings and its eventual decision to walk out of negotiations en masse — the moment when it appeared that her dream of effective resistance to the Social Contract might come to pass. It was, as she understood, a triumph of progressive organization, even if it failed its first real test of battle.

"You know," Barkley told me, "we had no rules at all for our first meeting. And not many afterwards, either. I was expecting about 10 people — from CUPE and OPSEU, mostly, and from various teacher organizations — but we ended up with 200 people, then 400, because there was no place else for them to go. The NDP wasn't there any more for us. And the OFL had split on the issue — far too many of its senior people were tied in with Rae's inner circle — and it also wasn't oriented much to the protection of public services. So the Coalition became our home to confront this situation. We ended up with 32 different organizations. We had everybody there: nurses and health workers, university faculty and support staff, college and university teaching assistants, LCBO employees, firefighters, police, transit workers, municipal employees, and the other teacher federations, in addition to OSSTF, CUPE and OPSEU. We went through 28 meetings over three months, with almost no rules, no structure to speak of, but in its strange form, it worked. Often we'd have standing room only. By the time the government started to the tables, after the May budget, all of the unions were on this side of the ramp.

"I can't tell you how tricky it was to get anything off the ground," Barkley continued. "It was always: two steps forward, four steps back. Who are we anyway? Are there hidden purposes here we're not all aware of? Who's talking to the government now and what are they saying? There wasn't much trust there at first, let me tell you, and it was never easy even after a few months. But as we went through it, the Coalition pulled the whole public service together. The staffs of the different unions started to work together, and even the leaders started figuring out what the others really meant when they said something. We learned to read between each other's lines. I remember when the doctors asked me if they could come in. I went to CUPE — I knew all the difficulties there were between hospital workers and doctors — and said that since we had no criteria for membership, the doctors should at least be able to come and sit down. 'OK, let them in for a while,' CUPE said. And eventually it worked out. As much as they could everyone put their old grievances on hold, and got along surprisingly well. Each organization took its turn paying for the meetings, and they learned to listen to each other, too.

"Then on June 3 it really came together. It was so crowded and intense that night. In three days time, we all had to put up or shut up, and the place was just jammed. The government had told us loud and clear that the June 6 deadline was final. Because we were at the Royal York the Coalition meeting had 500 more people than usual there. There were the representatives of all 32 organizations, their support staff, and a number of other political leaders as well. And when you added the press and all sorts of interested onlookers, it seems to me there must have been a thousand people in the room and out in the hall and in adjoining rooms. As chance would have it, it was my turn to be chair, and I started out doing what we always did. I asked for a report on what was happening at the various sectoral tables. This was something that could never be manipulated — direct reports from the people doing the actual negotiations. Now in the past, as we went around to hear from various tables, organizations like the nurses and OPSEU had tended to keep us fixed on the present format. They were going to stay at their tables, they told us. This was the right strategy, they said. They were going to work something out. They insisted on it. There was no other option. CUPE, of course, had not turned up at the tables at all; its local presidents voted to accept 'fail safe' rather than participate in this fraud. All the teacher federations were negotiating — I hate to use that word — but two or three were now very uneasy about this decision. And as the weeks went by we found that many other organizations were getting more and more demoralized. Each time they reported to us from their tables their situation seemed worse, the government more oppressive, with the emphasis coming down more and more on downsizing and wage cuts. Still, they said, we have to hang in.

"Yet on that night of June 3 I had the strongest feeling things were going to go well. I started going around the table. I went first to the municipal workers and then to the health workers, and then to other sectors, and they all said the same thing: We can't take this anymore. This isn't bargaining. This has got to stop. And then I got to the nurses, and I'll be damned if they didn't agree. And people said, 'Oh, my God.' The nurses, you know, people figured butter wouldn't melt in their mouths. Then I got to the teachers. I'm in the chair, remember. I say, 'Well, we have to have a caucus.' This was a pretty major decision for all of us to take; don't forget, we're five unions. And OPSEU says the same thing. They need to caucus, too. When the teachers got together we didn't have any trouble with the sentiments going around the table. We made a few phone calls to check things out, but we knew we didn't have to go back to our executives. We knew we'd had enough. We went back into the room, and I was the first to speak. 'Well,' I said, 'these boots were made for walkin'.' And Margaret Dempsey from the women's elementary federation said the same thing, and then the others did too. We're all waiting now for OPSEU. They've been the ones, alongside the nurses, who have been most committed to staying at the tables till the bitter end. (They really figured they were going to get something out of this.) Then Fred Upshaw comes in and he sits next to me, and I take his arm and I say 'What are you going to do, Fred?' and he whispers to me: 'I'm staying with this Coalition,' and he gets up and makes a great speech saying just that. Then the doctors make a big speech. This is so extraordinary — people making $12,000 standing up with people making $240,000. It was so hard to believe. Then someone said, 'It's time for Solidarity Forever.' The problem was we only knew the chorus, but we went through it fourteen times.

"Now the press started to hear this. They could hear it through the doors, and I think somebody might have gone outside too. The press knew there'd been a breach with the government. They broke down the doors and got on the tables to take pictures. People just streamed in. What a mêlée. There were hundreds of people out there. It was such great release for us all. We all knew what a lousy thing this was — what an anti-social thing this 'Social' Contract was — and we didn't have any control over it. Our singing must have seemed a little strange to people, but in the end it was a real expression of how we all felt. A huge release, an absolutely passionate response: We can't accept this. We can't go through this any longer if we want to keep our principles intact."

As we know, these principles had to take another shaking down, as the Coalition eventually returned to the government's bargaining tables. But not everything was lost.

But before I go on, I want to say this: In singling out the work of OSSTF in the building of the Public Services Coalition, I don't want to forget for a moment the efforts of other unions and associations and many of their leaders and staff representatives. What I am simply stressing here is that OSSTF, as an organization, gave of itself more energetically and more systematically than any of the other members of the Coalition. At that moment in time, its structure, its wealth and its motivation had set it up for this kind of leadership.

It is also worth noting here that there are large problems still to overcome in OSSTF's relationship to labour (as there are with other teacher federations). OSSTF has continued to resist joining the Ontario Federation of Labour, though its non-teaching employees may soon have a formal relationship with the province's house of labour. And in organizing these non-teaching employees, OSSTF has the additional problem of raiding charges, especially from CUPE; these issues have not been worked out. More importantly, there is the fact that the Federation has yet to develop and mobilize support for the structural and curriculum reforms that might really help working-class kids. And this hurts its relationship with labour most of all. If teacher organizations had stood up for such reforms at school boards and labour councils — laying out detailed suggestions for high-quality egalitarian schools and helping to organize pressure to make them happen — their ties with working people and the organizations that represent them would be far closer than they are today.

As we shall see in Part 2, however, the current policy direction of OSSTF is such that there is a good chance that these divisions with the labour movement can be successfully overcome.

In all of this, we mustn't forget that Ontario's teacher federations have stormy relationships among themselves. Bitter membership disputes have gone on for many years between the men and women's elementary teachers and between OSSTF and the English Catholic Teachers' Association. The latter two are also split, again bitterly, over the issue of Separate School funding for the final years of high school. And it is still in contention whether the Association des enseignants français de l'Ontario should be organizing all French-speaking teachers in Ontario or only French-speaking separate school teachers.

OSSTF's answer to these disputes, and my own, is that the province needs one big teachers' union (with tough provisions for gender parity in its constitution) as well as a local board structure that integrates as much of the Catholic and public systems as it can without being unconstitutional. The recent history of these struggles as they have made their way through the labyrinth of the teacher umbrella organization, the Ontario Teachers Federation, suggests it will be many years before they can be resolved. A number of months ago, it appeared as if the women's elementary federation was poised to join OSSTF which would have broken the logjam towards one big teachers' union. That possibility now seems to have fallen through as the women's federation pursues its Supreme Court case against women teachers' right to join the men's elementary organization. As this book goes to press, however, it seems the women's elementary organization is now closer to joining their male counterparts in a combined elementary federation.

It is easy, in retrospect, to see what a stroke of genius it was for the Tories to have set up The Teaching Profession Act in 1944 — separating the province's teachers into five different federations. They have been feuding ever since. If one thing has come out clearly in this Social Contract struggle, it is that a strong teacher-labour-community alliance can only emerge with one integrated teachers' organization. Individual federations like OSSTF cannot be expected to do the job on their own. Such an alliance requires integrated policies as well as an integrated organization. Labour and community activists have to know where all of Ontario's teachers stand, just as teachers have to know where their organizations stand.

Biting The Bullet

Once the momentum of the walkout had ended, going back to the negotiating tables was a hard moment for OSSTF. Its powerlessness — and the powerlessness of the Coalition it had tried to build — was there for everyone to see. Panic was now abroad, as individual organizations bolted from the Coalition to save what they could from the strips Bill 48 had taken from their contracts. By the time the province's five teachers' organizations met for a final strategy session on July 21, there was no stopping this tide. Already, six health-care unions had signed on as had two big CUPE locals. So too, with even greater impact, had their colleagues from the English Catholic Teachers' Association. And on the day before the teachers' meeting, Michael Decter boasted he had agreements or tentative deals with 600,000 out of the Coalition's total of 950,000 employees. Then, just hours prior to the meeting, 100,000 municipal workers had signed on the dotted line.[2] Any real choice for OSSTF to continue standing its ground had gone out the window.

But it wasn't just this retreating tide that moved the Federation in the end. It was also the hard numbers at stake. As OSSTF's chief negotiator, Jim Ross, puts it: "If we'd stayed away at that point, and taken 'fail safe,' our members would have killed us. 'Fail safe' brought an automatic twelve days unpaid leave, a frozen grid for salary and merit increases, and the possibility of unilateral employer action on working conditions, vacation time, leaves of absence, severance pay and notice of layoff. By going in," Ross argues, "we plugged these management possibilities, and we got something like a 50 percent reduction in the government position as it was written into Bill 48 — that's 50 percent fewer cuts in a framework agreement we had to live with for three years. You can't walk away from that. You just can't. We got the 20 percent off the top that came with signing what the government called 'an agreement.' We then negotiated a better deal on the pension-offset monies, which removed another $325 million from the government target, which was another 20 percent. At the same time, our presence prevented the government from threatening the integrity of our pension plan. And then there were a whole lot of other things that mounted up to another 10 percent. The most important among them was that we freed up our wage increment situation somewhat. Under Bill 48, teachers couldn't change categories, as they had in the past, with increased seniority and educational qualifications. The whole grid was frozen. Under the new agreement, the increment ended up being negotiable. The boards didn't have to agree with it, but the change let us in the door. That was a big deal for us."

OSSTF also had to ensure that its non-teaching members, who bargained under the Ontario Labour Relations Act, didn't get done in at the education workers' table. (This was commonly referred to as the OLRA table.) Indeed, OSSTF was so worried about a sell-out at the OLRA table that they slipped into its bargaining process a day early to make certain this didn't happen. Federation negotiators had received reports, accurate as it turned out, that OPSEU and SEIU were ready to accept a settlement on the lines agreed to by the province's municipal workers. The settlement would automatically have been imposed on OSSTF members, and it was significantly below what the Federation figured was possible to achieve. After a flurry of arm-twisting that kept their allies from an early signing, OSSTF negotiators made a very strong intervention — *The Globe and Mail* called them "tough-minded crusaders" in this action[3] — and they came away with some real gains, though not of the order they achieved for their teaching members. At the OLRA table Federation negotiators couldn't use a pension plan to get the target reduced, because the workers' pension plan (OMERS) wasn't in partnership with the government and nothing could be worked out at this level. They did, however, manage something: When an employee took a Rae Day, OMERS paid both the employer's and the employee's pension contributions for that day. OSSTF also got OMERS to pay an early retirement settlement. At the same time, OSSTF got job security provisions improved and the government agreed to a lot more flexibility in determining how board target figures were to be achieved for its non-teaching employees, which meant more room for successful negotiating at that level.

In all this, OSSTF could take some pride that they had fought while others had remained down-hearted and that they had regained some of the ground that others had given up as lost. Still, when all was said and done, it remained a bitter defeat, and Liz Barkley didn't pretend it was otherwise. As Susan Kastner reported it in *The Toronto Star*, this was "the most difficult final offer Barkley has ever had to swallow.... Minutes before the government's final deadline, the leaders of Ontario's five teacher unions were giving terse, bitter assent to the agreement: Yes. Yes. Yes. Yes. F__ yes, Liz Barkley snapped."[4]

Back In The Trenches

Liz Barkley would have been even angrier had she realized that a number of the major items promised in the framework agreement would never come to pass as the Federation now turned to negotiating with the local boards.

Under the framework agreement, for example, the local boards undertook to provide their teachers with complete financial accountability. It was time to open the books. In everyone's eyes, this was only common sense, given the level of cutbacks now being contemplated as part of the negotiating process. Yet nothing of the sort happened. Board accounts remained as closed to teachers (and to the public) as they had always been. The framework agreement also said that all new jobs would be posted, and it was assumed that these new jobs would go to those laid off and, hopefully, according to seniority. As it turned out, the boards declared they didn't have to take their new employees from an official list and could "cherry-pick" whomever they pleased.

No less important was the fact that board negotiators failed to honour what Jim Ross calls a "restructuring" agreement. This would have improved school board efficiency with minimal effect on classroom quality: "A sectoral task force was set up under the framework agreement," says Ross, "and it was committed to some definite responsibilities. These included a review of procurement, contracting systems, board operations and administrative procedures. Were they effective, were they efficient? The task force was also to explore sector-wide bulk purchases — things like software or capital purchases such as vehicles. And it was to assess and make recommendations for streamlining senior administrative structures. That would have included a consideration of what OSSTF calls a 'confederated structure' for the Ontario school system — a structure designed to solve at least some of the fiscal and administrative insanities and waste that comes from having two school systems in the province. None of this has happened. There were also supposed to be local task forces, to consider the same items as the provincial task force, but which were to be focused much more directly on their local boards. A few of these local task forces have met, but nothing has come of them. The whole cooperative effort the government talked so much about isn't anywhere to be seen. You know," Ross concluded, "at the time I thought this task force project might be the most important thing to come out of the framework agreement. As it turned out, it wasn't worth the paper it was written on."

This might also have been the case for some of the framework agreement's core provisions — like increment negotiation, the meaning of attrition, the actual length of the Social Contract and eventual exit from it — had it not been for widespread teacher resistance. In all of these areas, the boards pushed for a much harsher interpretation of the agreement than anyone could have imagined. Needless to say, these implementation troubles have ended in an extended, very messy and very expensive process of strike action and arbitration, in which the teachers have been constantly put on the defensive.

For OSSTF, the whole process has involved massive preparations for both negotiation and arbitration along with the need to build renewed determination among the membership (in even more difficult circumstances) to back their position with militant action.

What the government had in mind, in fact, was to use the boards as a battering ram against the province's teacher unions. Former OSSTF president Rod Albert, now a senior negotiator with the Federation, thinks "the only reason free collective bargaining was permitted to continue throughout the Social Contract was to permit school boards to claw back even more than the government had targeted."[5]

It was an especially comfortable strategy for the government, because it allowed them to play good cop against the boards' bad-cop persona. This was not a difficult task. A good number of boards were filled with angry representatives of the far right, and in comparison the government could present its Social Contract demands as a far more reasonable form of deficit reduction. Moreover, the use of the local boards in this fashion was a fine arms'-length technique for government revenge. In spite of his broad success at imposing the Social Contract, Rae badly wanted to hit back at the province's teachers. They had thoroughly outmanoeuvred, even embarrassed, his negotiators in resisting his strategy to make them special targets in the Social Contract process. They had avoided being split from the rest of the public sector so that they couldn't be nailed separately. And one teachers' union, OSSTF, ended up, as we have seen, giving the Public Services Coalition its most aggressive leadership. Then, to cap it all off, the teacher federations had come back to the bargaining table and done relatively well in the final version of the provincial framework agreement. As the premier and his Education Minister, Dave Cooke, considered the next stage of the Social Contract process for Ontario schools — its "implementation" at the local board level — it was understandable that they wanted to complete their offensive and to see the province's teacher unions experience more of the "shared pain" they had in mind for them.

What this required was little more than sitting on their hands. Once the framework agreement had been completed on August

9, all that was necessary was to give individual boards leeway to reinterpret this agreement in any way their lawyers thought possible. Often vague and full of holes, the agreement itself encouraged an emphasis on reinterpretation, as did the trustees' provincial organization, who had given up all pretence at cooperation with the teacher federations. Moreover, as the framework agreement was thrown into more and more arbitration battles, the perspectives of differing settlements could further loosen the ties its wording had put on board negotiators.[6] The province didn't need to provide so much as a wink or a nudge, although there is no doubt that the bureaucratic lines of communication between Queen's Park and senior levels of administration at the local boards were wide open during this "implementation" process.[7] It certainly didn't matter to the government that many of the boards' actions might violate both the spirit and the letter of the general agreement. If the boards went "too far," why then the province could intervene, as a "reasonable and caring" moderate, working for the good of the whole. But mostly, it could just sit back and watch.

This government strategy was particularly useful for those boards who were already in contract negotiations with their teachers. Under these circumstances, according to the legislation under which teachers bargain (usually referred to as Bill 100), the so-called "60-day rule" remained available for use by the boards, although Rae could easily have suspended it during the term of the Social Contract. It stands at the end of a process giving boards so inclined a free pass to unilateral contract-stripping. This is how it works: when (1) bargaining has broken down, (2) a "fact-finder" has reported on this breakdown, (3) the report has been made public at the request of one of the parties, and (4) 60 days have passed, all the terms and conditions of the contract become null and void. All a board needs to do, then, is stall negotiations, get a fact-finder's report, have it made public, and then wait for 60 days. After that they can strip to their heart's content. The teachers' only option in response is to strike. This was, of course, a very hard option in what Liz Barkley calls "the anti-worker/anti-education climate stirred up by the Rae government." In the past, Barkley notes, boards hadn't misused the 60-day rule, but in these circumstances a number of boards "figured it was time to recover all that teachers had gained over the last 50 years."[8]

As the implementation process opened up in such places as East Parry Sound and Windsor, the boards went after the weaker elementary federations first, using their contract-stripping rights under Bill 100. They were surprised at the fierce response. In spite of the hostile climate, these elementary teachers almost immediately went out on strike and stayed solid throughout.[9] It was hardly surprising that such militancy erupted, given the extreme level of contract-stripping to which they'd been subjected. Gene Lewis, the president of the elementary men's federation, estimates that as many as 70 clauses — everything from retirement gratuities to working conditions — had been removed from the East Parry Sound contract alone.

For OSSTF, one thing was certain: such attacks on Ontario's high school teachers, fuelled by the 60-day rule, would not be far behind. The Education Minister's consistent stonewalling of their pleas to suspend the rule had made that clear enough. (Later, when Dave Cooke was asked at an OSSTF assembly why he didn't order a suspension, he said he didn't want to open up the whole question of teachers' rights to collective bargaining. Surely, he smiled, the teachers didn't want that. They didn't want Mike Harris getting his hands on Bill 100, did they?[10]) As it turned out, Cooke was even unwilling to exercise his right under Bill 100 to impose arbitration. In Lambton County, when the board refused to join the teachers in an arbitration process, Cooke refused to insist on it, and thus forced OSSTF on to the picket lines. That was where he wanted them to be.[11]

Unleashing the boards against the teachers was not a simple matter of revenge for the Rae government. It was also pleased to support the boards' slash-and-burn agenda for far more practical reasons. Earlier the government had cut back on board transfers as part of its Expenditure Control Plan, and it had now further reduced these transfers by an additional 4.75 percent (as part of the Social Contract target). They didn't want local boards making up these losses from the local taxpayer, as some of the blame would obviously stick to them. (On this front, they needn't have worried. Local boards were even more adamant about keeping their taxes down, sensing a greater than usual public hostility both to themselves and to taxes generally.) Moreover, it was also important for the province to have its employees accept as tough a program of wages, job and service cuts as possible. The more the boards managed to take back beyond the demands of the Social Contract through their Bill 100 negotiations, the better. It would make the next round of provincial cuts a lot easier. A December 8, 1993 memo from the Ontario Public School Boards' Association estimates that "school boards in Ontario will save in excess of $500 million over and above the fail-safe arrangements of the Social Contract." This represents, says OSSTF, "a unilateral increase in board targets of about 25 per cent."[12] If that projection turned out anywhere close to the truth (and with current accounting procedures no one will ever know for sure), the government should be well pleased with the result.

The Fight For Increments

When the boards turned to contract-stripping in secondary education, they were somewhat more circumspect than in the primary schools sector. If the elementary teacher federations had reacted so strongly, what might they expect from an organization like OSSTF? It was a question that slowed them down a bit, but not as much as one might think. While a few boards decided to maintain reasonable relations with their teachers, they were very much in a minority. In districts like Peel, York Region, Brant County, Leeds-Grenville, Metro Toronto, the boards came on like gang-busters in an aggressive, frontal attack on teacher contracts.[13] As Earl Manners describes it, "it was like re-experiencing the Social Contract all over again. Our members were very shaken up by it. It was very traumatic. Teachers thought they had taken their hits, had tried to accept them and get down to work, and now they were looking at a whole new set of hits. We tried to meet this challenge through our efforts, along with the Public Services Coalition, to put 'a human face' on this assault, to get the public on side. But this campaign had a very limited effect. The next time we have to be a lot better at putting our case forward. What saved our bacon was the Federation's old tradition of tough collective bargaining. Even then it was nip and tuck. Many of these boards were out for blood. Our people had to be very determined to hold them back as much as we did."

The boards had already been smarting from significant reductions in provincial transfer payments in 1992 and again in 1993. Now the province wanted even more cuts, via the Social Contract, to fight the provincial deficit. Surely, many of them thought, they had suffered enough. Wasn't it time to really fight back? Not, of course, against the government, whose policy direction they generally supported and who had far too much power over them. Going after board employees, however, was another story. As the government had made clear to the boards, Bill 48 and its framework agreement provided a unique opportunity to deal with their unions and to clean house financially. It seemed an especially promising moment to attack their teachers, the "fat cats" of the public sector, who had consistently thwarted earlier cost-cutting exercises. For the first time in a long time, the public mood seemed to support such a move. Much deeper cuts than the Social Contract had envisaged might now be possible. As OSSTF's chief negotiator, Jim Ross, describes it, "There was just no cooling them out. With the Social Contract in place, many of the boards saw there had been a real breakthrough for them. The unions had made big concessions, and now was their chance to exploit these concessions."

"And nowhere," Ross continues, "did the boards try to follow up concessions more forcefully than in the area of increments." Ross was referring to the changes (increments) in salary for teachers that took place through additional qualifications and seniority over a period (or a grid) of up to thirteen years. As the Social Contract moved into gear, boards soon came to realize that increment cutbacks were, potentially, an extraordinary cash cow for the future. The boards' umbrella organization, the Ontario Public School Boards' Association, estimated that from 1994-95 to 1995-96 the increment provision of the Social Contract would save boards $535 million. And over the next ten years they would save an additional $1.6 billion.[14] It was just a matter of hanging tough.

For OSSTF the issue of the increment was especially threatening. Not only were its members looking at major salary concessions over a period of thirteen years, but its long history of support for member-equity was on the line. In Metro Toronto, for example, where the board insisted on a frozen grid (no increments to those who had not yet reached their maximum salary) it meant that junior teachers would end up contributing 8 percent of their salary in 1993-94 and 14 percent in 1994-95. Senior personnel would contribute only 2 percent in both these years.[15] And the actual financial ramifications for junior teachers, as Vice-President Jim McQueen put it, were "massive." "Over a thirteen-year span," McQueen estimated, "a beginning teacher could lose between $60,000 and $80,000. A senior teacher at the top of the grid would only lose about $6,000 during the Social Contract." Under these circumstances, the Federation faced the possibility that it could tear itself apart in a civil war between the generations, and they wanted no part of it. If the Social Contract hits had to be accepted, OSSTF determined, they would have to happen in other areas of local board budgets. In the end, that meant (over and above the Social Contract targets) a focus on staff cuts to take the place of increment cuts. The staff cuts would also be easier to take back in the future, OSSTF judged, when the public could be brought on side once more.

The increment issue, however, was a very tough nut to crack.

Not only were many boards gung-ho about it, but it was also evident that the provincial government was quite prepared to back the boards should they hang tough on the issue. In the framework agreement, the province had been obliged to abandon a frozen grid, but it had still managed to insist that the local boards should also have a crack at it. It was perhaps, as a provincial arbitrator noted, the first time in Ontario history that the government had forced this particular issue on to province-wide bargaining tables.[16] And with good reason. Dividing teachers while slashing their salaries was exactly what the government had in mind for this stage of the Social Contract. At a 1992 cabinet retreat, Rae is reported by one source to have indulged in "a long rant on the high salaries of principals and teachers and their evil increments." A year later he seemed equally adamant on the issue when confronted on a local hotline show. It was to be punishment for lack of cooperation.

An OSSTF member had phoned to complain that he would "lose $40,000, while some of my colleagues, making at least $20,000 more than I do, will lose nothing." In reply, the premier told him that the Federation had made its bed and would now be obliged to sleep in it. "But do you think this is a fair way to share the cost of the pain we're all in?" the teacher asked. In Rae's answer, we can hear not only his deep hostility to labour and its traditions, but we can catch something of his continuing determination (as the province's "good cop") to go after Social Contract resisters like the teachers: No, Rae said, it wasn't fair, but such inequity wasn't the fault of the province or the boards. It resulted from the "attitude" of union leaders, who weren't listening to their members and who hadn't been cooperating in finding fair ways to share the pain. "What we had from the trade union leadership — in the case of many of the unions — were some very rough tough aggressive speeches that might have made some sense in the '50s or '60s but don't have a whole lot to do with what we're facing in Canada in the '90s. [They] are reluctant to sit down and say, look, this is not going to work this way, but it is going to work this way, and this is how we can best protect the services and protect the kids, and accept the fact that we are all going to get a little bit less and we'll live with that. I haven't had too much success in getting that kind of response, but when people start getting speeches out of the French Revolution and singing songs and walking out of negotiations, I'm not sure you've been well-served by that process."[17]

As OSSTF entered the increment battle, it had the good fortune to achieve its bargaining strategy peacefully with the Sudbury board. Sudbury's OSSTF local achieved full restoration on the grid effective April 1, 1994. Its teacher salaries would be restored to the level they would have occupied had the Social Contract not occurred. The money to do this was achieved through extra staff cuts and by eliminating a number of paid positions of responsibility. A number of months later, again without the need for mediation or arbitration, local OSSTF negotiating teams achieved a somewhat similar pattern in Hamilton and Waterloo and then in Nipissing. In all instances, the Federation accepted further staff reductions (from 1 to 1.5 percent over the Social Contract's 4.75 percent target) in return for full status on the grid. In addition to showing other boards that such arrangements were possible, these cases set an important arbitration precedent when the Federation finally had to stand and fight on the issue.

These weren't, of course, the only precedents. Indeed, they were the exceptions to the rule, though crucial ones. With the vast majority of the boards the going was a lot rougher. A number of OSSTF locals, faced with board intransigence and wanting to avoid further escalation in the conflict, decided not to call in the provincial office for help[18] and accepted less satisfactory settlements. None, however, denied the principle of holding on to at least some restoration of the grid. A number of separate school and elementary teacher settlements, on the other hand, had entirely signed away all restoration of the increments lost during the Social Contract period. As OSSTF well knew, these contracts would be influential in the minds of arbitrators and would stiffen the resolve of board negotiators. Still, in all but two cases, where OSSTF reached a settlement in this first year of negotiating, they achieved a restoration of increments for at least one or two years. These settlements, however, were few and far between. The vast majority of OSSTF locals were still getting nowhere in their negotiations. Stonewalled by their boards, most were now preparing themselves for a long and possibly fruitless fight. It wasn't a happy thought.

It was a problem that couldn't be solved at the provincial level of the framework agreement, where a definitive interpretation, accepted by both sides, would have settled a number of local disputes. Before the ink was dry, the boards' strategy had been to challenge clause after clause of the agreement in order to push these clauses into the courts, where they are stalled to this day. The boards had no interest in a collective solution and refused all attempts at mediation. What they wanted was as much freedom of manoeuvre as possible. "Things are so jammed up in the courts," says Earl Manners, "they will never be resolved by the time the Social Contract ends, if it ends."

OSSTF was thus left with only local precedent as a way of moving forward. And here they have been remarkably successful, much more successful than the boards had predicted. In front of local arbitrators, federation grievances have succeeded on issues like benefit rollbacks and premium caps or unilateral wage rollbacks in lieu of Rae days. There has also been the occasional elementary arbitration that has helped. In Windsor, for example, the elementary settlement on how to count staff reductions turned out to be very helpful to the city's secondary teachers in achieving their contract. And this ruling has continued to be used by OSSTF negotiators in other jurisdictions.

In the end, however, though they were important enough in their own way, these grievances didn't touch the big issues. What OSSTF needed was a breakthrough settlement on the major items. The most important of these was, of course, the restoration of increment. In order to get this, however, they had to have a board agreement that would allow their negotiations to intertwine Bill 100 and the Social Contract and would at the same time guarantee job security. Finally, they had to protect benefit plans and establish the possibility of early exit from the Social Contract provisions.

In ways that no one could have expected, it was the OSSTF contract with York Region — built, of course, on the details of prior agreements with other boards — that settled every one of these issues, and provided the Federation with a realistic new target for future negotiations.

Turning A Corner In York Region

The York Region board certainly hadn't intended to be a breakthrough board for OSSTF. They had opened with a very tough position, from which, they said, there would be no backing down. It was a promise they kept.

The York board's toughness, however, proved to be their undoing.

This toughness was focused on a major reduction of teachers (via an increase in the pupil-teacher ratio or PTR) and a wage freeze. The level of savings envisaged, the board believed, would solve all their financial problems. Thus nothing else, it seemed, mattered. When the issue of intertwining Bill 100 and the Social Contract came up, the board at first resisted, and then said, Why not? Certainly the logic of what they wanted to do and what Rae wanted to do were compatible: both focused on downsizing and on wage reductions. Why not run the negotiations in sync? They also said, right at the beginning, that the teachers needn't worry about job loss. Teacher reductions, large though they might be, could be handled by attrition. York Region's rapid expansion of about 3 percent a year would make that possible. That left only the issues of increment, benefits, and early exit to be resolved, with the increment central to the board's proposed claw-back of teacher salaries.

In this way, OSSTF found itself with a straight run at the increment, with these other key issues attached, and within a framework of job security and integration of Bill 100 and Social Contract negotiations.

It was clear that these issues would not be settled peacefully and would finally come to arbitration, one way or the other. A judgement would eventually be made that would settle the options for the vast majority of OSSTF locals across the province. It now was win or lose for the Federation, and they prepared to mount the toughest fight they could.

As it turned out, the Federation didn't have to give it its best on the picket line. It was a combination of careful accounting, political smarts, and coolness under fire that delivered what the press called a major victory. On August 31, 1994, provincially-appointed arbitrator, Morton Mitchnick, chose the bulk of the teachers' position in a modified form of "final offer selection." The board had stayed too tough, he said. The teachers had been "more reasonable."

Headlines in *The Toronto Star* announced "We won, York teachers say," and "Ruling snubs social contract, board charges." The York "victory," said *The Star*, focused on teachers "winning the right to receive 'increments' ... while under the social contract.... When the social contract ends in September, 1996, teachers will be back on a 10-year grid without having lost three years' seniority." A total of 116 teaching positions would be forfeited but no jobs would be lost; the positions would simply disappear through attrition. Jim McQueen, the chairperson of the OSSTF negotiating team, was delighted with the decision. "The award," he said, "could set a precedent for teacher negotiations around the province by allowing full incremental raises, even while salaries are frozen under the three-year social contract. We're hoping this kind of settlement will have ramifications around the province."[19]

On the other side of the bargaining table, the chairperson of the York board's negotiating team, Harvey Nightingale, cried panic. The arbitrator's award, said Nightingale, "defeats the whole purpose of the legislation. The whole intent of the law was not have 'ballooning' at the end of the social contract." The board, he said, would "now have to pay an extra $4.4 million to secondary teachers to cover the payments. Similar monies paid to all staff could wind up costing the board $11 million." As a result, "in 1996 we're going to be facing massive tax increases and/or program reductions."

What is important to note is that this victory was much more limited than that suggested by *The Star*. Certainly, OSSTF had carried out its strategy successfully and had won an important part of this particular battle. But they were still losing the war and could not help but continue to do so. The Social Contract framework could have no other outcome. This is so, even though Harvey Nightingale was probably correct in saying that Mitchnick's decision went contrary to the intent (though not necessarily the letter) of Bill 48, and even though Jim McQueen was quite right to hope that it would have ramifications across the province. It did, indeed, prove a turning point for the Federation.

Underneath the headlines, as the contract clauses make plain, lay quite a different reality. OSSTF hadn't won anything. Their losses had simply been less than most people figured they would be. The York board, in turn, could hardly be described as the loser in this affair. All that had happened was that its winnings had been somewhat reduced. OSSTF doesn't pretend otherwise. As they describe this settlement, it was the York Board which ended up in good shape financially, not the Federation. "I do not trumpet York Region as a great victory for OSSTF," says Rod Albert, its provincially appointed negotiator. "The union made the difference between being assaulted and being raped."

But what of Harvey Nightingale's display of outraged surprise and gloomy predictions of future poverty? For OSSTF, Nightingale was only playing to the gallery in hopes of covering up a disastrous internal collapse of the York board's negotiating team. Harvey Nightingale had good reason, however, to be upset. The collapse, which was not his fault, had resulted in a situation that eventually undermined his Board's hard line and ended in OSSTF's official "victory." Nightingale had been hoping he could take home almost all the marbles, not just a majority of them. If it hadn't been for OSSTF's capacity to handle delicate and difficult negotiations, he might just have pulled it off.

I said OSSTF's relative success in York Region had come from a combination of careful accounting, political smarts and coolness under fire. Probably it was the latter two that counted most, but I want to take the area of careful accounting first, starting with the opening set of numbers crunched by the York Regional Board. These finances are a bit heavy going, I confess, and more than most readers will want to know about this situation. But these details are important nevertheless, if we are to capture some of the on-going reality of local board negotiations with their teachers.

Meeting The Bottom Line

The York Board began the bargaining in the spring of 1993, prior to the Social Contract. Its objective was to reduce its secondary budget of $105 million by $7.5 million. It was a figure on which they remained inflexible and it eventually cost them the final arbitration. At this point, however, the board's hard line, as the arbitrator described it, "set the mood for negotiations, and from there matters only got worse, as the passage of time and negotiation sessions only served to underscore the Board's statement that this was 'not a negotiating posture.'"

It was a mood, I should add, that was not especially friendly to begin with. The board was already angry at its teachers' refusal to reopen their contracts in 1992. In its last collective agreement (for 1991-93), the York board figured it had settled too early and had lost a good deal in the process. Its teachers had won an 11.2 percent wage increase over two years. Other boards had clearly done better, meaning their teachers had done worse. York Region teachers, the board complained, were now "the highest paid in the province," which was pretty close to the truth.[20] When the 1992 budget came on the horizon, the trustees realized this settlement was a lot more than they wanted to pay. The York Region system was expanding, and they were now facing a $13 million reduction in provincial transfers. Understandably, they wanted a wage roll-back. Understandably, the teachers didn't want to give it to them. When the board didn't get their roll-back, they ended up having to cut $18 million from other parts of their budget. Part of that cut — and part of their new determination to play hardball with their teachers — included unilaterally raising the pupil-teacher ratio (PTR), which took 72 secondary teachers out of the system. This move enraged the local OSSTF, who said it was illegal since the 1991-93 contract was still in force and there was no 60-day rule operating. The Federation immediately grieved the action.

When the chair of the York board opened negotiations for 1993, he declared that the situation was even worse than the previous year and that the board would be even tougher. "Enrolments," he said, "continue to climb. Provincial contributions will be less than 1992. The Board's operating costs are greater. Without cutting expenditures, the tax increase would be approximately 12%. The community cannot afford this. The Board will cut expenditures. Despite these cuts the tax increase will be considerably greater than inflation. Morally," he went on, "the Board, as a member of the community, must make sacrifices. The budget increases must be restrained. This will unquestionably affect all of us. Realistically, there is no alternative.... The reality is that the Board needs to reduce its annual costs of this collective agreement by $7.5 million. I emphasize, this is not a negotiating position. It is our position for settlement. It is the Board's view that these dollars can be found in two significant ways. The first is a wage freeze. The second is an increase in the pupil teacher ratio of 1.0."[21]

It was an approach that would turn out to be an exact replica of Bob Rae's Social Contract style: pick a number, don't budge from it, don't discuss it, moralize about sharing the pain, and as negotiations proceed, focus entirely on *how* the cuts should take place.

For OSSTF, the board's $7.5 million figure was always

what Rod Albert called "a political number." Nowhere did they effectively defend it. "You can see it's soft," says Albert, "when you consider the board's view that the PTR increase would be made without layoffs, through attrition and expansion of the system. Our figures showed that without layoffs, the board would only come up with a cut of 70 or 80 teachers in the 1993-94 school year, not the 116 teachers as they planned and said was crucial."

All of this, don't forget, took place before the Social Contract. When the Social Contract was introduced, the board realized it would lose another $5 million in transfer payments from its $105 million secondary budget. And since it didn't want to increase taxes or cut from those areas which had already taken an $18 million hit the year before, the board decided that its entire $12.5 million loss (the new $5 million plus the original $7.5 million) should come out of the secondary teacher budget line. It was a position made stronger by Tory and Reform Party activists on the board, who were especially concerned that York Region as a whole maintain its low commercial property taxes, in order to draw industry from other parts of the Greater Toronto Area. They also saw the cuts as part of a broader right-wing emphasis on downsizing government. The only area in which the position softened — partly when they worked out that it would be more effective to fuse the earlier Bill 100 negotiations with those of the Social Contract — lay in the method for calculating the 1.0 increase in PTR. The provincial staffing roll-back of 4.75 percent amounted to a 0.75 increase in the PTR, and the York Board decided it would allow that to be included in its 1.0 increase. The board could make up the difference, trustees figured, with a three-year increment freeze.[22]

OSSTF continued to hold fast to its strategy of grid restoration and an acceptance of staff reductions, when cuts could no longer be avoided. During these months of negotiations the Federation continued to make various offers following this strategy — offering to save money through more Rae days, more unpaid leave, more early retirements — but the board wasn't biting.

By the spring of 1994, with the parties still miles apart,

OSSTF knew it had to take the first level of strike available. A work-to-rule was called, and it eventually resulted in Morton Mitchnick being brought in as the provincial mediator. The mediator's job, in his own words, was "to kickstart the negotiations." He had some initial success. The board now made its first (and it turned out its last) move from its original savings target. It offered the teachers payment of increment in the first year of the collective agreement, which reduced its savings by $1.877 million. However, it still demanded "a permanent roll-back of the PTR by 1.0 (115/116 teachers), and permanent non-payment or credit of increment for the second and third years."[23]

For OSSTF, it was a completely unacceptable offer. The Federation once more dug in its heels and prepared for more traditional strike action. It was at this point, said the mediator in measured tones, that "with the prospect of an escalation on the sanction side, [the parties] elected instead to allow this matter to be resolved through the voluntary mediation-arbitration process...."[24] But beyond its first-year payment of increment the board was not prepared to go. Certainly it was not prepared for any restoration on the grid, which it continued to argue was in contradiction to the Social Contract Act and its Framework Agreement "to effect *permanent* savings in cash outlays (over and above the mandated 4.75 percent reduction in staffing), and perhaps more importantly ... from a labour relations point of view will only lead the parties in 1996 back into the same situation they were in in 1993."[25]

OSSTF continued to offer "reasonable" solutions. Both parties recognized that with the rapid growth of the York system, the board was likely to reach its Social Contract staffing target of 4.75 percent through attrition by September 1994. With even 75 percent of this amount, the mediator reports, York Region and its teachers "were a long way along the road to meeting their annual 'cash' target of $5.045 million as well." Both parties agreed on these figures. So why not an "early exit," OSSTF asked, adding further sweeteners which included a proposal to exceed the 4.75 percent staffing cuts mandated by the framework agreement by 18 teachers. In this area, the Federation's offer was now quite close to the board's position. With its additional teacher cut, the Federation was prepared to lose about 100 teachers overall. The board's demand for a 1.0 increase in the PTR was the equivalent of 115/116 teachers. Only 15-16 teachers separated them. Yet still the board hung tough on its 1.0 increase in pupil-teacher ratio. It also stayed firm on its demand for complete increment-withholding in the second and third years of the contract. On this latter issue, the teachers now proposed "to *defer* the payment of increments, in the first year only, to June 1, 1994 — a 'cash' savings for the Board of 90% of the increment in that first year."[26]

When it eventually accepted final offer selection, the board held on tenaciously to its position. Not only did it retain its offer on PTR and the increment, but its costing proposals forbade teachers any credit for reduction in staffing over the 4.75 percent Social Contract cut or for saving on increment payout beyond the first year of the agreement. Even when board negotiators saw the teachers' final offer, after which they might have been expected to moderate their own, they did not budge. It was, in fact, the position most trustees wanted to put before their public. It was central to their neo-conservative politics. The same politics now told them that they had to hang on to this position, however much it went against the grain of the arbitration in which they were now participants.

The teachers, on the other hand, were operating entirely within the logic of final-offer selection and were especially careful in crafting their final position. After much deliberation, they decided to swallow the board's entire 1.0 increase in PTR, primarily to be the "more reasonable party." At the same time, however, they were already living with an illegal cut of 72 teachers from 1993, and whatever they said those teachers would be lost to them for at least this year. They also knew that attrition wouldn't cut much more than that figure in the first year of a new agreement. So simple short-term realism was also a factor in the acceptance of the 1.0 increase in PTR. But Federation "reasonableness" on this issue was what really counted. For with this concession in place, the Federation figured it could then "reasonably" present the increment, benefit and early exit package they wanted, not only for York Region but for the province as a whole.

On the benefit front they asked for a Unemployment Insurance bridge for parental/pregnancy leave and 100% of the Ontario Dental Association dental plan rate, which would kick in on January 1, 1996, the date on which OSSTF expected to exit from the York Region Social Contract. On the restoration of increment, the Federation proposed two "lump sum" payments of 10 percent of the increments they would normally have received during the first two years of the Social Contract. Full restoration would come with teachers' first pay cheque in early May 1996, just after the freeze period specified by Bill 48. Thus, for the final year, the board would pay about 31% of that year's normal increment. Here's how these figures add up:[27]

		Teachers' Position	
	Normal Increment	Payout	Board Savings
1993-94	$1,877 million	$ 187,700	$1.689 million
1994-95	$3,754 million	$ 375,400	$3.379 million
1995-96	$5,631 million	$1,732,659	$3.898 million
		$2,295,759	$8.966 million

It was, in fact, a very "reasonable" proposal: "The total of this cash-proposal 'pay-out,'" Mitchnick noted, was "only some $400,000 more than the Board's own proposal of $1,870,000 (the cost of the first-year payout)."[28]

Overall, the teachers' position saved the board over $20 million for the three years of the Social Contract over and above their Social Contract target of $10,613,768. Divide that $20 million by 3 and you get a number pretty close to the board's starting figure of $7.5 million (which was to go on top of the Social Contract). In Mitchnick's words, the board was left with "a very substantial cushion" for future years. That's especially true since the province won't likely be as punitive in holding back transfer payments as the board has suggested, though these days you never can tell.

Rod Albert is particularly conscious of the savings the board will achieve because of its increase in the PTR. "The first year after the Social Contract," he says, "the board will save $7.65 million based on cutting 116 teachers at $66,000 [an average teacher salary]. In later years, it will be higher as the York system expands. This year, in fact, that 116 is probably 122 or so. That's because there are more kids in the system. I dare say by August 1996, the York board will be 135 to 140 teachers under-staffed in comparison to where they would have been with the original PTR. Multiply those figures by $66,000 and you get about $9 million in savings. The York board is going to do very well out of all of this."

"Of course," Albert continued, "we're going to try to get some of that staffing back after the Social Contract is over, if a new version isn't forthcoming. But it won't be easy. You win improvements in PTR in very small amounts. It's always been 0.3 or 0.4 a year. Nothing like a 5 percent change." To this, Jim McQueen adds the Federation's suspicion that the York Region board has hidden a certain amount of its future revenue, and it will be a long time before the Federation can put its finger on it. "Take the provincial decision last spring," he says, "that made it legal for boards to apply lot levies for education. There are a great many new buildings going up in York Region, and I would think a lot of new money is being taken in from lot levies. The board is saying it's just peanuts. We can't prove them wrong at the moment, but it seems to me there are probably millions of dollars going into its coffers from this source."

At an individual teacher level the York Region settlement certainly hurt. But it hurt a lot less than it could have, had OSSTF not won the increment settlement it did. And it is here, of course, that we see the reason for the Federation's big sigh of relief in the York "victory." Take, for example, a teacher in York Region between 1992-1993 and 2003-2004, with two years experience and nothing added from new negotiations or new qualifications. In these years, following OSSTF's York Region settlement, this teacher will lose $14,406. Had he or she received two out of three years of increment, as had happened with a number of other boards, this teacher would have lost $24,154. The York Board's final offer, had it been accepted, would have driven that figure up to $48,309. Finally, had the grid remained frozen, as Bill 48 originally intended, the loss would have ended up as $72,464.[29]

Teachers also lost, as their students did, on the size of the classes in which they had to work. But it is hard to say how much. Raising the PTR certainly puts pressure on class size growth. But OSSTF is fighting hard to have this growth as small as possible, mostly by arguing for a better balance between administration and classroom teachers. The "teacher" component in PTR includes school administration, which can be restructured or done by non-teachers, thus freeing more teaching personnel for the classroom. How much this will happen in York Region is still up for grabs. The Federation understands, however, that such a fight is essential in York Region and elsewhere, if it is to build a serious alliance with parent, student and community groups. Decent class sizes are key to an effective and popular public school system.

Down-Home Politics

On the more political front, OSSTF largely out-manoeuvred the York board. And this was certainly at the core of the success they achieved.

First, the Federation managed to get the board to integrate Bill 100 and the Social Contract negotiations. There was a certain logic to the board going this route, since their aims were so similar to those of the Rae government. But as a negotiating tactic it made little sense, particularly if they were expecting a lengthy strike or lockout, as it seems they were. OSSTF isn't sure what actually persuaded the board to take up their suggestion of fusing the two sets of negotiations. Perhaps board negotiators were convinced by Federation arguments that this was the most efficient way of proceeding, the best way to strike a deal on all the issues. Or perhaps it was simple arrogance, the trustees figuring they didn't need a backup argument denying arbitration for Social Contract matters, which was still legally a grey area. They could simply hammer home their two issues of increment and PTR to public acclaim. Whatever OSSTF did, it certainly had the good sense not to let the board know how worried they were that this legislative fusion wouldn't take place at their level of negotiation. They knew only too well how difficult it would be for them if they had to fight this battle on two fronts. They needed the established Bill 100 pattern of teacher sanctions to fight the Social Contract. Besides, Federation negotiators expected a long strike or lockout. If at the end of it, the arbitrator bought a board argument that he could only deal with Bill 100 items (a legal possibility) then that would mean that the issue of increment, which came under the Social Contract framework agreement, would simply be left in abeyance. Their strike would have been for nothing. (It was only on the day of the York Region settlement that the ERC (Education Relations Commission) came down with a decision in Grey County that insisted the board deal with both Bill 100 and Social Contract issues. And even this decision is on shaky legal ground and could still be challenged in the courts.)

The second important political factor in OSSTF's success in York Region was its democratic form of negotiating. Prior to OSSTF's central office team coming to York, a strong local negotiating team had already built up a solid operating procedure, a good network of contacts and a trusting relationship with their membership. Jim McQueen, as takeover chair, was very insistent that these local strengths be built upon and that the new teacher negotiating team function as one. Local pressure from York teachers was always available at every step of the Bill 100 process in which sanctions were called for. However tough the board was, OSSTF knew it could respond to this pressure. When the strike vote came, it would be very much a local decision, not manipulated from the top, and much stronger for it. McQueen's democratic style also involved a process whereby local negotiators could keep on negotiating informally with whoever wanted to talk to them. As his chief negotiator Rod Albert put it, "We figured that if the York people had their own ways of shaking the tree, more power to them. We wanted to keep things loose and open. All that mattered was that we kept in close contact."

On the other side of the bargaining table, it was the issue of contact — or lack of it — that finally destroyed the board's negotiating team. The story of this team's collapse is a very complex one, which we can hardly begin to cover here. All I can offer is a summary of how OSSTF negotiators told it to me:

"The first thing you have to know about the York board at the time of the Social Contract," they told me, "is that it was no longer being run by its director, Bob Cressman. Cressman was a local powerhouse and a guy who liked to wade in there to make the big deals. Not a bad guy, in fact. At least from our point of view. From the board's perspective, though, he had recently dealt himself a big problem. He was the guy who had finessed a contract which had given York teachers a 11.2 percent raise in 1991-93. The board was so mad about it, they bought Cressman out of his last year of a five-year contract. Threw a quarter of million dollars at him, just to see him out of there. Then they brought in Bill Hogarth, who had been a supervisory officer in North York, and who they figured would be much more compliant than Cressman. They didn't want a director-led board anymore; they wanted someone they could control. The trustees pushing for this were politically motivated right-wingers, who had the votes on their side. People like Harvey Nightingale and Bill Crothers, the new chair of the board. They were determined that trustees, like themselves, were going to be in charge for once. A new tough-minded politics would now set the agenda.

"In the end, though," the story continues, "when it came to our negotiations, nobody, it seemed, was in charge. The new hard-nosed politics went haywire. And it cost them. Boy, did it cost them.

"The first thing they did was to agitate against the appointment of our first mediator, David Fleet. Fleet was a former Liberal MPP in Peterson's government and Nightingale is a bag man for the Conservative Party. Nightingale was dead set on getting rid of Fleet, and eventually he succeeded. The Education Relations Commission pulled Fleet, but then they turned around and gave us Mort Mitchnick, who was probably much better for us at this critical stage of bargaining.

"The other thing that happened was that the new chair, Bill Crothers, and the new director, Bill Hogarth, decided on a secret alliance and tried to pull off their own secret set of negotiations with us. At the time, though, we didn't realize that this was happening and that the meetings our people were having with these two were especially secret. Of course, we expected everyone to be discreet. But we figured the board was acting like we did — using different combinations of negotiators to shake out different concessions from their opponents, yet always operating out of a strategic centre. Checking things out with each other. As it turned out, they were doing nothing of the sort and were trying to develop a side deal that would end up as the main settlement. They kept everything that was said to themselves. Not a peep to the rest of their negotiating team. And it was this that did them in.

"Now, we should say here, that Crothers and Hogarth weren't selling out their side on any of the major issues. Really, they were just putting forward a different version of the board's original hard line. What they were offering, in fact, would have been worse than what the board eventually offered us. The main thing these two were pushing was a scheme for low-seniority teachers to handle extra classes. Not only was it unfair in terms of workload, it would also have upped the PTR by more than 1.0. We didn't want anything to do with it. But we believed in keeping all the channels open. And to some extent we took what they said into account when we were making counterproposals at the main negotiating table.

"By April it was clear that we weren't getting anywhere. The talks with Crothers and Hogarth continued to lead us into dead ends and the main set of negotiations weren't functioning much better. Finally, we got so fed up with it all, we said the hell with it. We're going to have to go out on a work-to-rule. Which is what we did, and the members were really solid. Now the board would have to react. In June, two weeks before the end of school, they started to move. The word came down that all the final marks must be collected from the teachers. No exceptions. That was on a Monday. At the same time, they asked for an arbitration session for Thursday or Friday. We figured they were going to lock us out on the next Monday at the regular board meeting. That was certainly the information we received from our board sources. And it seemed logical enough, given the board's determination to hang tough on their position.

"Then something happened that was just fate. One of those really strange things that occur sometimes and you just have to go with it. In the sidebar discussions our people were having with Hogarth and Crothers, there were many items discussed, and there was one of them we figured could easily fit into the larger package we wanted to see in place. When we were alone with Mitchnick during the arbitration session, we told him about this. We did it almost in passing. Nothing at all heavy about it. Later, we realized Mitchnick was astonished that we'd been having these discussions. But at this point, he was very low key. Did we have documentation? he asked us. Sure, we said, a whole raft of it. Crothers and Hogarth had given it to Lynn Johnston (the local president) and Ron Gable (the local's chief negotiator), who were doing most of the talking during these sessions. So we handed the stuff over to Mitchnick. And he went off to see the board caucus. Talk about throwing the cat among the pigeons.

"It was about 10:30 at night. Despite having given the board a revised offer, our negotiating team was still expecting a lockout on Monday morning. Around 1:00 a.m. we phoned the board's caucus room. What the hell are you waiting for? we asked. But nobody would tell us anything. Then around 2:00 a.m. Mitchnick phoned and said he was coming up with the board negotiator, Colette Nemni, and Harvey Nightingale. A few minutes later there they were at our door. We were then treated to an extraordinary apology. They hadn't seen a word, Nightingale told us, of the proposals we'd been discussing with Crothers and Hogarth. And they didn't know what the hell to do about it. There had been so much deceit, they couldn't put themselves together. They had no idea how to proceed. Their entire negotiating position has collapsed. At the end they said that all they could do was to leave the hotel and go back to the board on Monday night. That was Mitchnick's conclusion too.

"But we couldn't leave it at this. We turned to Nightingale and said, Look, we have 1,700 teachers coming to the board meeting Monday night because we're convinced you are going to lock us out. What are we going to say to them? Nightingale said he couldn't guarantee there wouldn't be a lockout, but he promised that if there was, he'd resign as chair of the York negotiating team and hold a press conference where he would level with everyone about what really happened. With that, we agreed to hold back our demonstration. It was the right move. The board met in private, and once they heard what had happened, they passed a motion that said the board chair couldn't talk to anybody about negotiations. Everything had to go through the vice-chair. And they made us a proposal: Rather than have a straight arbitration, as we had suggested, they wanted final-offer-selection arbitration. This process involved two days of arbitration, and if the parties failed to settle, both sides would submit a final offer and the arbitrator would pick one or the other. (In this case, there were some stand-alone items, as well, on which both sides also put forward positions, one of which would be chosen by the arbitrator.)

"This offer was high-stakes poker for us, but we knew we had no alternative but to go for it. If we don't, we told our members, the board will lock us out and we'll walk the picket line — maybe all summer — and they'll make a fortune on our lost wages. That was their plan to begin with. With the public on side, the board figured they could break us. What really worried us was what would happen with a new arbitrator, who would come in after we had been legislated back to work. There was no guarantee he wouldn't hang us out to dry on the Social Contract items. At that point we hadn't had the ERC ruling from Grey County that said it was OK to fuse Social Contract and Bill 100 negotiations.

"Just as important for our decision to go with final-offer selection was that we had confidence in Mort Mitchnick because of his role as our mediator. He knew the figures and the issues. It seemed likely to us that the board would try to hold its hard line when they made their final offer. Final offer selection let them stay tough, and if they lost, they could scapegoat the arbitrator. Which is what they did. They accused Mitchnick of breaking the law in choosing the teachers' position. It was too bad that papers like *The Star* supported that argument. Anyway, we knew we were being a hell of a lot more reasonable in the context, and that Mitchnick was no fool. Most important we knew our figures were solid. When we saw they hadn't moved from their figures — Mitchnick had us exchange our two final positions in hopes of last-minute changes — we felt pretty confident. Though, God knows, we still had our hearts in our throats the day the announcement came through that we'd won. It's always chancy."

Beginning A New Politics

I have taken some time with the York example, not only because it proved a turning point for OSSTF in its negotiations with its local boards, but also because it tells us something about what it is like to be in the trenches these days as a teacher unionist.

It's crazy, it's intense, and it's all-encompassing. As you can see, struggles with local boards have become impossibly complex in both their financial and their political implications. Teacher negotiators and local activists are constantly having to fly by the seat of their pants to meet crisis after crisis. And they live daily schedules that would kill most of us.

Before the York outcome, these struggles were taking a very heavy toll on local negotiating teams. Many of the complexities and the difficulties experienced in York County were being repeated for OSSTF, in many different forms, in district after district across the province. And no one could find much light at the end of the tunnel. A serious demoralization was beginning to set in. Then York happened and a new realistic target became possible. Here was something that could actually be won, not just received as a gift from a few of the less punitive boards.

York was the first real test of what what could be achieved within the Social Contract legislation, and it brought OSSTF locals back into the struggle again with renewed energy and determination. Sometimes the result was as favourable as the York settlement, sometimes not. But on the whole the Federation has been remarkably successful in its bid to restore increment payments on their salary grids. By March 1995, nineteen public boards had agreed to give their high school teachers full restoration on the grid by September 1996, while another seven accepted two-out-of-three years restoration (with an additional board offering a cash payment instead of these two years). Four boards have agreed to pay only one out of three years.[30] But on no occasion has the Federation had to walk away from the table entirely empty-handed on this issue. Even in the area of non-teaching employees, where the framework agreement did not permit a strategy of grid restoration, OSSTF managed to get three settlements in which there was full restoration by September 1996.

Bob Rae will not be pleased.

OSSTF hopes that with the success of these settlements, the bargaining process may be a little easier for those districts that have yet to sign a contract. But not for a moment can it afford to let down its guard. Over the next year the Federation must continue to hang very tough on the issue. In the language of the OSSTF newsletter for Federation negotiators, school boards "continue to see the opportunity to generate savings from not paying increments and are quite prepared to be unyielding if Bargaining Units fail to make them priority items."[31]

There are still many battles to go. But there is every reason to think that the increment issue will continue to be solved, as well as can be expected, by Federation negotiators as these local conflicts come to their various conclusions over the next year or so.

In the wake of this success, however, there remains the growing issue of class size. This too will have to be resolved at the local level. Having given up teachers for increment, the Federation now feels the heat on pupil-teacher ratios.

In response to this heat, what the Federation proposes is the kind of restructuring Jim Ross hoped would emerge from the sectoral task force set up under the Social Contract framework agreement.[32] On many different fronts, local OSSTF negotiators are approaching boards with suggestions for a more efficient school organization in order to keep class sizes stable. As noted above, there are a good many teachers and administrators included in the pupil-teacher ratio who are not actually in a classroom, and OSSTF is trying to find ways to return more educators to their primary role. "Too many boards," says Earl Manners, "have tried to isolate their senior staff from the cuts. We have to press hard for a classroom-focused restructuring." In places like Grey County the Federation has succeeded. In its last contract with the Grey County board, the PTR went up while the class size stayed the same. Indeed, this contract insisted on a ceiling for both class size and teacher workload. The problem with this solution, however, is that it reduces the range of programs available to students, many of which had been developed by OSSTF members. And local teachers have found it very hard to let their programs go. But, however painful, it appeared to make the best of a bad situation. (The real solution was obviously fewer cuts.) OSSTF has also, with less success, been pushing for board efficiencies on a wide range of administrative and social services so that these too can be turned to classroom support.

As we move into the issue of class size, we move into the larger question of quality education. It is here that the "down-home" politics of money and power meet the broader politics of what that money and power are for. The defence of small class size is a defence of strong teacher-pupil relationships. If these relationships don't matter, class size doesn't much matter, either. If the interaction between teachers and pupils doesn't count in the quality of what is learned, then any number of kids can be squeezed into a room for "efficient" instruction and testing.

If OSSTF is to effectively fight for class size, and for the money that makes that possible, it must be fighting for a particular kind of curriculum and pedagogy: where human relationships count most of all. In many respects, it is a new kind of politics, though these can never be divorced from an older political focus on decent funding and democratic process.

As we saw in Chapter 1, OSSTF was in no position to mount such politics as the new NDP government assumed office. The Federation had helped to defeat David Peterson from the perspective of its old-style "politics of money." More is good for kids, it said. And, *sotto voce*, more is good for teachers. When the Social Contract hit the Federation in the third year of Bob Rae's mandate, the world, as we have seen, was a different place. Schools and teachers were now on the defensive as they had never been before, and not simply as a result of tax-payer grumbling. Much more fundamental issues of what should and should not to be taught were now on the table. A massive corporate/bureaucratic media campaign, focused on both the deficit and a "back-to-basics" curriculum, had managed to shift the emphasis in public debate away from support of public schooling. Much could no longer be taken for granted. More was not necessarily better. Massive cutbacks were not necessarily bad. Public support for Ontario teachers standing against the Social Contract was not necessarily there, though polls continued to show a surprisingly high level of such support in actuality.[33] There was every likelihood that the public would not back a full-scale resistance to Bill 48's impact on education, as it would not back such resistance in support of public services generally. And organizations like OSSTF figured they had no option but to pull in their horns.

By the time the NDP government released the report of its Royal Commission on Learning in the final year of its administration, however, OSSTF had had the opportunity to collect its thoughts. It was not as much time as the organization needed, but it was enough to open up a much more serious level of resistance than it had managed in the initial round of the Social Contract battle. For the first time in its history, OSSTF began to integrate into one coherent policy a position on the economy, on school democracy, and on classroom curriculum and teaching practice. The Federation is at a very early stage in this activity — many of its complexities have yet to be faced — but there seems no reason in the immediate future for this policy process not to continue to grow progressively stronger.

A good many of these policies have been developed in conversation, over a number of years, with the Federation's public sector allies and with the labour movement as a whole. Sometimes this conversation has been heated, but it has always been valuable for both labour and teacher activists, and there is now a growing degree of unity on many fundamental questions.

In the next chapter I want to consider these developing policies in the context of OSSTF's response to the Royal Commission, which, as I understand it, is a direct extension of the original Social Contract assault on Ontario schools.

FOOTNOTES

1 French, Larry, "Memo to the Provincial Executive, re: Public Services Coalition: The Way Forward," September 14, 1993.

2 Papp, Leslie and Ferguson, Derek, "Teachers' unions end boycott of key talks," *Toronto Star*, July 22, 1993.

3 Mackie, Richard, "Social-contract talks full of plot twists," *Globe and Mail*, July 24, 1993.

4 Kastner, Susan, "Liz Barkley's 180-degree turn," *Toronto Star*, August 9, 1993.

5 Albert, Rod, Interview with George Martell, September 19, 1994.

6 See Jewell, Duncan, "Report from OPSTF," *OPSTF News*, February 1994, p. 24.

7 A good example of the Education Ministry's capacity to communicate to local board officials during the Social Contract can be found in the York Region Separate School Board's decision to issue layoff notices to 300 teachers. See Moloney, Paul, "Teacher union says province behind layoffs," *Toronto Star*, April 30, 1994.

8 Barkley, Liz, Interview with George Martell, January 4, 1994.

9 See Duffy, Andrew, "Teachers blame Rae for school strikes," *Toronto Star*, Nov. 25, 1993.

10 Cooke, Dave, Question-and-answer period, following his speech to the OSSTF Annual Assembly, March 14, 1994.

11 In a letter to Betty Ann Bushnell (OSSTF files), March 2, 1994, Dave Cooke not only refuses to suspend the 60-day rule, he makes its clear that teacher strikes and back-to-work legislation will be considered routine activities within the framework of Bill 100.

12 OSSTF Political Action, *Factsheet*, Trustee Elections '94, "Social Contract and Local Education, Social Contract: Pretext for Contract Stripping."

13 The Ontario Education Relations Commission (ERC) reported that "there were 10 uses of the 60-day rule during the seventeen years from 1975 to 1992. From 1992 to September 1994 there have been 10 additional uses...." OSSTF Political Action, *Factsheet, Trustee Elections '94*, "Social Contract and Local Education, Social Contract: Pretext for Contract Stripping."

14 Ontario Public School Boards Association, "Financial Impact of Increment Provision," January, 1994.

15 Here is the analysis produced by the OSSTF Political Action Committee of Metro Toronto in a document entitled "The Road Back from the Social Contract: Recommendations for removing bargaining inequities caused by Bill 48," May 27, 1994.

> Bill 48 (48.6) suspends movement on the grid for teachers and other board employees (Professional Student Support Personnel, support staff, etc.) as of June 14, 1993. The Sectoral Agreement Schools Sector for TPA Members (7.2, 1.d) freezes grid movement 'unless by agreement of the parties' see attached Framework Agreement). Boards thus have a veto on negotiating grid movement, which a large number of them are using. To restore equity in this area the government should amend Bill 48 and produce accompanying regulations as needed to force boards to negotiate grid movement if employees desire this approach, and to allow arbitrators to make awards in this area if necessary.
>
> The extent of the present inequity is outlined [below] on the impact of the increment freeze on junior teachers. In the Metro area, junior teachers will contribute up to 8% of annual salary in 1993-94, while the Director, senior superintendents and teachers at maximum salary will contribute up to 2%. In 1994-95, junior teachers will contribute up to 14% of annual salary, while other

senior personnel will contribute up to 2%. This inequity cannot be justified.

Junior Teachers have contributed more this year:

Position	*93 salary*	*$$ lost*	*% salary lost*
Director (at max)	148,855	2,858	1.92 (5 unpaid days @261 days)
Senior Super	130,051	2,305	1.92 (5 unpaid days @261 days)
Cat. 4 Max teacher	65,153	1,153	1.77 (3.4 unpaid days @ 194 days)
Cat. 4, Step 5	47,976	3,712	7.73 ($2863 lost increment plus 1.77% of salary)

Junior teachers will contribute even more in 1994–95. (Note: assuming same number of unpaid leave days.)

Position	*93 salary*	*$$ lost*	*% salary lost*
Director (at max)	148,855	2,858	1.92 (5 unpaid days @261 days)
Senior Super	130,051	2,305	1.92 (5 unpaid days @261 days)
Cat. 4 Max teacher	65,153	1,153	1.77 (3.4 unpaid days @ 194 days)
Cat. 4, Step 5	47,976	6,751	13.7 ($5722 lost increment plus 1.77% of salary)

Their total loss is $90 million dollars, as high as $80,000 each.

The Metro Boards agree that this total (minus the increment credit which saved us all 2 unpaid days) represents their actual profit if they do not restore secondary increments for the 3 years of the Social Contract, and we fail to negotiate catch-up after 1996.

Needless to say, they are delighted with these windfall earnings that the Ontario government has handed to them at the expense of our on-grid teachers!

The Metro Boards would love to keep these millions and pay for capital construction or rising elementary enrolments with the money. Let's tell them NO. That money belongs to the teachers entitled to it.

We must not let our Boards keep these unfair profits gained at the expense of junior teachers.

The Metro teachers go on to ask: 8 other boards have restored at least one year of increment. Why has our Board refused?...

If the grid inequity continues during the three years of the social contract, metro's junior teachers will contribute a total of $90 million, which the board would like to keep as windfall profits beyond the social contract target. This irresponsible behaviour is made possible by the terms of Bill 48 and the government's attitude to increment freeze.

Although other non-education groups are affected by Bill 48's freeze on grid movement, not all groups have grids as long as those of teachers and some other board employer groups. This means that the salary difference and number of persons affected is enormously greater for teachers and other board employees than for those employee groups with shorter grids.

Ontario is the only province imposing this sort of inequity on a sub-group of employees in education, and should immediately take steps to remove itself from this invidious position.

16 See Morton Mitchnick, "Award: In The Matter Of An Interest Dispute Between OSSTF and The York Region Board of Education, 1993-96 Collective Agreement," pp. 15–16.

17 Quoted in Barkley, Liz, "Memo to OSSTF Representatives re: Lobby of Policy and Priorities Board of Cabinet," May 30, 1994.

18 In OSSTF language this provincial assistance is called "a takeover." It considerably ups the ante in the level of resistance being offered. A member of the provincial executive takes over as chair of the negotiating team, which integrates the local team with central office negotiators. At this point, the negotiating team has behind it OSSTF's very considerable strike fund.

19 Daly, Rita, "We won, York teachers say," *Toronto Star*, September 1, 1994.

20 Morton Mitchnick notes that "the Fact-Finder [in the Social Contract/Bill 100 dispute] ... to some extent ... accepted [that judgement even though] York region ranks substantially lower than that on some of the off-maximum positions on the grid, and, because of the teacher mix, in actual average teacher salaries as well." See Mitchnick, Morton, "Award: In The Matter Of An Interest Dispute Between OSSTF and The York Region Board of Education, 1993-96 Collective Agreement," pp. 2–3.

21 In Mitchnick, Morton, "Award: In The Matter Of An Interest Dispute Between OSSTF and The York Region Board of Education, 1993-96 Collective Agreement," pp. 1–2.

22 See Mitchnick, Morton, "Award: In The Matter Of An Interest Dispute Between OSSTF and The York Region Board of Education, 1993-96 Collective Agreement," p. 5.

23 Mitchnick, Morton, "Award: In The Matter Of An Interest Dispute Between OSSTF and The York Region Board of Education, 1993-96 Collective Agreement," p. 5.

24 Mitchnick, Morton, "Award: In The Matter Of An Interest Dispute Between OSSTF and The York Region Board of Education, 1993-96 Collective Agreement," p. 6

25 Mitchnick, Morton, "Award: In The Matter Of An Interest Dispute Between OSSTF and The York Region Board of Education, 1993-96 Collective Agreement," p. 8

26 See, Mitchnick, Morton, "Award: In The Matter Of An Interest Dispute Between OSSTF and The York Region Board of Education, 1993-96 Collective Agreement," pp. 7–8.

27 Mitchnick, Morton, "Award: In The Matter Of An Interest Dispute Between OSSTF and The York Region Board of Education, 1993-96 Collective Agreement," p. 13.

28 Mitchnick, Morton, "Award: In The Matter Of An Interest Dispute Between OSSTF and The York Region Board of Education, 1993-96 Collective Agreement," p. 14.

29 York Region Statistical Analysis of Grid Placement (Prepared by Rod Albert, OSSTF negotiator, York Region). Assume a teacher with 2 years experience as of August 31, 1992.

School Year	*Normal Grid (Placement)*	*Restoration Deal*	*Taking 2 of 3 Increments*	*Board Offer*	*No Restoration*
1992-93	$43,468	$43,768	$43,768	$43,768	$43,768
1993-94	$46,789	$43,768+302=44,070	$43.768	$43,768	$43,768
1994-95	$49,811	$43,768+604=44,372	$46,789	$43.768	$43,768
1995-96	$52,824	$43,768+2807=46,575	$49,811	$46.789	$43,768
1996-97	$55,846	$55,846	$52,824	$49,811	$46,789
1997-98	$58,866	$58,866	$55,846	$52,844	$49,811
1998-99	$61,887	$61,887	$58,866	$55,846	$52,824
1999-2000	$64,904	$64,904	$61,887	$58,866	$55,846
2000-01	$67,923	$67,923	$64,904	$61,887	$58,886
2001-02	$67,923	$67,923	$67,923	$64,904	$61,887
2002-03	$67,923	$67,923	$67,923	$67,923	$64,904
2003-04	$67,923	$67,923	$67,923	$67,923	$67,923
	$706,386	$691,980	$682,232	$658,077	$633,933*

On a "no change" grid basis, a teacher with 2 years experience would have earned $706,386 between 1992-2001 without the Social Contract intrusion. With the Social Contract deal negotiated in York Region that same teacher will lose $14,406 and earn $691,980. If the York deal had paid 2 of the 3 years of increment starting in 1994, the same teacher would have "lost" $24,154 and earned $682,232. The York Region Board of Education's offer would have seen this teacher lose $48,309.

* Without restoration to the proper grid level, the grid is actually lengthened by 3 years to reach maximum in 2003-2004. This scenario results in the teacher losing $72,464.

30 OSSTF, *The Negotiator*, "The Struggle for Grid Restoration," March 1995, p.3.

31 OSSTF, *The Negotiator*, "The Struggle for Grid Restoration," March 1995, p.3.

32 See p. 133 of this chapter.

33 The last decade of public opinion surveys conducted by the Ontario Institute of Studies in Education (OISE) show this support. See, for example, Livingstone, D.W., Hart, D., and Davie, L.E., *Public Attitudes Towards Education in Ontario, 1994: The Tenth OISE Survey*, Toronto, OISE Press, 1995.

Part Two

Towards a New Education Politics: A Response to the Royal Commission on Learning

Introduction

> Don't they know this struggle is about people, that it's about preserving the social fabric of our lives?
>
> –Liz Barkley, OSSTF President, 1990–95

In denying the need for Bob Rae's Social Contract and the recommendations of the Royal Commission on Learning which follow in its wake, OSSTF and its public sector allies make this core argument: Liz Barkley's view stated above — shared by labour and community activists across the country — is not a sentimental response to the economic and political realities of global capitalism. At bottom, they say, it is the most tough-minded approach possible. For it opens up the one real alternative to corporate-sponsored illusions about the workings of the new international economy and a market-driven society.

For teachers and workers in Ontario, the Social Contract battle — whether it's about an efficient economy, an effective decision-making structure, or a really useful set of state services — has to be focused on the relationships we establish between flesh-and-blood people. In spite of corporate language to the contrary, we cannot be reduced to extensions of machines, faceless producers and consumers, commodities to be bought and sold (to). We remain complex, thinking beings, who insist on love, however much we hate, however much we may be defined and treated as less than we are, however dark our lives may be. We all require human purposes — a continuing sense of the fulfilment of our human potential. Otherwise we die, in all the slow (and not so slow) ways the world allows us to die. If this is not recognized, then both our wealth producing capacities and our abilities to create and maintain a strong and loving society will wither. It is not recognized in the "corporate agenda" for our economy and our political system.

In other words, we cannot separate our personal lives and loves from the larger structures in which we earn our living, function as citizens, or send our children to school.

This is a hard message for organizations like OSSTF to get across, when the corporate media — with the support of politicians like Bob Rae — are trumpeting the view that only the market's "hidden hand" can be counted on to make things right. Real people can't do it. Only abstractions can be trusted. Governments (and those they represent) have to let something called "international competition" determine what and how goods will be made, who will make them, how much they will be paid (through salaries or social wages), and how the goods they produce will be sold. And everything else we call "social" must fit within this competitive framework.

In response, OSSTF and its allies say that it really doesn't work this way. The economy — both national and international — continues to be run by real people who make enormous profits and salaries for themselves, while at the same time they promote the most widespread human suffering and an incalculable waste of the world's resources. Furthermore, to borrow a line from Brecht, these allies insist that "capitalism has an address." International corporations, however "stateless" they may appear, still carry out most of their activities within the framework of the nation state, which supports their most fundamental operations. These corporations can still be resisted by nation states in alliance with other nation states. Business's mobilization of capital and labour and the public policies it advances can still be controlled and turned back in the name of a larger public good. We do not have to stand by and let "global interests" destroy what all the generations of this country have built. We can do something right now — in Canada, in Ontario — to build an effective resistance to the corporate agenda in our society, and most importantly for OSSTF, in our schools.

And in this resistance, the most important thing to remember is that we are dealing with people — not things. This is as true in the economy as it is in the classroom. Whatever the specifics of its various policy stands, OSSTF has increasingly begun to argue, this focus on the relationships between people has to be at the centre of its political vision.

With this approach in mind, in the next three chapters I deal with the Federation's response to the Royal Commission on Learning as an extension of the government's Social Contract policies.

But first, two short notes on the limitations of the analysis in these chapters.

The first of these is about rhetoric. In the Social Contract, Rae's language of "partnership" and "negotiation" was designed to be explicitly divorced from reality. Nobody believed it for a moment, and it was not meant to be believed. The ruthlessness of the Social Contract was there to be seen. Fear was the order of the day. The insistence on a signed settlement was meant for the future, when only the official text would matter, removed from its oppressive context. The rhetoric of the Royal Commission is another matter. Dealing more directly with kids, the Commission could not afford the same hard detachment the government might express towards its provincial workforce. Public sentiment demanded a tone that said "we care." The commissioners (and those who wrote for them) were obliged to wear on their sleeves an abiding concern for children and their "heroic" teachers. And for some of its members, the Commission's expressed ideals may indeed be an honest reflection of the views they hold. But however passionately these ideals may be held by certain individuals, an alleged openness to the human reality of students and teachers doesn't survive a quick first reading of the report, and particularly of its official recommendations. Much of the press, however, didn't attempt even that and ended up merely repeating the Commission's official press releases.

When OSSTF's leadership got its first look at the Commission's report, they were appalled. Earl Manners called it "a thick shell of rhetoric around a rotten centre." Later, Liz Barkley wrote that "It has a warm fuzzy exterior, but cloaks a nasty anti-union core."[1] This was also the view of Jim Turk, the

Education Director for the Ontario Federation of Labour. In notes circulated among labour educators, Turk observed that "labour and progressive educators ... get the commentary and the Right gets the recommendations that will be acted upon."[2] In this section I'm going to pay very little attention to the Commission's rhetoric, and I'm sorry about that. The actual text needs a lot more analysis than I can give it here. It is obviously the product of many hands, and a detailed examination of their contributions will prove a valuable approach to help sort out some recent shifts in Ministry politics.[3] In what space I have available, it seems best to focus on the main lines of the Commission's recommendations, apart from its various expressions of good will to all. And even with this focus, there are a good many important topics that must be left to one side.[4]

My second note is to say that the analysis before you offers perhaps too optimistic a picture of OSSTF's prospects in taking on the Social Contract and its logical extension in the Royal Commission. The policy directions I'm outlining are real enough — the newly elected leadership of the Federation and its recent Provincial Assembly support these directions, and they are there in the official documents. But the pressures on the Federation are heavy, and will get heavier, and it is always possible that a deeper right-wing current will make a dramatic appearance in Federation ranks.

As the assault on all aspects of public education grows, and as the new College of Teachers is poised to add its energy to destroying what unity remains among Ontario's warring teacher unions, there is the possibility of major splits on such fundamental questions as teacher education, curriculum reform, the role of teacher unions and the meaning of school democracy. There will increasingly be teacher leaders, including those at at all levels of OSSTF, who will encourage acquiescence in Bob Rae and his successors' new world order for Ontario education. Teachers, they will say, must avoid confrontation. All they can hope for, these voices will insist, are the crumbs that come from cosying up to whatever government is in power. How strong these voices will be is hard to say. Certainly, the next decade will be a very painful time for Ontario teachers, and it will require extraordinary leadership and grass-roots organizing if OSSTF is to survive as a united union, bringing together a strong program of curriculum reform, tough collective bargaining and effective political action.

Moreover, the future for its membership will hinge on more than OSSTF's ability to stay united. It will depend even more on the capacity of all five provincial federations to figure out the structures through which they can effectively speak and act together — some form of one big teachers' union. And it will depend too on whether a rapprochement can be worked out between OSSTF and other public service unions over the organizing of non-teaching board employees, who now make up some 15,000 of OSSTF's 50,000 members. (With the massive restructuring of school board boundaries beginning in September 1995, we could see some very bloody turf wars in the near future, adding further and perhaps irreparable damage to the already fragile infrastructure of the Public Services Coalition.) At the same time, along with labour and community groups, OSSTF, like teachers everywhere, must also build a political party they can call their own. Such future possibilities are, clearly and regretfully, beyond the scope of this book.

It is time to return to the Royal Commission and OSSTF's response to it, which is still in its early stages. The critique presented in these pages will be much more thoroughly developed in the future — and perhaps significantly changed — as the Federation moves into its Provincial Assembly's "Action Plan"[5] to deal with the full implications of the Commission's recommendations.

We begin with the issue on which the Social Contract itself centred: Are major cuts required in public services to save us from an ever-expanding public debt?

The Royal Commission on Learning takes the same position as the provincial government on this question, and in situating OSSTF's response to it within this section of the book, I hope to kill two birds with one stone. Whether responding to the Commission's cuts or the government's Social Contract cuts, the Federation's answer is the same: They are unnecessary and destructive. There is a real alternative. We now turn to this response.

FOOTNOTES

1 Barkley, Liz, "Where we stand: The Royal Commission on Learning," *OSSTF Education Forum*, Spring 1995, p. 4.

2 Turk, Jim, "Comments on Report of The Royal Commission on Learning", unpublished, p. 1.

3 In his "Comments on Report of the Royal Commission on Learning," unpublished, February 12, 1995, David Clandfield deals with the Commission's text in this fashion. Hopefully an extended version of these notes will eventually be published.

4 The Commission's very limited response to the issue of race, for example, is an important area for study. So too is its non-reponse to gender questions.

5 OSSTF Provincial Executive, "Recommended Action Plan on Royal Commission on Learning Report and Minister's Initiatives," Annual Meeting Provincial Assembly, March 11, 1995.

Chapter Four

Finding The Money

Expanding The Cuts

For all intents and purposes, the Royal Commission continued where the Social Contract left off: stripping the public school system of more of its basic funding and opening up a new front for union-busting. We'll look at the union-busting in the following chapter when dealing with the Commission's broader assault on school democracy and a purposeful curriculum. Right now I want to focus on funding and on OSSTF's response to the Commission's recommendations on that issue.

OSSTF estimates that, in addition to the Social Contract/ Expenditure Control Plan cutbacks, the Royal Commission's recommendations could remove hundreds of millions of dollars from the public school system. The Commission doesn't lay this out in any detail, but that is the inevitable result of at least three of its recommendations.

First, there is the recommendation (#159) for a new funding system based on pupil enrolment for public and separate (or Catholic) boards. This system would entail pooling property taxes now levied by boards on both residential and industrial-commercial tax bases. It is hard to estimate exactly how much the public system will lose to the separate system, because we do not yet know what the new per pupil ceiling will be. But the loss will evidently be substantial. "Education budgets," as then-Minister Dave Cooke made very clear, "are not going to grow."[1] This means that the richer public system has to lose money in the new pooling arrangements. Thirty-nine of the 40 poorest boards in the province (in terms of local assessment) are in the separate system. The Commission itself makes this transfer of funds perfectly clear: "In the past," it says, "when resources were more readily available, the inequities could be dealt with by increasing the level of 'have nots' to that of the 'haves,' but this is no longer possible. Instead, the same pie must be sliced and distributed differently."[2] And the pie, of course, will be getting smaller as part of the NDP government's Social Contract initiatives and its Expenditure Control Plan and the continuation of such policies by the government elected in its place.

One obvious part of the solution, which OSSTF has promoted for years, is to fuse the administrative structures of the separate, francophone and public systems, while taking into account the necessary constitutional protection for Catholic and French education. Many millions of dollars would be saved, OSSTF estimates, by integrating a vast array of services and personnel into Confederated School Boards — everything from purchasing, transportation, program coordination, negotiating and financial planning to trustee arrangements, small schools, school board workers, and senior management.[3] The Commission, intent on reaching out to the Catholic hierarchy, would have nothing to do with it.[4]

The second Commission recommendation likely to result in fewer dollars for the public system is its proposal (in Recommendation #160) for a cap of 10% on over-the-ceiling expenditures. That is, local boards will be able to add extra property taxes up to only 10% of provincially recognized expenditure for their board. In the new scheme, we do not know the per pupil ceiling (which produces the recognized expenditure), and so we cannot judge the extent to which the 10 percent cap will hurt the public boards, many of whom currently tax far above this cap. (Across Ontario, school boards are currently taxing, in total, at 25 percent above ceiling, with the public boards taking up most of this amount. A 10 percent cap, all things remaining equal, would result in a shortfall of $1.5 billion,[5] which could, of course, be softened by a rise in the ceiling.)

The Commission also insists that any of this 10 percent above ceiling be levied entirely on residential property tax rather than on the much broader base on which boards currently tax, which includes industrial and commercial properties. Forcing boards to focus on the residential base for extra money makes it much tougher for trustees to go that route, since this means that their voting residents will be paying the entire shot. In company towns like Sault Ste Marie and Kapuskasing, where a large industry dominates the local economy, such a focus becomes absurd. But more generally, since the public boards are the greatest users of extra taxation power, this concentration on the residential taxpayer will hurt them the most.

A third recommendation to pool "undirected" taxes (Recommendation #161) will also result in a significant loss for the public system. Throughout Ontario's history, taxpayers who wanted to support the separate system were responsible for "directing" their school taxes to that system. For all others, the public system was assumed to be the system they supported, and their taxes were applied accordingly. It was an approach, OSSTF argues, that "recognize[d] the primacy of the public system as the only one whose doors are open to every student in the province and which must meet the needs of any student regardless of ability or background...."

At present, the Federation is investigating the constitutionality of this last recommendation. "The exemption of public ratepayers from the need to designate their taxes," says OSSTF, "has been part of the fundamental bedrock of the financing of Ontario education from pre-Confederation onwards, and should not be subverted now. The constitutional protection of access to residential property taxes is enshrined in the Ontario *Education Act*. Separate boards cannot access the public residential property tax base. If public ratepayers for the first time are required to direct their tax support, those who, for whatever reason, fail to do so, would find part of their residential tax redirected to the separate board. Such an eventuality would be a violation of their constitutional rights." (A well-placed source tells me that the Ministry's legal department has ended up agreeing with OSSTF's position on this matter and that this recommendation will not be included in any Ministry response to the Commission.)

In all of this, it is the large urban public boards, containing the bulk of the public system's poor and working-class students, which will be the hardest hit. In Metropolitan Toronto, for example, OSSTF estimates that "the elementary panel would lose up to 20.33% on per pupil expenditure, depending on the funding model, with a corresponding rise of 7.84 % on the mill rate. In the secondary panel, the board would lose up to 18.73 % of the per pupil expenditure while the mill rate would rise by 1.83 %. The Ottawa board would lose up to 19.73% and 7.65% in elementary and secondary per pupil expenditures respectively."

Given the Commission's lack of expertise in school finance and the political minefield such fiscal restructuring entails, the Education Ministry's final response to these recommendations might end up with quite different details.[6] The general direction, however, will be the same: substantially less money for the public system. And, lest we forget, this will be in a context of less money for education generally, under the terms of the Social Contract and the Expenditure Control Plan.

As if to underline the point, the most progressive (and most expensive) recommendation from the Commission — that the schools provide early childhood education for all children from 3 to 5 years of age upon demand from parents or guardians[7] — was almost immediately dumped by the government because of its financial implications.[8] (Its costs had been estimated to be in the neighbourhood of $1 billion.[9]) From its inception, Ministry insiders understood this recommendation as a public relations exercise to help sanitize the reactionary core of the report and didn't take it seriously for an instant, even though it had some support from individuals in the Premier's Office.[10] The Ministry knew perfectly well that the system, as currently funded, couldn't even support the Peterson government's reduction in class size for Grades 1 and 2 or its mandatory extension of junior kindergarten. Indeed, the NDP had already exempted 23 school boards from that extension for another three years.[11] This did not, however, stop the government from going on to declare, once it had abandoned its early childhood initiative, that it would substitute a full-day kindergarten for 4- and 5-year olds by the year 2000. This was flagrant dishonesty, even for this government, since the pilot projects put forward, linking full-day kindergarten with childcare, were a drop in the bucket. Only 500 students were provided with places for fall 1995.[12] There is now little prospect that even these pilot projects will be maintained, at least in their original form. Such projects may, of course, offer Mike Harris' new government an opportunity to replace reasonably paid kindergarten teachers with badly paid early childhood staff, and we will see the eventual expansion of such arrangements. The companion piece to the early childhood flip-flop was a new government literacy plan for Grades 1 to 3. It is no less worrisome than the prospect of kindergarten teacher reduction, and we shall deal with it later.

OSSTF's main response to the Royal Commission's cuts, as well as to those of the Social Contract/Expenditure Control Plan, is that they are wrong-headed. Not only do they undercut serious education for the province's youth (with the larger social costs inherent in such a move), but they also do nothing to help the economy. They hurt it. It is this latter argument to which I now turn.

What OSSTF says is that a well-funded public school system — as part of a larger well-funded state system — is a solid benefit to the economy. Government funding structures must be rearranged to take this into account.

The main thing to realize is that these are things people can do. We don't have to sit by and let things happen to us.

In particular, governments can act to get our economy moving again and in a way that makes life better for everyone. We can put money back into the pockets of working people so as to improve demand in the short run. And there is much work to be done for effective wealth creation, to insure a higher long-term standard of living, which includes a stronger framework of effective public services.

Furthermore, most Canadians agree we should try this route.

Despite their widespread anger over what they perceive as government waste and mismanagement, a solid majority of the country's citizens continue to support government activism. In *Rethinking Government*, for example, one of the most comprehensive studies ever carried out on Canadian attitudes towards government, most citizens of this country are reported to "strongly believe that Ottawa must do whatever is necessary to ensure jobs for people willing and able to work and generally to invest in people." Interestingly enough, "the public's top priority for federal activity is education, [even though this] is a provincial jurisdiction, and [the public] still supports institutions aimed at building Canadian identity." Moreover, while "the deficit increasingly concerns Canadians, they seem disinclined to give up much in fighting it. They see a major role for the government in developing human resources and in helping to create jobs regardless of fiscal pressures."[13]

Here is how OSSTF understands that role.

More Jobs, Fairer Taxes, Better Services: A National Program The Provinces Could Use

The Ontario government obviously does not stand alone in being responsible for the well-being of the provincial economy. The federal government has also a very large role to play. And over the last decade it has played this role badly, as Bob Rae consistently made clear to his Ontario voters.

One of the major reasons Ontario is in a bind over its deficit is the federal government's practice of down-loading its financial problems to the provinces. Between 1982 and 1993 federal caps on transfer payments under Established Programs Financing and the Canada Assistance Plan amounted to a loss for Ontario of $15.8 billion. As a direct result, the province's debt in 1992-93 increased by $11 billion, or 28 percent.[14] On a broader front, an Informetrica analysis found that "Ottawa's attempts to control its deficit by shifting program costs to provincial governments increased Ontario's debt by almost $23 billion from 1985 to 1993, almost 50 percent of the debt the province incurred over the period."[15]

In the Social Contract fiscal year of 1993-94, the NDP estimated, that Mulroney's last budget "cost the province $3.6 billion directly in transfer payments alone ... and nearly $1 billion indirectly." This was a good deal more than the Ontario government saved in its "social" contract-stripping during the same year. It amounted to almost half the provincial deficit of $9.7 billion. At the same time, Ottawa made fewer people eligible for unemployment insurance and thus substantially increased the number of people on Ontario's welfare rolls.

Then came the federal Liberals' 1995 budget. According to Dominion Bond Rating Service, the transfer cuts in this budget will result in further losses to Ontario of $180 million in the fiscal year 1995-96, $1.24 billion in 1996-97, and another $600 million in 1997-98. Bob Rae's figures are even higher.[16] Ontario treasurer Floyd Laughren estimated that these cuts would increase the province's unemployment rate by 0.5 percent, resulting in the loss of about 90,000 jobs.[17]

In response to this Liberal budget, an "outraged" Ontario premier declared that "Mr Chrétien was not elected to impose some neo-conservative, right-wing agenda on the people of Canada." Rae went on to say that this was probably "the most reactionary budget the country has seen in my lifetime."[18]

Bob Rae may well have been right. The 1995 federal budget may have been the most reactionary budget the country has experienced in Rae's lifetime. Its long-term implications for Canada's survival are truly frightening. Not only will some $3 billion be taken from transfers to the provinces in health, post-secondary education and welfare, but there are also major cuts in transportation (50 percent); natural resources (31 percent); industrial, regional and scientific support (38 percent); cultural programs (23 percent); unemployment insurance (10 percent). Forty-five thousand civil service positions are to be slashed across the board. All told, the 1995 cuts added up to a $11.9 billion reduction in federal wages and programs.[19]

Still, Bob Rae need not be modest in assessing his own capacity for "right-wing reaction." With his removal of $8 billion from a provincial economy in 1993 and his continuing assault on public sector collective bargaining, Ontario's premier remained a fully paid-up member of Paul Martin's neo-conservative finance club. A pioneering member, even. And he wasn't elected to impose such an agenda either.

For OSSTF and its allies Rae's hypocrisy here didn't really matter much. What did matter was that Ontario's premier could not lead the battle against this kind of thinking in the national government, because it was his kind of thinking too.

What Ontario needed, they insisted, was a government that

would develop an alternative agenda applicable to both federal and provincial funding arrangements. And when it did, that government must spearhead genuine opposition to the Paul Martins and the Jean Chrétiens of this world. Needless to say, that will not be the government of Mike Harris.

By the time the 1995 federal budget rolled around, OSSTF, along with many other organizations and individuals across the country, was ready to say what it thought an alternative budget might look like at the national level.

The process by which this alternative budget was developed involved fourteen working groups on a wide range of budgetary issues and extensive consultations with social, community and labour organizations across the country. It wasn't an easy process; "trade-offs and compromises" had to be made by everyone. The discussions, the early drafts and the final text were brought together by the Ottawa-based Canadian Centre for Policy Alternatives and Winnipeg's CHOICES: A Coalition for Social Justice. OSSTF took an active role in these policy groups, participated in the general consultation process, and attended meetings of the project's steering committee. What emerged in this process was very much consistent with OSSTF's thinking on these matters over the last few years.[20] When *The 1995 Alternative Federal Budget*[21] was presented to the public a few days prior to Martin's budget speech, Federation leaders took the trouble to attend the Ottawa press conference at which it was introduced. They wanted their support for this approach to public financing to be loud and clear.

It was a budget, OSSTF stressed, that put people first, because it was right, and because it was more efficient.

The 1995 Alternative Federal Budget began with a number of basic principles:

1. The creation of jobs and the prevention of job losses should be the no.1 economic concern of government, with the reduction of youth unemployment given special attention.
2. Income and wealth must be distributed more equitably, through fairer taxes and more effort and resources put into eradicating poverty and inequality.

3. All individuals and families must be treated equally, including same-sex and non-traditional families.
4. The rights of collective bargaining, organizing, workplace safety, job security, and other essential rights of workers that have been eroded in Canada, especially in the public sector, must be restored and strengthened.
5. Greater priority must be given to safeguarding and improving the environment, both nationally and internationally.
6. Policies proposed to help Canadians should not exploit or take advantage of people in other countries.
7. The crucial and constructive role of public services must be recognized, and steps taken to protect and enhance these services.

These principles are not cheap. In opposition to Martin's eventual 1995-96 cut of $11.9 billion, they require an increase in federal revenue of $14.3 billion over the amount raised in 1994-95.

Where does that money come from?

Most of it, says *The Alternative Budget*, would come from the normal increase in revenue that comes from economic growth. The government, this budget says, projected about $9.3 billion from this source, and then built this figure into its calculations. That leaves $5 billion to be accounted for. From this amount *The Alternative Budget* takes $1.4 billion for back taxes, as recommended by the Auditor General. (This is a relatively small percentage of the back taxes owed; arrears in income tax alone stand at $6.6 billion.) There is now $3.6 billion to be found. About half of this would come from "job creation and economic stimulus strategies," whose costs are already accounted for in the projected $14.3 billion, and the other half from "new taxes and reductions in federal grants and subsidies."

The "job creation and economic stimulus strategies" are to insure that an additional 1.2 million jobs are created over the next three years.[22] This is in sharp contrast to "the government's forecast of 900,000 new jobs over this period which does not take into account that every $1 billion cut in government spending will destroy up to 30,000 jobs." *The Alternative Budget* includes an additional $1.5 billion a year for a National Job Creation Strategy, $500 million a year on a National Infrastructure Program, and $600 million for social housing and energy retrofitting of homes. A National Child Care Program will also have major job-creating spinoffs. In addition, the budget makes proposals for more effective research and development in both the public and private sectors and for the creation of a National Industrial Strategy, in which government plays a major role. A Federal Industrial Development Bank will also be established. At the same time, the budget insists that an expanding economy must pay more attention to the lives of all its workers. It calls for regulations to insure that existing work be spread more widely among the country's workforce, while provisions for both paid and unpaid family and educational leaves are institutionalized. Income tax and Canada Pension Plan provisions which encourage flexible leave, retirement and working arrangements must also be introduced, and benefit protection extended to part-time workers.

In approaching the issue of new taxes and reductions in grants and subsidies, *The Alternative Budget* was careful to stay within accepted "international norms." Canada's current level of taxation, it argues, "is not excessive by international standards. In the European countries, for example, taxes account for as much as 45% of GNP. The problem in Canada is that *our tax system is unfair*, in forcing middle-income Canadians to pay the same share of their income in total taxes as the very well-off. It also lets many thousands of profitable corporations avoid paying corporate income tax." To make the system fairer and to recoup the extra $1.8 billion required from this source for 1995-96 (as well as to support additional revenues in following years), *The Alternative Budget* proposed the following changes to Canada's tax laws.

Corporate income taxes must be increased by 0.35 percent of GDP over the next three years, mostly by closing tax loopholes. Two more tax brackets are added to federal income tax rates: 31 percent on taxable income over $75,000 and 33 percent on income over $100,000. A national wealth transfer tax on inheritances over $1 million is imposed, with complete exemption for a surviving spouse. A limit of $10,000 per farm is set on annual federal payments to farmers, substantially reducing overall payments to large agribusiness. For the future, RRSP/RRP deductible limits are lowered for high-income earners as of 1997-98. The federal tax on gasoline is increased by 1.5 cents a litre in 1995-96, and the federal tax on cigarettes is restored to the $10.85-per-200 rate still applicable in Newfoundland and Western Canada. At the same time, the budget eliminates the 3 percent surtax on the basic federal tax for those with incomes below $20,000, giving them an extra $500 million. It also introduces a new low-income tax credit for families with children, in the form of monthly payments based on the previous year's tax returns, giving them an extra $1 billion in 1995-96 and $2.4 billion over three years.

"The outcome of all these tax changes," *The Alternative Budget* concludes, "is that middle-income earners and small businesses will see no increase in income taxation, while low-income families will get income tax reductions of some $1.5 billion in 1995-96."

While tax increases on business and the rich in this budget are quite minimal, a number of large corporations and financial institutions may still decide to put pressure on Canada and threaten to withdraw their money and put it elsewhere. For the future, *The Alternative Budget* notes, "these problems should be resolved through international agreement on a common set of rules and standards for the taxation of income from capital. We need new international financial institutions and agreements to preserve the principles of fair taxation on which the social consensus of democratic societies is based." In the meantime, however, "as one of the countries most adversely affected by the flight of capital, Canada should be in the forefront of a campaign to impose taxes on international currency transactions." The budget foresees the possibility that Canada might be obliged, on its own, to impose a very small transactions tax, though ideally such a tax should be implemented by all countries.

What would Canadians get for the extra $14.3 billion that is paid for in this fashion? A lot, as it turns out.

In addition to its job creation programs, *The Alternative Budget* halts cuts to health care and adds an estimated $1 billion to its funding over the next three years. The 20-year monopoly on the sale of new drugs given to the big drug companies is rescinded, reducing health care costs by up to $7 billion. $50 million is allocated in 1995-96 to promote alternative delivery models.

The budget also tackles high poverty rates. In addition to the tax cuts noted above, transfers to the provinces for social assistance are boosted and Unemployment Insurance benefits are modestly improved. The budget restores the UI benefit to 60 percent of insurable earnings, and includes, once again, those who have quit their jobs. The duration of benefits will also be adjusted to eventually reach one week for each week of work. UI will also be extended to part-time workers.

In post-secondary education, *The Alternative Budget* reinstates federal funding to its previous level, adding another $150 million over the next two years as well as allocating $400 million in 1996-97 and $800 million in 1997-98 to a system of national grants to help students cope with the rising costs of tuition, books and other expenses. The budget also proposes a new Canada Post-Secondary Education Act that will guarantee accessibility to post-secondary schooling for all qualified students.

By 2005 *The Alternative Budget* expects a high-quality, not-for-profit National Child Care Program that will increase the number of regulated child-care spaces by 1.5 million.

Finally, this budget advocates important new advances in assisting people with disabilities, improving funding for the Women's Program, assuring a healthier environment, shoring up Canada's cultural sector (particularly the CBC) and promoting crown corporations like Via Rail and Canada Post (especially in rural areas).

In all of this, of course, it isn't just Canadians generally that benefit from such a budget. It is also provincial governments. Reversing the policies of the Mulroney and Chrétien governments which reduced transfer payments for health, post-secondary education and social assistance, would, as we have seen in Ontario, make an enormous difference in provincial deficits and debt. Improving federal contributions to childcare and Unemployment Insurance would also make a significant contribution to provincial treasuries. So too, would the two new tax brackets the budget added to the federal income tax structure, which is, of course, shared by the provinces.

Not only do we get all of this, but at the same time the national debt and deficit would be declining substantially. *The Alternative Budget* projects a "significant fall" in the deficit, "meeting Mr. Martin's target of 3% of GDP in 1995-96" and declining to "about 2% GDP by 1997-98. The debt burden falls steadily, from 73.6% of GDP in 1994-95 to 68.8% in 1997-98, and the relative size of the debt charges also falls, from 6.1 % of GDP to 5.3% by the end of the period."

Is there any reason Bob Rae's government in Ontario couldn't have gone the same route? And while he was doing it, couldn't he have been organizing Ontarians to put pressure on the feds to follow suit?

Substantial job creation programs have been worked out for Ontario. Rae could have moved on them. Instead, he backed away. After a weak effort in his first budget, he withdrew almost entirely from from this area, except for a certain amount of rhetorical window dressing. David Peterson had done more.

The premier could also have gone after unpaid taxes and imposed a modest tax increase, as *The Alternative Budget* suggests, on the corporations and on the rich. He'd promised such action in opposition. As we saw in the Introduction, Ontario-based corporations were making handsome profits and contributing a pittance to the public purse. The same can be said of the rich. There was room for the government to move here.[23] Nobody was stopping it. Indeed, the outcry from these quarters might well have been quite muted. Ontario's business community expected something of this sort from an NDP administration. A modest tax increase might have been received with relief that it was not larger. And surely a move to collect back taxes could not be presented (even if it was understood) as the beginning of the revolution. Rae's government, however, did next to nothing.

These two broad policies made as much sense in the Social

Contract spring of 1993 as they did in the election Summer of 1990.

They would have made a big difference in the state of the Ontario economy and in public services offered its citizens.

The problem is that Bob Rae and his inner circle of bureaucratic and party advisors didn't believe in them. For the past five years, they were marching, as I have argued, to a very different drummer.

A Low Interest Rate For Ontario

From the same corporate perspective, the Rae government supported a set of federal and provincial monetary policies that were every bit as destructive of a healthy economy and the public sector as the Social Contract package was.[24] *The Alternative Budget* offers an alternative position in this area of public finance as well.

"The excessively high interest rates that have been maintained since the early 1980s," *The Alternative Budget* argues, "have given us 15 years of slow growth and two very severe recessions." This can't go on. Interest rates have to be brought down. For every percentage they rise, the federal government "has to pay $1.7 billion more in interest payments, and more as time passes."[25]

The Bank of Canada, this budget argues, has some real room to move on the question of interest rates, whatever the conventional wisdom, and the government can help it do so. Facing pressure, a small transactions tax on speculative foreign exchange outflows may be necessary, hopefully in concert with other countries. But once the willingness to put such a tax in place is evident, there are two major policy directions in which the government should move.

First, *The Alternative Budget* says, the country "should be reducing the degree to which we rely on foreign borrowing, since foreign debt results in significant flows of capital from Canada to foreign-bond holders and restricts our ability to control our own economy. Foreigners cannot be obliged to invest in Canada, but measures can be taken to limit outflows. This will require stronger economic growth to reduce the deficit, a higher trade surplus, modest increases in the proportion of government debt held by the Bank of Canada, greater reliance on Canada Savings Bonds, and a reduction in the proportion of registered pension funds which can be invested offshore from 20% to 10%. Consideration should also be given to requiring those enjoying tax breaks on pension and retirement savings plans to invest a minimum portion of such plans in government bonds."

Second, the Bank of Canada has to be pressed to use the power it has to lower interest rates within its own bailiwick. "The Bank of Canada," says *The Alternative Budget*, "... could significantly reduce short-term interest rates, through adjustments to its system of short-term debt management (conducted primarily through Treasury-bill actions), and through its influence on the overnight lending rate offered to the banks. Longer-run interest rates could be lowered by several methods, including increasing the share of the debt financed through the Bank of Canada and through Canada Savings Bonds. As respected economist Pierre Fortin has stated, 'the Bank of Canada has all the leverage it needs to lower the whole structure of interest rates — if it wished to do so."

The Ontario government levers on monetary policy are not as powerful as those of the federal government. Still, there are areas in this field in which Queen's Park could effectively move to stimulate economic growth.

The province has a number of large pension plans in which the government either exercises control or is a major partner. It could do a lot to insure that more of our pension monies are invested in job-producing activities here at home in Ontario. Big funds like those from the Ontario Teachers Pension Plan or the Ontario Municipal Employees Retirement Savings Plan (OMERS) need imaginative government leadership and solid financial assurances in order to move into this field.[26]

The government could also do a lot more with Ontario Savings Bonds, which are available only to Ontarians, and are another valuable means by which our debt can be repatriated. As Thomas Walkom pointed out, they turned out to be a "good deal both for taxpayers and potential buyers. In recent months," he noted in March 1995, "the province has been paying 9 per cent interest on the money it borrows from foreigners and large investors. The guaranteed rate on the Ontario Savings Bond is 8 per cent for the first year. That not only costs taxpayers less in interest, it also represents a better return than most individuals can get on similar financial investments."[27] In February of the same year, the provincial treasurer had finally got around to putting out an issue of these bonds. It was the first time in Ontario history that such a sale had been made. But bad timing (they parallelled a new offering of RRSPs and followed a major issue of Canada Savings Bonds), a poor publicity campaign, and the resistance of major financial institutions, which didn't want competition for their own bonds and RRSPs, led to a relatively small sale of $1.6 billion. Despite a limited effort, made far too late in the day, this sale was an important step in the right direction. And the amount sold was really quite respectable. The future for such bonds could be very significant indeed. Walkom reported that some of the Ontario treasurer's advisors — they must have been very junior — encouraged "a kind of wartime-style mobilization that would appeal to the patriotism of Ontarians in order to persuade them to buy government bonds and get the province over the hump of recession." This would be a much bigger step in the right direction. One can only hope that these officials survive to serve a government committed to a such a direction.

Lastly, there is the Province of Ontario Savings Office (POSO), a child of the United Farmers of Ontario in the early 1920s. POSO could turn out to be the most important monetary instrument the province has under its control. Unlike the Bank of Canada, POSO can't print money, but it can and does take in deposits (without offering loans) through offices which are open to the public and are spread (very thinly) across the province. By 1994-95, these deposits had ended up contributing a total of $2.1 billion to provincial funding. That $2.1 billion was the equivalent of a loan the province would otherwise have had to borrow on the market at much higher rates, and which for all intents and purposes does not have to be paid back, unless there is a run on the bank. Even with all its costs included, POSO delivers cash to the government at a rate substantially less than the current bond interest rate of 9 percent. This kind of "loan" is called a "contingent liability" and is even viewed by bond rating agencies as less distressing than direct debt.

POSO is open to considerable expansion. One analyst I spoke to suggested that its 24 branches might be doubled within the next five years if the organization was given its head by the Treasurer. And there is no telling what a real campaign to encourage Ontarians to bank their savings in a publicly controlled institution would bring by way of customers and future contributions to the provincial debt. It is an obvious need in hundreds of small Ontario communities which have no local financial institutions of their own. And the present agency model, developed by POSO out of the experience of Alberta's Treasury Branches and now functioning in five communities, is a cheap and effective means of responding to this need. The need has been most obvious in the north, but now that the banks are starting to leave depressed areas of eastern Ontario, there would an immediate demand for POSO agencies here as well if they were made available.

Under Bob Nixon as Treasurer, the Liberals had looked somewhat kindly on the Savings Office and had encouraged a little expansion, including a new capacity to offer its own GICs. The NDP was not so interested, however. While Rae's administration let some new products, agencies and branches already in the pipeline go through, it encouraged no further activism. It didn't have the money, it said, and couldn't listen to the argument that POSO would deliver much more money than it cost. There was also, it seems, pressure from the credit union movement, which was worried about competition, although there is no reason why these two institutions could not flourish together, particularly with government encouragement. The chartered banks and the trust companies — in their collectivity — have succeeded well enough, although they too have added their much more powerful voice against POSO's expansion, just as they have in the past. POSO owes much of its exceedingly low profile in Ontario to the heavy hand of the Canadian banking industry and the trusts. In its last months of office, however, with the transfer of POSO to the new crown agency, the Ontario Financing Authority (OFA), the NDP government was having second thoughts about the usefulness of an institution like POSO, and some small-scale reforms had been predicted. As with the recent sale of Ontario Savings Bonds, such reforms were unlikely to make much difference in the short run. But they too could have been an important, if small, step to financial solvency for the Province of Ontario in the years to come.

FOOTNOTES

1 Lewington, Jennifer, "Ontario to slash number of school boards by up to half," *Globe and Mail*, February 25, 1995.

2 *Report of the Royal Commission on Learning, For the Love of Learning, Vol. 4*, Queen's Printer for Ontario, Toronto, 1994, p. 129.

3 OSSTF, Submission to the Ontario Fair Tax Commission, "Fair Taxation for Responsible Education: Report of the Funding Initiatives and New Directions Committee," September 22, 1992.

4 See the section entitled "Religious minorities," pp. 88-89 and recommendations 115–118, *Report of the Royal Commission on Learning, Vol. 4*, cited above.

5 OSSTF quotations in the following paragraphs are from OSSTF, *Royal Commission Fact Sheet #3*, pp. 1–3.

6 The NDP decided to put off any major decision on fiscal restructuring until after the 1995 election. NDP Education Minister Dave Cooke asked a number of his "stakeholders" to participate in a high-level "working group" on education finance, which would not report until November, 1995. And now to a Conservative government.

7 *Report of the Royal Commission on Learning*, Vol. 4, see above, p. 167.

8 Duffy, Andrew, "NDP decides against school for 3-year-olds," *Toronto Star*, February 21, 1995.

9 Lewington, Jennifer, "Full-day kindergarten vowed for four-and five-year-olds," *Globe and Mail*, February 22, 1995

10 This policy direction had long been one of the pet projects of Julie Mathien, Co-ordinator of Social Policy in the Premier's Office, who had accompanied government delegations and tours of the *écoles maternelles* in France. While she went along with the right-wing thrust of Cooke's new policies, she seemed determined to push a progressive early childhood education reform through. Although turned back in the Cabinet approval process more than once, this policy had an astonishingly long shelf-life thanks largely to her efforts and those of Ross McClellan the Premier's Special Advisor on Social Issues who also supported it. The Commission's Report represented its last gasp.

11 Hawaleska, Dan, "School's still out for some youngsters," *Globe and*

Mail, June 11, 1994.

12 Lewington, Jennifer, "Full-day kindergarten vowed for four-and five-year-olds," *Globe and Mail*, February 22, 1995.

13 Greenspon, Edward, "Maintain services, Canadians tell survey," *Globe and Mail*, February 25, 1995. The survey, *Rethinking Government*, was carried out by Ekos Research Associates and was sponsored by ten federal departments and agencies, two provincial governments and two private-sector companies.

14 OSSTF, *Trustee Elections '94*, "Factsheet: Federal Transfers."

15 Mackie, Richard, "Rae to demand Ontario's 'fair share'," *Globe and Mail*, November 8, 1993.

16 Ferguson, Jonathan, "Debt rating agency places Ontario 'under review,'" *Toronto Star*, March 2, 1995.

17 See Walker, William, "Irate Rae lashes 'betrayal' of ideals," *Toronto Star*, February 28, 1995, and Rusk, James, et al., "Provinces cry the blues in spite of feeling relief," *Globe and Mail*, February 28, 1995.

18 Walker, William, "Irate Rae lashes 'betrayal' of ideals," *Toronto Star*, February 28, 1995.

19 Editorial, *Toronto Star*, "Martin performs fiscal exorcism," February 28, 1995.

20 See, for example, OSSTF, "Adequacy, Equity and Democracy: A Proposal for Education Funding in Ontario," submitted to the Ontario Ministry of Education, January, 1993 and "Deficit Counterattack: Taxation and Interest Rate Strategies to Tame Deficits and Debts," Presentation to the House of Commons Standing Committee on Finance, November 4, 1994.

21 Copies can be ordered from the Canadian Centre for Policy Alternatives, 251 Laurier West, Suite 804, Ottawa, Ontario K1P 5J6, tel: (613) 563-1341 or CHOICES, A Social Justice Coalition, 5th Floor, 275 Broadway, Winnipeg, Manitoba R3C 4M6, tel: (204) 942-0343. ISBN: 0-88627-131-2. A summary is also available.

22 In 1993 the cost of unemployment to the Canadian economy was estimated at $109 billion and to extra health care at $1 billion. The direct government tax loss from this unemployment was put at $23.7 billion and its indirect loss at $15.4 billion. See OSSTF, "Strengthening Canada's Social Safety Net, A Brief to the Standing Committee of the House of Commons on Human Resources Development," December 1994, p. 9.

23 One entirely untouched area is that of wealth taxes. In Canada, as whole, Richard Gwyn writes, "of out total tax take, just 0.03 percent comes from taxing wealth, This is one-twentieth the proportion in Britain (0.64 percent), even after a dozen years of Margaret Thatcher. It is one-twenty-fifth the 0.77 share in the U.S., despite a dozen years of Ronald Reagan and George Bush. It's an amazing one-hundredth the 3.06 percent share in Switzerland, a country not widely known for being nasty to the wealthy. We have no wealth

tax." See Gwyn, Richard, "This is one of the best countries to be rich, study finds," *The Toronto Star*, May 28, 1995.

24 On the day prior to Rae's calling the provincial election, his treasurer, Floyd Laughren, introduced a "budget plan," which finally called on Ottawa and the Bank of Canada to lower interest rates. "You have to ask," writes Thomas Walkom, "why Laughren and Rae chose to wait until the last possible moment before making this point; both the problem of high interest rates and the arguments for easier monetary policy have been well-known for years. And the nagging suspicion you're left with is that the NDP government doesn't mean it. To put it bluntly: if Rae woke up tomorrow as the prime minister of Canada and Laughren as the Bank of Canada governor, we know they would not lower interest rates. We know it. Instead, they would talk about the dangers of re-igniting inflation or the perils of deliberately lowering the currency." Walkom, Thomas, "NDP budget plan like a deathbed repentance," *The Toronto Star*, April 28, 1995.

25 Buzz Hargrove, the president of CAW-Canada, writes, "Since the 600 percent increase in real interest rates starting in 1981, the average rate of economic growth has been cut in half: to 2.4 percent from over 5 percent during the first 35 years after World War II." See his "Notes for an Address to the Summit on the Future of Public Services," Toronto, February 12, 1995.

26 The Ontario Teachers Pension Plan alone was worth $35.1 billion at the end of 1994. See Myers, Adam, "The big gorilla of pension funds," *The Toronto Star*, April 16, 1995.

27 Walkom, Thomas, "NDP's savings bond idea gets shortchanged," *The Toronto Star*, March 4, 1995.

Chapter Five

Democracy vs. Central Control

If the main line of OSSTF's response to the economy is "to put people first," it is also the major thrust of its approach to school governance.

This has been a tougher road to take, however, as the issue of educational democracy involves a much more complex set of administrative problems and teacher fears. A good many of these fears are well-founded — rooted, for example, in the mobilization of right-wing parents' groups or in the very real prospect of political deception. The fruits of countless meetings and discussions at local schools could be left to wither in bureaucratic limbo. In the end, OSSTF has increasingly judged that whatever dangers lie in wait along this road, it is worth taking the risk of following it. Not only do teachers, parents and students have an honest commonality of interest, but a governing alliance among them is essential if the public school system itself is to survive.

It boils down to a matter of trust.

Do you trust people to make the decisions that matter about their lives?

With some fear and trembling, OSSTF says "Yes, we do." Despite assurances to the contrary, the Royal Commission, on the other hand, offers an unequivocal "No."

For the Commission, this stance is perhaps its most direct expression of both the letter and the spirit of the Social Contract. Bob Rae not only didn't want to hear the ideas of the province's public sector unions on government debt and the means for economic recovery, but he also proceeded to rip up the legal framework through which these democratically run unions functioned. Although the Commission offered more democratic rhetoric when dealing with parent and teacher input into school management, it thoroughly failed to listen to the teachers and parents whose lives it touched. And it saw to it that the governance structures it proposed would strip what little was left of popular control in Ontario educational decision-making.

The Commission's assault on local democracy is very widespread. Let me start with its attack on the local boards: on their financial powers and on their curriculum responsibilities.

Money And Curriculum: The Province Takes Control

Framed by the government's deficit-slashing focus, the Commission pressed for a much greater level of provincial activity in taxing and spending the education dollar in Ontario. It was an activity it clearly wanted out of local hands, and the commissioners were frank enough about the reason: "The relatively low level of direct provincial support for elementary and secondary education," they argued, has meant "that the province has *less control* [my italics] over school-board decision-making, particularly with boards that have the capacity to raise entire budgets from local taxes."[1] The Commission's solution to this lack of provincial control is to have Queen's Park take over all education funding (including what's received from the local property tax) with the exception of the 10 percent over-ceiling board levy on residential property we touched on earlier. "We recommend," it says, "that equal per-pupil funding across the province, as well as additional money needed by some boards for true equity, be decided at the provincial level, and that the province ensure that funds be properly allocated."[2]

Within the elementary and secondary school sector, this recommendation will allow the government to direct money away from the public system towards the separate system and eventually, as the commission seems to hope, towards a more private zone of "independent" schools catering to the well-to-do and to religious special interests.[3] It also permits the Commission to shift funds away from the urban public boards, with their expensive labour-intensive streaming systems now increasingly deemed archaic alongside cheaper high-tech substitutions. Finally, and most importantly, the recommendation provides the province with the hammer it needs to nail down its centralization of curriculum and the curriculum "reforms" it envisages.

OSSTF has consistently resisted this approach. It supports a strong local property tax, which can be made considerably more equitable than it is at present and which insures a major degree of local power. At the same time, the Federation proposes — as all three parties have proposed over the last two decades — that the province increase its share of elementary and secondary funding "to a level that would approximate 60 percent of the real operating costs of school boards ... excluding pension and capital payments."[4] Such a level of provincial funding, OSSTF argues, provides a realistic balance between financial equity and functioning local democracy.[5]

At the same time as the Commission recommended that local boards' financial power be replaced by provincial control, it also recommended a thorough gutting of the boards' curriculum responsibilities, again on behalf of the Education Ministry at Queen's Park.

At the outset, it is worth noting that this provincial centralization is taking place in the context of a national effort — led by provincial governments in alliance with the corporate sector — to standardize curriculum in Canada's schools through national tests designed to furnish "indicators." "Over the last two years," the Commission favourably reports, "the first national assessment program, organized by the Council of Ministers of Education in Canada, has been established, and we have begun to see interprovincial co-operation in developing curriculum at the regional level. Whether this interprovincial co-operation will become a driving force in creating a national curriculum remains to be seen; certainly, it seems to have been possible to reach an agreement on testing in spite of the lack of a uniform curriculum." It is a process, the Commission writes, that is "plausible" pedagogically and has widespread public support. With such a "national curriculum," there might be no improvements in learning, but "there might be a greater sense of consistency and unified purpose in education."[6]

At the core of what is being centrally controlled is something called "learning outcomes." What these outcomes mean in both theory and practice we'll deal with later in the chapter on curriculum. Right now it is important to get hold of the level of centralization involved.

The Commission recommends that the provincial government set "the standards" against which we can assess student performance in school. They are to do this by setting up "outcomes that describe what students should know and be able to do." Such outcomes, says the Commission, have already begun to be developed by the Education Ministry in "language/literacy and mathematics/numeracy." These are based on the "learner outcomes" within the official "*Common Curriculum* for language and mathematics and which suggest different levels of performance such as 'limited,' 'adequate,' and 'proficient' for students at the end of Grades 3, 6, and 9.... The math standards, for example, are built on areas within math that are specified in *The Common Curriculum* as 'measurement,' 'problem solving,' 'algebra and patterning,' etc."

"These standards," the Commission continues, "are intended to provide descriptions of expected levels of achievement by which students' learning can be assessed.... Learner outcomes and standards must be very clear for all foundation subjects: language, mathematics, science, computer literacy and group learning/interpersonal skills. As these standards are developed and refined, they will become the yardstick against which teachers and the public can measure student performance."[7]

The Commission does not mince its words in insisting on the deepest possible level of provincial control over these "standards."[8] The Education Ministry, it says, must "develop a guide, suitable for parents, teachers and other caregivers, outlining stages of learning (and desirable and expectable learner outcomes) *from birth onwards* [my italics], ... [which will] link to the common core curriculum, beginning in Grade 1. This guide, which would include specific learner outcomes at age 6, would be used in developing the curriculum for the Early Childhood Education program." From this point, the Commission continues, "learner outcomes in language, mathematics, science, computer literacy, and group learning/interpersonal skills and values [must] be clearly described by the Minister of Education and Training from pre-Grade 1 through the completion of secondary school, and ... these [will] be linked with the work of the College Standards and Accreditation Council, as well as universities; and ... clearly written standards, similar in intent to those available in mathematics and language (numeracy and literacy), [will] also be developed in the other three areas."

By Grade 7, every student must have "a Cumulative Evaluation Plan." This plan includes the student's "academic and other learning experiences" and is to be "the major planning tool" in shaping the student's educational future, up to and including college or university. Tight curriculum guidelines in each subject must also be developed "to assist teachers in designing programs that will help students achieve the learning outcomes in *The Common Curriculum*." And, as students come to graduate, they will be tested on a set of graduation outcomes from the Ministry, both "subject and skill oriented," which will "cover common learner outcomes for all students as well as supplemental learner outcomes for the OAcC [academic] and the OApC [applied] programs." Some of these students will also have experienced ministry-sponsored "challenge exams and other appropriate forms of prior learning assessment ... to be used up to and including the granting of diplomas and degrees."

For parents, the Ministry is "to create a brief and clear document that describes ... what their children are expected to learn and to know, based on the developmental framework of stages of learning from birth to school entrance, *The Common Curriculum*, and the secondary school graduation outcomes.

Succinct information on college and university programs should also be included."

All that will be left to the local boards are some small additions to *The Common Curriculum*. Such "options" must "meet provincially developed criteria" and are permitted only so long as "at least 90 percent of instructional time is devoted to the common curriculum for Grades 1 to 9."[9]

It is worth recalling, I think, that these new financial and curriculum powers will now be in the hands of those neo-conservative bureaucrats who directed the first Social Contract onslaught against the Ontario school system, and whose masters will be a Conservative government with an official new-right agenda.[10]

The Information-Technology Bandwagon

The centralization of curriculum via control of provincial "learning outcomes" is securely linked to provincial control of the information-technology structure for Ontario schools.

The Royal Commission makes this point abundantly clear.

The Ministry, it recommends, must "be responsible for overseeing the increased and effective use of information technologies in the province's schools." It must "determine the extent and nature of the computer-related resources now in use in schools across Ontario" and must function "as an information clearing house for these resources." It must facilitate "alliances among the Ministry, school boards, hardware and software firms, and the private sector" and "develop common standards jointly with system partners, for producing and acquiring technology." It must develop "licensed protocols that support multiple remote users accessing centrally held software in a local area network (LAN) or wide area network (WAN) structure," and it must co-ordinate "efforts, including research and special projects, to refine effective educational assessment programs."[11]

In creating a centrally controlled structure for information technology, the Commission's perspective clearly includes corporate as well as government control. Like the Social Contract, this new structure is to be the product of a business-bureaucratic alliance. Big international corporations are to be central in developing Ontario's school-based information technology.

It is a perspective the Commission was pleased to present in high profile.

It wants us to know that major corporate players have a large interest in the development of this technology. "The education system," it says, "has become a major target of the gigantic information technology industry, which has a huge stake in every kind of software and hardware, and is taking aim at schools across the continent in an effort to expand its markets. While the Canadian push is being led by such large firms as Rogers, Southam, Core, Unitel, and Stentor (an alliance of Canadian phone companies), the international drive is being conducted by some of the most powerful corporations in the world: Time Warner, Paramount Communications, Microsoft, the computer manufacturers, as well as the dominant players in the gargantuan computer and video-games industries. Indeed, some of the biggest Canadian concerns have formed links with vastly larger American corporations; AT&T, in concert with Rogers and CP, owns 20 percent of Unitel, while Stentor has a marketing agreement with MCI Communications Corporation."[12]

It is also clear from the Commission's report that this level of big-time corporate involvement in education doesn't worry them very much. Education, when all is said and done, is set out as an appropriate target for these information-technology corporations. Our schools should be considered a legitimate marketplace for such companies as Rogers and AT&T.

Nothing, the Commission implies, need really disturb us about this corporate involvement. There is, it says in passing, a "fascinating issue" concerning this involvement: the question of whether it is "talking about an information highway where the public interest prevails, or about an information mall where commercial concerns dominate."[13] This issue, however, is not fascinating enough to be pursued and is left entirely up in the air. With its support of corporate control already in place, the Commission was presumably wondering about the extent to which it could rely on good corporate citizens not to pursue their bottom line on the Internet. This was not a question the commissioners seemed anxious to resolve.

Even when it comes down to the specific school content of corporate-produced information technology, the commissioners remain undisturbed. This is really an astonishing omission. There is a mild disclaimer saying technology isn't "an automatic good in the learning process" and that "machines must be at the service of human kind — not the reverse." But after that the Commission gets on to worrying about whether teachers will have the proper techniques to use information technologies appropriately.[14] "Higher order learning skills," it tells us, "... are not developed unless the right software is being used in the right way. Similarly traditional didactic approaches are left behind only if there is enough equipment and if the particular teacher using the technology feels comfortable with the changes involved.... Information technology by itself does not lead to change: the determinants are the ways it is used and integrated into all learning and teaching, the quality and appropriateness of the software that is chosen and the abilities and interests of the teachers."[15] There is not a peep about the dangers of corporations helping to construct the curriculum which will be embedded in this new technology.

As David Livingstone puts it, the Commission seemed to be "oblivious" to the issue of corporate control of the information highway in our schools. "Much of the computer hardware and a lot of the software now promoted for educational uses," he writes, "grew out of the research on military computer-based command-and-control and weapon systems, mainly in the U.S. The field of 'cognitive science' emerged out of military research aimed at reducing troublesome 'human factors,' and the field is still largely military funded." This "legacy and its possible hazards for democratic education," Livingstone argues, must now be faced. "In spite of their military origins, the Internet and other forms of the information highway still retain the potential *of aiding and expanding* democratic discourse between human beings. But as PCs proliferate, the information highway is rapidly being commandeered by commercial interests." Since the Commission has given us no help in meeting the corporate challenge on this front or in finding ways for teachers and students to obtain "really useful knowledge" and not be swamped by "information glut," Livingstone continues, the issue is once more before us in need of an answer. The good news, he reports from his recent OISE Survey of *Public Attitudes Towards Education in Ontario*, is that there is solid public support for educational institutions, functioning like libraries, to maintain and expand our democratic access to the information highway. The only "real dissenters [from this position] are corporate executives."[16]

While Livingstone is quite correct to say the Commission is "oblivious" to the dangers of corporate-produced curriculum, there may be an occasional unconscious recognition of these dangers buried in the text of its report. At moments its cheerleading for the world of information technology becomes so extreme that its language seems to break down on its own. Initially this seemed a rhetorical collapse that came mostly from overheating. Now, I suspect, these passages may be telling us something.

Listen, for example, to these concluding lines: The Commission's "vision" of high-tech education, it tells us, "is both exhilarating in its possibilities and daunting in its uncertainty — terrifying in the sense that much of it is being driven not by human needs but by the imperatives of technology or commerce. But if society at least acknowledges the phenomenon, it can attempt to shape it. In fact, no-one has the remotest idea of what tomorrow's schools will look like; we can confidently assert only that they will not look like those of today — thanks, in the main, to evolving technology."[17] Get past the contradictions of this "vision," and what emerges, it seems to me, is an acceptance (indeed, largely a joyous acceptance) of the deepest sort of powerlessness, a chaotic plunge into the dark. At an individual level we would ascribe this attitude to those pursuing a very dangerous love of death. At a societal level, it reflects nothing less than an acceptance of the country's death or perhaps that of society itself.

Another of these moments comes with the Commission's strange view of books. We must remember, it says, that "computers and the related technology are nothing more than machines — even if their ability to process information still dazzles the human imagination. In fact we doubt they will ever replace the joy of reading a great book as a form of continuing education." Whatever we may think of technology's power over the imagination, the *possibility* of a machine *in itself* replacing the joy of human communication (in a book) is really a very chilling thought. I cannot imagine such a possibility. Putting good books on the Internet involves quite different questions, of course, which the Commission doesn't deal with. It does tell us, however, that students should continue "to read books, not just computer screens," because "books have a different smell and feel and that must not be lost, no matter how attractive technology may be." With defenders like this, Canada's publishing industry is in deep trouble. But perhaps I'm being unfair. With their plunge into the technological dark, the commissioners may be trying secretly to warn us that what our children will find on their computer screens won't be much to our liking, and that we'd better keep some of those old books around. We can tell the authorities it's just for the smell and feel of them.

The Place Of Teachers

This centralization of computers in corporate-bureaucratic hands isn't just for curriculum and market control. It is also part and parcel of a process for deskilling Ontario teachers, which in turn contributes to Social Contract-style downsizing and wage reduction. We'll deal with this issue later on. But there is a point David Livingstone makes about the introduction of technology into education and the role of teachers that is worth repeating in the context of curriculum centralization.

"School systems as a whole," Livingstone writes, "have typically introduced new learning technologies slowly and in limited ways. The Commission's recommendations are not only narrowly focused on microcomputers to the exclusion of other alternative technologies, they appear to have bought the advocate's pitch, hook, line and sinker, without the benefit of careful study.... The most thorough review of the related evaluation research to date has found that most of these studies are of poor quality and typically overstate moderate effects."

"In the past," Livingstone continues, "teachers have usually altered classroom behaviour selectively, to the extent that certain technologies have helped them solve important problems without seriously eroding their classroom authority. Teaching is one of the most difficult jobs there is. In addition to subject knowledge, it requires substantial imagination, improvisation and pacing, all combined with sufficient sensitivity to establish student rapport. Teachers are not 'technopeasants' as the Commission implies. Like most university graduates, they are generally now fairly computer literate. The reluctance of many teachers to embrace computers more fully in their classrooms may be quite intimately linked with a knowledge of the intangible human dimensions that they and their students could be losing. As Larry Cuban puts it:

> At a deep level that often goes unspoken,.... many teachers may sense how the introduction of machines into classrooms endangers those intangible, highly prized rewards that count so heavily in why teachers decide to endure in a most difficult but intensely satisfying job.

"Most teachers," Livingstone concludes, "are probably now quite willing to use computers as an *aid* to classroom learning. But the school's many publics continue to insist that the schools pursue several inherently contradictory goals (i.e. socialize all children, but nourish individual creativity; teach the best of past traditions, yet ensure that each child possesses currently marketable practical skills; demand obedience to authority, but encourage critical thinking and questioning; cultivate cooperation, but prepare children to compete). As long as we do so, teachers' multiple knowledges, negotiating skills and intuitions are likely to be central to the task. Even the most sophisticated future computers will not be up to it."[18]

In responding to the Commission's emphasis on high-tech schooling and the need to computerize now, the government, like the Commission itself, paid no attention to teachers' responsibility for the introduction of technology. Within days of the Commission's report, Ontario's Education Ministry declared, with no classroom teacher consultation, that the province's educational system would now become "a model user of information technology." The ministry would "coordinate [public] investment of up to $500 million over the next five years to update information technology." There would, of course, be no new money,[19] but a "reallocation" from existing budgets to buy computers, link classrooms to information networks, and develop resources such as curriculum-based software. Most of the money is to be spent on purchasing 40,000 computers each year for the next five years. And overall, "government, business and school boards," said the Ministry, "will invest $100 million a year to make sure Ontario schools are kept up to date."[20]

The future for teacher involvement in this area looks no brighter than its present. The Ministry's focus, it told us, will be in "developing partnerships with local businesses and high tech companies." No teachers need apply. "With the knowledge and support of private business," the Ministry declared, "students can get hands-on experience in the use of current technologies." These partnerships will be "stimulated by matching any funds contributed by boards or private companies for improving classroom technology." The most recent stimulation involves "a new agreement between IBM Canada and several Ontario school boards. [They] will focus on developing new technologies to support innovative learning methods — especially those that can be developed as models for easy implementation across the education system. Wasting no time at all, the Ministry announced five major projects to be brought on stream within eighteen months."[21]

It is also clear that with these new technologies in place, teachers' jobs will increasingly be on the line. Here is how a recent Ministry-sponsored background document put the problem: "In addition to lingering reluctance about acquiring the range of skills needed to integrate Information Technology (IT) in their teaching, teachers/professors are concerned that any projected cost savings achieved by IT will be effected through job loss: i.e. that 'two teachers plus classrooms' will become 'one teacher plus computers.' While attitudes to IT are becoming much more positive among all stakeholders, any residual resistance must be appreciated and effectively addressed. Similarly, any lingering reluctance to use parent and private sector resource personnel needs to be overcome."[22] With such responses to their concerns, it is easy to see why teachers are so worried about IT-job loss.

The Commission is firm that teachers will be obliged to accept and to learn these technologies within the context of this corporate structure. It is exactly the same process by which the Commission would force teachers to accept and to learn the structure of the Outcomes Based Education within the "common curriculum." The Commission recommends that its proposed College of Teachers (a central body for certification and accreditation) "require faculties of education to make knowledge and skills in the educational use of information technology an integral part of the curriculum for all new teachers." It further recommends that professional development in IT "become a condition of recertification."[23] Regular classroom teachers have now five years to shape up to this new technological imperative or ship out of the profession.

As we might expect, OSSTF stands resolutely opposed to this kind of curriculum centralization — whether in information technology or the Liberal Arts.

Following publication of the Royal Commission's report, the Federation opened up a new front in opposition to bureaucratic and corporate control of what's to be taught in Ontario schools.

"The time has come," said its Provincial Executive in its 1995-96 statement of priorities and program, "for OSSTF to take professional control of curriculum development."[24] This initiative must involve all aspects of the Federation's activities. "Curriculum, collective bargaining and political action must be recognized as interdependent if OSSTF is to establish effective strategies in the public arena. A new approach to curriculum is necessary. The traditional sources of support — the Ministry of Education and Training and boards of education — lack the resources and the will to respond effectively.... Now is the opportunity to press government to set broad-based education policy, and to return to the professionals the authority and resources to develop curriculum and resource material, to organize and facilitate professional development and to design assessment and evaluation techniques."

"OSSTF," its executive continues, "must be actively engaged in development of subject specific guidelines, the appropriate implementation protocols and resource books. OSSTF possesses the experience and the skills to shape the curriculum of the province, thereby providing members with the best available materials. An essential component of this approach will be the development of a proposal to the Ministry of Education and Training for OSSTF to be contracted to provide curriculum and resource materials for both the Transition and Specialization Years. Assessment and accountability issues — such as the latest version of the mathematics and language standards — should be addressed through OSSTF resource documents. School-based research and exemplary programs would be the primary motivations for change."

A second major initiative in curriculum development, says the Provincial Executive, "would be the establishment of a publishing house under the auspices of OSSTF. Our resource books are the most successful endeavour of their kind on the continent. The Federation has a great number of skilled authors and experienced trainers available. Now there is an opportunity to broaden OSSTF's role in this area not only for educational and financial reasons, but also as a means to counteract foreign influences in Canadian publishing." In addition, the Federation proposes to undertake and develop an action plan for OSSTF involvement in professional development, pre-service and additional qualifications courses.

At the same time that OSSTF is calling for new professional responsibilities in the development of what's taught and how it's taught, the Federation also recognizes that even in the area of "broad-based planning," curriculum development can't be left to central government officials. This level of policy development has to be reached through a much wider political process. "OSSTF," its executive argues, must "continue our public education campaign with our communities. In an effort to refute the myths about public education, and to respond effectively to the government's implementation strategy with regard to the Royal Commission on Learning, the campaign will promote the importance of stronger links between the school, parents and community organizations. Emphasis will be placed on the principles of public education (universality, comprehensiveness, proficiency and accountability), and the role that public education plays in the wider society."

The Provincial Executive statement was looking ahead to the impending provincial election. For OSSTF, the strategy meant that "the Federation [would] work with OTF and its affiliates, the Public Services Coalition, the CAW, OPSEU, CUPE, the Coalition for Social Justice and other like-minded groups to ensure that educational and social policy issues are at the forefront of the election campaign." The leadership encouraged OSSTF locals and bargaining units to join these groups in working for the election of candidates sympathetic to the Federation's policy platforms.

Finally, such a strategy involved a much more systematic approach to community coalition building: "The defence of public education and the preservation of public services requires that OSSTF, at both the local and provincial level, widen our sphere of influence through support and participation in coalitions. The Public Services Coalition continues to play a vital role at the provincial level and in many of our communities. Groups like the CAW, ACTRA, The Social Planning Council of Metropolitan Toronto and seniors' groups, have reached out to OSSTF to join in activities to promote education, health, social services and Canadian cultural activities. Outreach to local parent advisory groups is also vital."

Coalition-building won't be cheap, and the Provincial Executive knew that the Federation must bite the financial bullet if such organizing was to get off the ground. Thus it recommended establishing "a fund to assist local districts/divisions and bargaining units to build and extend their relationships with other unions, local labour councils, Public Services Coalitions, Social Planning Councils, Parent Advisory Councils, Arts Councils and other like-minded organizations committed to the preservation of public education, social services and Canadian culture."

An Official History Of Centralization

As in its approach to stripping financial and curriculum power from the local boards (and their teachers), the Commission is remarkably straightforward in its overall position concerning these moves. It does not hesitate to frame its increased centralization within a general pattern of centralization in Ontario education.

There are no tears shed here for the one-room school.

There is, in fact, not one ounce of sympathy for 150 years of remarkably successful struggle by Ontario's rural communities to hold on to the schools they built. Our present system of school governance, in the view of the Commission, has been the result of straight-ahead progress. "Ontario schools," it says, "were originally established and controlled by local citizens. With an eye on efficiency and equality of opportunity, however, successive governments slowly developed larger units, culminating in 1969 with the amalgamation of more than two thousand small boards into less than 200 larger school boards, most based on the provincial county as the administrative unit.... It was at this point that the one-room schoolhouse, relic of Ontario's pioneer past, finally became part of history."[25]

This not a perspective shared, I should note, by most of the historians who have written on this question. Among them, the majority conclusion is that for Queen's Park this process of centralization had little to do with equity or efficiency. Rather, it was about financial and curriculum control over rural and working-class students, their communities and their teachers. It was also about reproducing the divisions of social class within the Ontario educational system. Per pupil costs, in fact, skyrocketed during this process. This was the price governments were prepared to pay — to friendly contractors, of course — for these new levels of control and reproduction.[26]

In setting out its "equity and efficiency" version of education centralization in Ontario, the Commission also incorporates its own additions to the official line on centralized/decentralized decision-making.

"The challenge," it says, "is to find the appropriate balance of power and control at the school, community, Ministry and provincial levels." A "reallocation" of power has now become necessary, the Commission argues, and it recommends "a stronger voice for students and parents; greater decision-making authority for principals, with involvement of teachers as well; clarifying the role of school boards; and articulating a strong policy leadership role for the Ministry of Education and Training."[27]

What the Commission does, in fact, is give a pittance to students, parents and teachers, wipe out most of the responsibilities of the local boards, and vastly increase the power of the Ministry in all areas of educational decision-making, with school principals acting as central-management personnel. Its justification for doing this — and the government's justification in carrying out this agenda — is framed by the Commission's history of maintaining a "balance" in Ontario education decision-making.

The first part of this history goes as follows: "The Ministry, like other government agencies," says the Commission, "has traditionally exercised highly centralized control over Ontario education, relying primarily on regulation and monitoring to ensure compliance from boards and schools. In the 1960s and 1970s, however, control was so decentralized that school boards had a high degree of autonomy in the way they organized, set programs, and made a host of other educational decisions. Consolidating school boards, eliminating provincial school inspectors, and abandoning provincial Grade 13 examinations contributed to a shift of the balance of power towards school boards...."[28]

There are a number of problems with this analysis. First, as I've indicated, there was no "tradition" of "highly centralized control." Whatever the legal niceties concerning provincial power in education, Queen's Park had to hammer the local boards decade after decade before it eventually won significant control over the province's school system. Second, centralization came to fruition in the late 1960s with the consolidation of the local school boards and the implementation (via the Robarts Plan) of a much more widespread and sophisticated streaming system directed to social class division. Third, in the late 1960s and early 1970s, the province was not restructuring in aid of any kind of serious local board "autonomy," though classroom teachers themselves experienced some significant relaxation of curriculum guidelines. As Loren Lind writes, "what was happening was a basic shift in the method of control." What William Davis offered, says Lind, was a particular kind of "curricular and inspectoral autonomy," which actually increased the power of Ontario's educational administration. "He forced the school boards to amalgamate in such a way that both curriculum and inspection would come under bureaucratic control. The new larger school boards were expected to do for themselves what the province had imposed upon them. By and large they accepted bureaucratic control and self-inspection after the provincial model as a feature of 'equal opportunity.' That was, after all, how the big city boards did it."[29] Most of the directors of the new big boards, I should add, came directly from the provincial bureaucracy and the Ministry maintained Regional Offices to help keep the locals in line.

It was a decision-making structure that once went under the broad category of "corporate liberalism." It assumed considerable largesse both in promoting an expensive streaming system and in allowing a certain level of creative teaching and affirmative action — on race, gender, even class issues (as in "inner-city" formulas). Boards were given their heads on these questions. It was a time for imaginative "legitimation" of a prosperous capitalist society. That time, however, has now passed, as the government responds to what it understands to be the new reality of the global economy. It now wants to run a tighter ship, operating within a narrower, more explicit business agenda. At this point, we return to the second part of the Commission's historical analysis, which in itself is accurate enough.

A large property tax base, the Commission argues, has provided so much financial independence among "some large urban boards, especially in Metropolitan Toronto and Ottawa" that it has led in recent years to "confusion about leadership in the education system." These boards have been able "to act on their own to some extent, without getting Ministry approval for all projects, or even to ignore Ministry policy directives. Some of these boards developed innovative educational programs, such as schools for the arts and for sciences, alternative schools, and other special programs which make them leaders in the province's educational system. Although policy autonomy was not officially sanctioned, the Ministry seemed unable, or unwilling, to ensure compliance with many of its directives."[30] Now, says the Commission, as we face such "uncertain times" — with a growing emphasis on fiscal restraint and the need for a stardardized curriculum — "the Ministry must set the priorities for Ontario education, clarify goals and define the desired outcomes."[31]

But the point is that in the model of centralization which emerged in the late 1960s and early 1970s, the boards were *meant* "to act on their own" to develop such innovative programs. That was what "corporate liberalism" in Ontario schools, with its Hall-Dennis window dressing, was all about. The system worked within a two-tiered board/Ministry framework of bureaucratic control. What the Commission now recommends is a reduction in the lower tier and an increase in the upper tier of that earlier framework, and this, of course, results in an even smaller level of teacher and parent input. The Commission isn't "balancing" an earlier impulsive move towards increased local "autonomy" that got somewhat out of hand. Under its recommendations, bureaucratic-corporate control of education is simply intensified. In making this point, I don't mean to underestimate the significance of the Commission's recommended changes in this area. As we shall see, major new curriculum and streaming initiatives as well as deep financial retrenchment are part and parcel of this administrative restructuring.

One More Kick At The Local Boards

Having significantly reduced the power of the lower bureaucratic tier of educational governance in Ontario, the Commission decided against significant amalgamation of school board structures themselves. Such amalgamation, it judged, was liable to incur some high initial costs, and there were constitutional problems, but most importantly, Ontario boards were already big enough. On average, they were larger than the boards of any other province, including Ralph Klein's Alberta. More than thirteen Ontario boards had more than 40,000 students. It was a size beyond which, the Commission judged, boards "may be in danger of losing their connection to the community."[32] By this the Commission meant that when boards get larger, their bureaucratic structures tend to become too unwieldy. In order to direct 5000 schools from head office, the Commission argued, the Ministry required a manageable local board bureaucracy to translate provincial policies into effective action on the ground: "Through their supervisory officers and other professional staff, boards can provide direction and focus for schools, communicating clear policy guidelines and helping them set priorities.... School boards can assist principals and teachers to establish professional networks outside their own schools, and can mediate in school-community conflicts. The increased emphasis on monitoring and reporting on student learning and on other indicators will make it particularly important for boards to help schools act on the results of board-wide program reviews and student testing programs. Schools will need assistance in using the results of such monitoring to improve their programs and teaching."[33]

Under these new structural arrangements, and particularly with the province taking over the financial control of Ontario education, even the amalgamated/federated structure of the Metro Toronto School Board could be dissolved. It would be replaced, said the Commission, by an "administrative consortium," which would handle useful economic integration and carry on collective bargaining with Metro's various teacher unions.[34]

But what about the elected trustees in all of this bureaucratic restructuring? What are they supposed to do in this new "balanced" version of democratic school governance?

As it turns out, not much. There are no surprises here.

The Commission was very anxious to reduce the role of school board trustees as much as possible. It took particular pains to separate the trustees from the "operations" of the board, leaving them the task of setting "broad parameters" and letting "staff get on with managing the system within [these parameters] ... to be held accountable for the results they achieve." The trustees are to articulate "the mission or vision of the board, which usually includes some indication of the values the board wishes to infuse throughout the system." (Like some of Bob Rae's pronouncements on the Social Contract, this one may also be beyond irony. What in God's name could a board's "mission" be in a provincially controlled system of "learning outcomes," measured by externally designed standardized tests, and delivered by a provincial financial structure?) Trustees are also supposed to "set limits" on such things as ethical behaviour or on the specific costs of certain budget items. And that's about it.

Now, anyone who has spent more than an afternoon at one of the more active local boards will know that good trustees pay special attention to the actual operations of the boards and very little to the official "vision" that surrounds it. Much of the best work from these elected representatives — especially in the big-city boards — comes in hand-to-hand combat with bureaucrats at all levels of the system. The trustees' main job is to fight for very specific policies to make life better for students or teachers or parents and then fight some more to ensure that these policies do not get sandbagged during implementation. Trustees are there on behalf of a constituency who have no other serious representation in education decision-making: students and parents, and also teachers. (Teacher unions are as far removed from most policy loops as Home and School Associations.) As an outspoken Conservative trustee, Herb Barnes, put it at the Toronto board over twenty years ago, his job as a trustee was to be "part of the loyal opposition." The administration was "the government."

I recognize that many trustees don't do the kind of job many of us would like them to do. But wouldn't we say the same thing about our Members of Parliament? I think few of us would suggest we remove our MPs' capacity to dig as deep as they can into the government of Canada to ensure effective and honest administration. Yet that is exactly what the Commission recommends for elected trustees. Indeed, to make sure that trustees spend as little time on the job as possible, the Commission put a $20,000 cap on trustee salaries, insuring their part-time status — in a job clearly demanding full-time attention. At the same time as it shortened their hours, the Commission increased their workload. There should be "continuing efforts to reduce the number of trustees," it said, "once consistent criteria have been developed."[35]

The NDP government's response to this section of the Commission's report was interesting. It seemed to have no problems with the Commission's diminishing of trustee power, its capping of trustee salaries at $20,000, and its emphasis on reducing the number of trustees. But it didn't buy the Commission's subtleties on the need for a reasonably sized middle-level bureaucracy operating out of the local boards on the Ministry's behalf. Riding a right-wing wave of school-board criticism and deficit phobia, the government opted for a massive program of school board amalgamation. Education Minister Dave Cooke established the Ontario School Board Reduction Task Force with a mandate "to reduce the number of school boards in Ontario by between 40 and 50 per cent." The Task Force is to move quickly, suggesting new school board boundaries by September 1, 1995, going through a consultation process in the Fall, and then submitting its final recommendations on new boards to the Minister by December 31, 1995. "The new board boundaries," said the Ministry, "will be put in place in time for the 1997 municipal election."

Exactly what the government had in mind here is not entirely clear. Perhaps, for them, it was just an election gimmick, responding to public dissatisfaction with their local boards, and wanting to seem in charge of a reform agenda, without much consideration for its larger implications. But if the government was only concerned with electioneering, I suspect the political fall-out from amalgamation among such seasoned campaigners as school trustees would have given it pause so close to going to the polls. What is more likely, it seems to me, is that Ministry bureaucrats designed the policy as part of a much broader and more aggressive attack on local government, both for its "waste" of resources and its unruly citizen and teacher politics. Certainly, the premier would have been comfortable with such a direction, and would not have worried unduly about its political implications. He also knew that amalgamation would bring no short-term savings to boast of on the hustings.

The backgrounds of the Task Force members tended to lend weight to such a conclusion. To chair it, the government nominated John Sweeney, a former right-wing Liberal cabinet minister, who used to be the director of the Waterloo Region Separate School Board. To fill the remaining three seats, the government named Jean-Louis Bourdeau, a Franco-Ontarian who gave up teaching to become a businessman, Dorothy Wight, a right-wing former school trustee with a varied business career, and Duncan Green, once an assistant deputy minister, who as a "liberal" director of the Toronto Board of Education worked overtime to prevent citizen democracy from finding its way into his board's activities. The Task Force's chief executive officer is Assistant Deputy Minister Mariette Carrier-Fraser, a former Regional Office director, who comes from a conservative background of school financial administration. Its project head is Brian Fleming, a former director in the separate system and an unabashed conservative on school board matters. All in all, it is a Task Force that should fit in well with the bureaucrats already in place and planning a new round of education downsizing and restructuring.[36]

In responding to the Commission's gutting of board responsibilities and to the government's amalgamation plan, OSSTF finds itself between a rock and a hard place. It would prefer relatively small boards, offering good access to teachers and parents. And it certainly wants the boards to keep their current financial and curriculum responsibilities. It is a position which reflects the Federation's growing commitment to school democracy, as we shall see in the following section on community-schools. It is a position that also makes sense in terms of a province-wide bargaining strategy, which sets up the Federation to play one board off against the other. On the other hand, the Federation is desperate to deal with the increasingly high level of education cutbacks in the public schools. It is especially conscious of how Catholic school funding will increasing bleed the public system. Consequently OSSTF has stressed, as we noted earlier, cooperation between co-terminous public and separate boards to prevent unnecessary duplication of services. And it has offered a restructuring proposal for "confederated school boards," which integrates services for public, Catholic and francophone boards, while at the same time preserving their constitutional rights. These boards could be relatively small, but the likelihood is that they would turn out to be monster boards, much like those the government proposed, however much OSSTF might wish it otherwise.[37]

The government, however, following the Commission, had

no intention of any such "confederation" of school boards as part of its amalgamation scheme. It would continue to preserve the religious and language structures already in place. One possible outcome, says an OSSTF analysis, would be a system of "25 public, 25 separate, 15 Francophone boards with boundaries similar to Ontario Training Adjustment Board (OTAB) zones."[38] Thus, in many ways, OSSTF would get the worst of all possible worlds: new boards that are far too big, but which at the same time support a structure that will draw funds away from the public system. Once the amalgamation has been put into place, however, and OSSTF has worked out the various labour problems facing both its teaching and its non-teaching members, it will have to sit down to rethink the whole business of school governance and the place of the local boards within it.

Before we move on to the next section, I should briefly note the Commission's recommendations for more student involvement in education decision-making.

At one level, the Commission proposes to actually increase student power. It says there should be "at least one student member" on the local board, who is "entitled to vote on all board matters." Student Councils should "be given the responsibility for organizing students' views on all aspects of school life, and for transmitting these views to teachers and principals with responses sent back to students in a systematic way, and [for providing] advice to student trustees." There should be a Student and Youth Council to advise the minister "on all educational matters, to seek further ways to involve students in decisions that affect their lives, and to sponsor research about what students can do to improve learning in schools." The province should also set up "a collaborate process for developing a Students' Charter of Rights and Responsibilities," which would "include a significant role for students." Students should be involved as well "in developing and regularly reviewing codes of behaviour and other selected policies and procedures that flow from the Students' Charter of Rights and Responsibilities at both board and school levels."[39] All of this seems to be an advance on what presently exists in the current system, although how much the Commission sees this new student involvement as an exercise in self-policing is hard to say. The main problem with it, however, is that it will drop into a new governance system in which the institutions through which students are now to have these additional responsibilities — school boards (as we have seen) and school councils (as we shall see) — are to be stripped of any power to actually improve the effect of schooling on students' lives.

Extending Provincial Power To The Local School

At the end of the governance line in Ontario schools, the Royal Commission proposes a form of "school-based management" for local schools. This structure, as well as the larger structure of school governance we have just examined, appears to be inspired somewhat by the basic shape of the reforms carried out by the Alberta government, and particularly those of the Edmonton school board, "a pioneer in school-based management." The Edmonton board, the Commission reports, has allowed principals to "make decisions that elsewhere in Canada are usually made by school boards. However, control of such broad policy matters as budgets, province-wide testing, and curriculum remains in the hands of the provincial government, while hiring, special services, and budget allocations are the responsibility of a reduced number of boards of education. Alberta's Premier Klein's 1994 restructuring initiatives centralized Ministry control, while creating the option of parent councils."[40] Nailing down this structure as the Commission has designed it for the Ontario context is difficult, however, since it has been reshaped to fit the complexities of the most industrialized sector of Canada and to defer, in certain respects, to the province's continuing culture of local control in educational matters. Indeed, the Commission has made every effort to camouflage this central management with a blanket of democratic rhetoric and heartfelt concern for the overworked teacher, who must be returned to her fundamental role of teaching academic subject matter. And sometimes the blanket is so thick it becomes next to impossible to figure out what the Commission has in mind. All I can hope to do here is to pull out the main lines of the structure being proposed.

At the centre of Commission's recommendations for school-based management is something it calls the School-Community Council.

The first thing we have to learn about the School-Community Council is that will be an advisory council that is going to be run by the principal, even though parents will make up a majority of its members.

It is most definitely not going to be an institution through which parents will be seriously involved in running the school. Contrary to most opinion polls,[41] the Commission says that "only a small minority of parents want to participate in school governance or decision-making." It draws this conclusion because only a "very small number ... are active in home-and-school associations." What most parents want instead, it says, is for schools to tell them how their kids are doing, and if they are not doing well, how to improve. Besides, the Commission adds, the only kind of parent involvement that really counts in student success is keeping an eye on your kid's progress and helping with homework, attending school events, and being a classroom volunteer. While parents' active participation in a parent organization may be "valuable ... for the school in general," it doesn't cut so much ice in producing those "happy results" all parents want for their children. Such happy results, says the Commission, are "the touchstone for all our deliberations."[42]

Instead of parental governance, the Commission expects the leadership of these councils to fall on the shoulders of the school principal, who will "devise an action plan for the establishment and implementation" of the council in his or her school," and who will play "a pivotal role in convening the council and in motivating its work."[43] A parent council with real decision-making power would place "an unneeded additional burden on principals."[44] On the other hand, the Commission gave no thought whatsoever to structuring substantial teacher power into these councils. Under the guidance and control of their principal, teachers are to focus on their students' "learning outcomes" and, it appears, on building friendly relationships with parents and community. In school management, they should be consulted only in those areas of their "professional" expertise, and their involvement in the council should be limited to a few representatives.[45]

The government accepted the Commission's recommendations on School-Community Council representation pretty much as they stood, with only a few small changes. When parents' organizations complained about the lack of parent power being proposed by the Commission, Rae said a parent could chair the School-Community Council instead of the principal. But nothing else changed for parents, and the leadership role for the principal remained. When the unions complained about lack of representation, Rae said that support staff could elect one representative on the council and that labour could be one of the community representatives. At the same time, the premier reduced the power of teacher representatives. Where the Commission had said several teacher representatives were possible, Rae insisted that it be only one. The number of students (from Grade 7 on) who will sit on these councils still remains to be worked out.[46]

Whatever the breakdown of representation among parents, teachers and students turns out to be, the main point is that these are not governing councils. "We do not see these councils as having a decision-making role in relation to school management," the Commission says, "although we would expect them to participate and be consulted in many aspects of the life of the school."[47] Principals should have "maximum flexibility to organize and operate their schools as they see fit."[48]

What the councils actually turn out to be are institutions through which the school principal can bring together what the Commission calls community alliances: "We conceive of the school-community council as an essential underpinning or resource in aiding principals in the determination of the kind of alliances needed and resources available in a given community."[49] In this context, "community liaison staff" are assigned to principals to strengthen "school community linkages. These staff, who would not be certified teachers, would be responsible for helping to implement decisions and initiatives of the school-community councils as well as other school-community initiatives."[50]

There are two groups of people with whom alliances or linkages are particularly important for the Commission: social service agencies and business organizations. We will return to them in a moment. (There is also an emphasis on "religious groups" being represented in these councils, which I won't be dealing with here. Like the informal support the Commission gives to school funding for different religions — to match Catholic privileges — the extent to which this emphasis is for short-term public relations or is the product of a deeper alliance with the religious right remains unclear. We'll just have to wait and see.)

What is important to get straight first is the Commission's thinking in setting up these alliances.

The Commission makes a very firm distinction between the "academic" and the "non-academic" needs of students. Teachers are to focus on the "academic" needs, expressed through "learning outcomes." The "non-academic" needs turn out mostly to concern social problems of one kind or another as well as the need to be prepared for work. The school is to share the responsibility for these non-academic needs with community partners, whose resources can be "organized and mobilized" through the School-Community Council.

This external organization and mobilization of resources is necessary because the school can no longer handle all the social and work-related problems it faces. Teachers need a break from this kind of activity, so they can concentrate on their students' academic performance. They need help from such sources as "business and industry, health-care institutions, and social-work agencies, municipal infrastructure and services, community associations, [and] religious groups."[51]

In this context, the principal should now be understood to have two major management functions, a "new dual role." He must be "an instructional leader" and at the same time he must become "the active agent in the development, fostering, and sustaining of the alliances that form the heart of community education ... co-ordinating services that help students." He must be the "agent of change to establish a new understanding about the school and its responsibilities."[52]

There is no question in the Commission's report about the principal's power in the first of these two roles. Whatever teachers, parents and students may think about curriculum development in their local school, whatever their "input," it is the job of the school principal to make sure that provincial guidelines on "learning outcomes" curriculum and testing are carried out to the letter. The principal is to have "considerable autonomy" in this area. It is a "top priority."[53]

In line with this local management emphasis on establishing provincial curriculum priorities, departmental heads are now to function as sub-managers. They are not only to assist the principal in broad management functions, but they are also to supervise and evaluate teachers and to "take on a strong leadership role in developing and implementing the new curriculum we are recommending."[54]

The principal's role is equally strong in bringing together what the Commission calls "community alliances," and it is equally in the direct service of provincial policy. Such alliances are primarily to be built in the areas of social service provision and work preparation, and in both areas there is a powerful provincial (and corporate) agenda at work.

In the realm of social service provision, the Commission says it is concerned to "ensure an integrated approach to the care and nurturing of children." This is what the work of the School-Community Council is all about. The Commission looks to the local school to help develop a broader "restructuring in the delivery of not only educational but of all supports for children. This requires that together with families, a wide variety of community agencies, groups, and institutions can, and should, be brought to the table through the school so that they can determine how to best work together to support the development and learning of young people. It is not the school, and certainly not the teachers," the Commission continues, "who must assume prime responsibility for responding to the needs of young people. But, in our vision, the school must assume responsibility for bringing together the people, the groups, and the agencies who can respond to these needs...."[55]

This integration of the "care and nurturing of children" at the local school level is part of what the Commission sets out as "the direction for long-term systematic reform of the multiple, hierarchical, children's service systems that have evolved in the province. The redesigned initiative we propose reflects our conclusion that the expansion of the large children's service system already in place does not promise greater well-being for our children and youth. We have ... argued for a new direction that builds on the strengths of communities, families, children, and youth. The systematic changes in provincial children's services systems that we believe are needed to fulfil our vision of community education require significant political leadership committed to redesigning existing flows of authority, resources, skills, and capacities."[56]

What we have here are the code words for an unequivocal downsizing of children's services in the province: the "expansion" of the present system won't help; we have to have "a new direction" that builds on "the strengths of communities, families, children, and youth" (which is obviously a lot less costly); and we need "political leadership" to hammer the cuts and the sacrifices home.

The Commission and the government are dead serious about such restructuring.

The Commission recommends "that the Premier assign responsibility for reforming children's services to a senior Minister, in addition to his/her regular portfolio; and that this senior Minister be supported by an Interministerial Committee of Ministers responsible for children's services." This committee, in turn, should establish "through the regional offices of the Ministry of Education and Training, a leadership and coordinating plan between the school boards and other local providers of services to develop and help implement the mechanisms necessary to support the work of school-community councils."[57]

Not the least of the possible savings from such restructuring will come from the eventual replacement of teachers by what the Commission calls "differentiated staff — human-resource people who will not be certified as teachers, although they will be sharing in the education of students." These staff members include "volunteer parents, paid or unpaid, helping in classes, or other professionals and paraprofessionals, as well as aides."[58]

This restructuring and downsizing of children's services is part of a larger restructuring and downsizing of social services within the province as a whole. It is also linked with increased provincial control of these services. For a government that hopes — as the Rae government quite explicitly hoped — to extend the slash and burn agenda of the Social Contract and the Expenditure Control plan into the future, it becomes increasingly important to take over the social service sector from local government. The more control you have over a service, the easier it is to cut.[59]

In making its case that the school should be an institution integrating children's' service agencies, the Commission is not shy in fingering the main culprit for the recent expansion of social problems which have overwhelmed the schools, forcing them to "stretch their mandate" far beyond their current resources. Such problems have emerged, the Commission tells us, from the functioning of a capitalist economy in Canada over the last 30 years. Families are under much greater stress because both parents are now forced to work. Even if parents "live together … they [now] have less time for their children, unless they are unemployed." And this in a world, it adds, where kids need more parent support than ever. But "if changing socio-economic conditions of families have affected children," the Commission continues, "so have other socio-cultural factors such as the youth consumers' culture (and economy), or the anonymous urban life that has often replaced traditional communities' cohesion and support." Furthermore, there is the stark reality of poverty facing so many of our students. "One recent Ontario study," the Commission reminds us, "found that 'one in every six children is in a family receiving social assistance. About three-quarters of them are children of single-parent families, a majority of these parents being female. Child poverty in Ontario is on the rise, standing at 15.3 percent in 1990.'" This poverty, the Commission concludes, is clearly linked to significant "economic restructuring caused by automation in the manufacturing sector [which] is escalating at a rapid rate. The greatest victims in the slide toward low-paying and temporary jobs are young families — those with parents under 25, who have seen their incomes drop from the 1980s by nearly 20 percent."[60]

For the Commission, a restructured set of social services is to pick up the immediate fall-out from this economically-based fragmentation of family life.

But what of the future?

Where do we put our hope for a good adult life for our present generation of students?

Why, says the Commission, without a hint of irony (or even remorse), we think it should go directly into the hands of the folks who have done so much to destroy our family life over the last three decades: the business community.

It is the same sort of plunge into the dark we saw with the Commission's whole-hearted embrace of corporate information technology. It is a plunge which involves a major new business perspective and involvement in the provincial curriculum as a whole, which we shall turn to later, but it also entails lots of business action at the local school level. Getting this action into her school, via the School-Community Council, is the second major task for the school principal in her capacity as an organizer of "community alliances."

There is an exciting role, says the Commission, for business representatives on the School-Community Council: "We imagine local businesses in another domain of community life expanding their links with schools beyond providing part-time jobs for students who need them. Businesses may lend staff to augment teachers' efforts in conveying certain knowledge in particular courses, co-ordinating workplace visits by students, providing schools with equipment that has become unnecessary at work. They may even provide healthy communities through their internal practices by developing family-friendly policies that assure time for employees who are parents to maintain regular contact with their children's schools."[61]

What an extraordinary last line that is, offering a thoroughly new and unexpected avenue for the "soulful" corporation to reach out to the Canadian people: "We may destroy their jobs," corporate executives can argue, "slash their wages, pressure governments to cut their welfare, social services, education and health care, dismember their communities, slander them in our newspapers and television outlets, pump up the prices they pay in our stores and hammer them with advertising to get them there, but hey, when it comes to working folks finding a way to keep in contact with their kids' school, we're going to be there for them. Believe it, brothers and sisters. 'Healthy communities,' that's what we're about, all right. We're your 'family-friendly' corporate sector."

In line with the Commission's early frankness on the corporate impact on family life, was it too much to hope for a word or two on the role such a School-Community Council would play in promoting a business-oriented ideology in the local school curriculum? Or in the more practical preparation of students to willingly accept the future conditions of their work? The Commission might also have told us something about the significance of corporate logos on classroom and cafeteria walls. As Vincent Solek of Pizza Pizza puts it: "Whenever you can deal with a captive market, you can be very successful. Usually we have replaced a generic product and when students see a brand name, sales go up from 25 to 100 percent. The point is to develop brand loyalty while the students are in school."[62] Or maybe, remembering the big-time corporate players it noted were targeting the school system, the Commission might have favoured us with more analysis of the value of the education system as a marketplace and as a profit-making opportunity through privatization.

It is this last point — linking the new order in education with a new order for corporate profits — which gets me to the principal's final function in the Commission's outline for a system of school-based management.

As the Commission sees it, there are going to be more bucks spent at the local level, even if there are fewer of them available for the system as a whole. It recommends that "the Ministry phase in a policy requiring school boards to turn over an increasingly significant portion of the school budget to principals, on the condition that the school have a school growth plan...."[63] And, in this framework, "community alliances" are the order of the day. "Principals and school-community councils must be encouraged by boards to develop the kind of alliances best suited to their area, and must be given substantial support by supervisory officers acting as leaders at the municipal/county level. Principals and school-community councils will therefore require greater local autonomy and budget control."[64] The local representatives of the business community would do well to get in line.

Coming To Grips With Democracy

As we might expect, OSSTF remains opposed to all the fundamentals of school-based management as envisaged by the Commission.

OSSTF's position, like that of the Commission, is centred in the School-Community Council, but what it imagines for this council is very different from what the Commission has in mind.

The Federation begins with an understanding that local parents have to have real power within the school. This involves a good deal more than school flexibility, friendliness and open communication with parents, however important these aspects of school governance may be.[65] Parents have to be substantially involved in school decision-making. The Federation has yet to engage in a process for working out different formulas for such participation, and they would want to be very clear about preserving a high degree of teacher professional autonomy when doing so. At present, however, OSSTF argues that "the local school and community are the best judge of the form parental involvement should take. In one Ontario high school, a parent representative sits on the department heads' committee, the school budget committee, the school staffing committee and attends staff meetings. The representative functions within a school constitution and a parent association constitution. In another school, the parents meet on a regular basis to examine issues surrounding the school and education in general. In a number of jurisdictions, OSSTF members work closely with parents to defend the right of every student to a full-service education system. Whether the parental involvement is in a coalition, an association or an advisory body, OSSTF believes that the community is where the parental involvement should originate."[66]

At the same time as OSSTF supports a serious level of parent involvement in the schools, it also believes that the Commission has set up a straw man in the vision of the parent-controlled school that it rejects. The model of real democratic control of our schools, the Federation says, has to have a much wider base than the school's parents. For a start, the School-Community Council must have many more teachers involved than the Commission's recommended "minimal presence." "School-Community councils will work," it says, "because of, not in spite of, educators' involvement. The Commission seems to have accepted a very narrow view of the classroom and the teacher's role in it."

At the centre of OSSTF's version of a School-Community Council, however, is a much more complex structure than a simple alliance of parents and teachers. Such councils must also include older students, local officials, school support staff and interested community members working together, in different ways, to improve all facets of school life. They should function as a "cooperative." The last thing OSSTF wants is school councils to become "the captives of singular special interest groups."[67] In working out this kind of local democracy, the Federation doesn't deny the need for "overall standards" for Ontario schools, developed at the provincial level with solid input from a wide variety of community sources, including the province's teachers. At the same time, however, the Federation insists that the local community, operating through School-Community Councils and the local boards, must be given considerable freedom to implement provincial guidelines and produce "the curriculum necessary for [their] implementation."[68]

What is necessary, in other words, is a creative tension between local and central school governance, with honest power-sharing between different levels of decision-making. And nowhere is this truer than in the local school itself. "The principle of strong administration is power-sharing," the Federation argues. "If power-sharing is real, the power will remain with the leader. If the power-sharing of the leader is hesitant, frightened or overly assertive, the sharers will become aggressive, uninvolved or indecisive."[69]

This kind of democracy is not just necessary for the effective running of our schools. It is also necessary, OSSTF says, for the survival of the public school system itself. Honest parent involvement is especially important for this broader goal, as parents have "a natural alliance" with teachers for the well-being of their children. Parents of school-age children may be a minority, and a decreasing minority in the society, but "they do have considerable moral force." It is a force that must be roused. "Public education is in serious danger of becoming an anachronism by the end of this century. The forces of conservatism are actively pushing business control of the curriculum and management of schools. The disappearance of the concept of universality in social programs is part of their educational agenda under the guise of choice. Parents understand the need for public funding of education. But if they become convinced that they are better parents with user-pay education, as has happened in Australia and large parts of the US, then we have lost our last opportunity to preserve publicly funded education for all. It will have become simply a hundred-year experiment in social engineering."[70] Teachers and parents must struggle together for a public school system we can all be proud of. But not only teachers and parents. The Federation notes that "three-quarters of the people residing in the community do not have a family-oriented connection with the local school. Yet these people are also paying the tax dollars which keep our programs going. In order to continue to survive and indeed to prosper we need their support as well."[71]

At this moment, and particularly in response to the Royal Commission, the mobilization of parent, teacher, student and community forces must centre on the School-Community Council. In a call to its members at its most recent Provincial Assembly, the Federation recommended "that local districts and workplaces immediately begin working with their existing parent councils and associations to ensure that student, parent and staff interests are protected. Where there is no council or association in place, staff should immediately begin a community outreach program to assist families in laying the groundwork for effective associations which have real power and will be able to survive the school community council as envisioned by the Royal Commission's recommendations. OSSTF's models for school community councils or parent advisory councils have a constitution as their base. Setting up a school constitution may be the most effective immediate step to take."[72]

In responding to some of the specifics of the Commission's view of School-Community Councils, OSSTF notes the non-democratic aspects of the "community liaison staff" who will be attached to the school principal. There is, says the Federation, a "concern that there could be an attempt to create a kind of [government-sponsored] guerrilla force working independently of the community to oversee the Councils, the schools and the communities themselves."[73] Such democratic concerns, OSSTF argues, are to be seen throughout the entire report. "Given the anti-labour tone of the whole document," it says, "and the desire to create a mega-ministry to help the local councils achieve community partnership, we believe that local school councils will require the vigilance of parents and teachers to prevent this from becoming simply a way of introducing various economic and religious ideas into the classroom as well as a means of dumbing down and otherwise undermining the teaching function."[74]

Not only is the Federation concerned about the implications for democracy in the Commission's version of the School-Community Council, it is equally disturbed by the hard distinction the Commission makes between "academic" and "non-academic" functions in the school.

This distinction, alongside the Commission's emphasis on provincially controlled "learner outcomes," will be central to how these school councils function to "dumb down and otherwise undermine the teaching function." What OSSTF argues is that the content of what's taught must be infused with a larger sense of what matters in society, for individuals and for the society as a whole. Facts, however they might be expressed in "learner outcomes," can't be separated from values. Again, it is the fundamental relationships between people that OSSTF is stressing here, how they change and why they matter. They lie at the heart of the curriculum itself. Good teachers know this, whether they are teaching Science, History or English. Human values are woven into all their texts. To bring these values to the surface is essential for students to grasp both the larger meaning and the inner logic of what they are studying. At this level, a distinction between "academic" and "non-academic" understanding is meaningless and deeply destructive of good teaching.

At another level, OSSTF is also disturbed by the Commission's unnecessarily rigid distinction between these functions (described as looking after kids' "social needs") and the "academic" role of teachers. As David Clandfield writes in response to this section of the Commission's report, "Anyone who believes in the importance of teachers moving beyond their role as subject specialists or as providers of skills and knowledge will be concerned that new integrated services plans will soon return teachers to their narrowly defined professional roles as transmitters of knowledge and trainers of skills, and pass on *all* concern for the learner as a person to specialists in the 'relevant' discipline or profession."[75] The concern for the learner as a person, OSSTF judges, is central to a teacher's role. Relating subject matter to the real interests and experience of their students is at the core of good pedagogy. This judgement is also central to OSSTF's argument for smaller classes. They are essential if these personal relationships between teachers and students are to be maintained. Only shallow mechanical learning can survive large classes, with survival defined as the maintenance of standards measured by shallow standardized tests.

It was in this context of concern for the learner as a person that OSSTF put forward to the Commission its vision of "integrated services" within the school. When students need help from professional services, beyond the realm of the classroom teacher, OSSTF argued that these services should be centred at the local school and those who carry them out must be knowledgeable about the school program. Integrated services are to be *for students*. OSSTF was not at all anxious, as the Commission eventually recommended, to have the school function as an integration centre for other institutions dealing with children. "Those working in schools," it said, "develop different focuses and skills than similarly trained professional working in other settings. Advantages to educators include increased experience in dealing with school-related problems, preparedness and ability to provide relevant and practical strategies affecting education." This structure, the Federation judged, would also be the most cost-efficient.[76]

OSSTF does not see a passive or establishment role for

these school professionals. "The role of the professional student services personnel is to provide services and resources to assist classroom teachers and students to ensure equal educational opportunity for all."[77] The Federation has yet to come to grips with government use of its professional services sector to entrench social class divisions within the school system and the society as a whole. But the logic of the Federation's call to teachers to take up the cause of school and social reform would also apply to those professional staff within its jurisdiction. If professional services are often structured to disempower communities, it must be part of the professional workers' job, through their union, to resist this approach and to work alongside their "clients" for real equality.

This issue of school reform is particularly important for the School-Community Councils. Teachers, parents and students, community and labour groups have to work together to insure a productive direction for this reform within these councils. For OSSTF, there are two major aspects to real reform: the democratic thrust, which we have just touched on, and the development of a strong curriculum policy, which we will deal with shortly. The Commission's focus on "happy results" within the present system benefits only a limited number of kids, and then only in terms of their social class position and not of their knowledge and understanding of the world. The schools, the Federation understands, have to be made better for everyone.

What these School-Community Councils do not need, OSSTF says in response to the Commission's new centralized structure for children's services, is another heavy-handed administration looking into their affairs. "Children do not require even more bureaucracy," it argues, "to deal with their education, health and welfare.... The authority for overseeing services already resides in the appropriate ministries."[78] And in terms of the larger downsizing initiatives of the government, these councils must also not be used as vehicles to "contract out of services to voluntary agencies, social service agencies and private care providers at the expense of the school professionals already delivering such services."[79] This is now a common tactic among school boards. "A statement made by the Minister of

Education and Training," OSSTF told the Commission earlier, "has intensified this concern. He states in a letter to a trustee that 'school boards are not expected to pay for social workers, speech pathologists and other therapeutic services … these services remain under the jurisdiction of the Minister of Community and Social Services, and of Health.' The Federation is extremely concerned with this statement since many students who require professional services will not receive them. Other agencies are not staffed to pick up a new client load. In fact, hospitals and community agencies have never had as their mandate the provision of professional services specifically designed to help children to be successful in school and would find it costly and time-consuming to reorient their services to provide school support." The Federation calls for these services to "work within the school system as members of the educational team," and continue to be funded through the Ministry of Education."[80]

Finally, OSSTF remains determined to resist the Commission's emphasis on a major business presence in the public schools. The Federation has no problem with local business people, as individuals, being part of School-Community Councils. They welcome them. But it does not want them as representatives of a business "interest," with special privileges and responsibilities. The School-Community Council's primarily role, says OSSTF, is to help ensure that all students get as solid an education as possible, one that equips them to deal with all aspects of the world around them. Job-slotting, mostly for very limited jobs, is way down on the Federation's list of educational priorities. For most students, it argues, such "skills" can be picked up very quickly on the job and need not take up much classroom time. An education that empowers and enriches students in all aspects of their life has to come first.

A College Of Teachers "For The Government"

In what can only be described as part of a general strategy to centralize curriculum and to reduce the power of teacher unions, the Commission proposed what it called a "College of Teachers." It would be responsible for "determining professional standards, certification, and accreditation of teacher education programs."[81] With these new responsibilities, the College was the most aggressive anti-teacher-union recommendation by the Royal Commission. OSSTF was leading the attack on it within hours of the publication of the Commission's Report. This College of Teachers," as Liz Barkley put it, "is not there for teachers, it is there for the government."[82]

Contrary to Barkley's assertion, the Commission argues that it is giving *more* power to teachers, since the College's functions are currently framed by the Education Act and the Teaching Profession Act., a situation that is oppressive for teachers. "Governance," says the Report, "is currently exercised under the Acts by universities through admission to faculties of education and control of the pre-service program; and by the Minister through authority over certification and decertification, and post-certification qualifications. As long as these crucial areas of governance in teaching remain outside the control of teachers," the Commission concludes, "the profession of teaching will remain in a state of limited development."

OSSTF doesn't see it this way. It understands the College as a mechanism that will take control of their lives out of their hands. As things currently stand, teachers experience considerable freedom within the university context. While the Federation and its members are consistently critical of the program they receive at faculties of education, they can't imagine tighter Ministry control improving matters. The College is much more likely, they figure, to make things worse, particularly when it comes to the quality of the program they will be offered.

The province's teacher federations, through their umbrella organization, the Ontario Teachers' Federation, have had a fair amount of clout in bargaining with the Ministry over qualification. Indeed, OSSTF, like other Federations, takes over from the Ministry (in practice, though not in theory) the activity of judging teacher qualifications levels once a B.Ed. has been obtained. It is the Federation which determines for local boards whether the qualifications a teacher needs for each new step of the salary grid have been met, and the Federation's right to do so is embedded in its collective agreement with each board. With this new institution, says Barkley, we are all "at the mercy of a government bureaucracy,"[83] however many teachers may be elected to its governing bodies.

The tight policy framework under which the College of Teachers must operate will ensure it remain a consistent promoter of Ministry policy.

The Commission is determined, for example, that its particular approach to curriculum be translated, through the College of Teachers, into much tighter control of university courses for prospective teachers. Thus it recommends that "common undergraduate prerequisites be established for entry to pre-service teacher preparation courses, with decisions about specific prerequisites to be made by the College of Teachers, with input from faculties of education and school boards."[84] The Commission obviously doesn't want any more of those loosey-goosey arts programs for teachers if they are to aspire to be tough-minded "gatekeepers" for the new economic order. Pre-service training itself, of course, is to be firmly directed by such curriculum goals under the aegis of the College. But equally important for the Commission is that the present cadre of classroom teachers also buys into its new "learning outcomes" curriculum.

In this curriculum area the College has another major role assigned to it. It is to oversee mandatory professional development for all regular classroom teachers. This professional development is quite explicitly to make sure teachers know and teach what the government wants them to know and teach; it is to be distinguished from "what might be termed professional renewal, which is a more personal and individual notion."[85] It will have no automatic salary increments or certificates associated with completion of its programs. Every five years regular teachers will be simply recertified by the College, and they will be out on their ear if they don't perform "satisfactorily" or "participate in professional development recognized by the College."[86] In this context, the College of Teachers joins Ministry and board management to "emphasize that principals are accountable for satisfactory teacher performance in their schools, and that supervisory officers are responsible for ensuring that principals take appropriate action in dealing with teachers whose performance is not satisfactory."[87]

What about the teacher unions in all of this?

In setting up the College, the Commission was very clear it must not be "an extension of the teacher federations and associations." "Certainly," it says, "some of the educator councillors could be elected from their membership by OTF affiliates during their individual annual general meetings. However, we think it very important that the College reach out to educators through other mechanisms: direct elections might be held, or representatives might be elected by provincial subject councils, by curriculum co-ordinator groups, and from private schools.... Whatever mechanisms are adopted, it is critical that no one interest group have undue influence in the College."[88]

The main argument the Commission uses to keep the teacher federations at bay on this front is that they cannot overcome their "special interests" in order to work for the good of the whole system. In spite of the federations' excellent work on professional issues, the Commission argues, their "role in collective bargaining has gradually emerged as their essential defining activity." The unions have thus been "constrained" in "promoting teaching as a profession and in addressing broad-based educational issues." Union "contractual imperatives" — such as salaries and working conditions — "may sometimes undermine professional interests and educational reform."[89]

OSSTF has two responses to this argument.

The first is that the teachers' unions do much better work on the professional front than do the boards and the Ministry. The bureaucrats who run these institutions, and who will soon be working for the College of Teachers, have never envisaged any serious reform of the province's educational system, except, of course, for those who carrry the torch for a neo-conservative agenda in Ontario schools. And that's worse than doing nothing. A lot worse.

The second and more important response from OSSTF says that teachers really do care about the well-being of their students and of the system as a whole. That concern is central to how they want their federations to function. Teachers' worklives and larger sense of purpose depend on such an attitude. This is the deepest sense in which teacher unions have a "natural alliance" with parents and community activists. OSSTF knows it can get sidetracked on money questions, which are still of great importance to its membership, but in the end teacher unions still have to come back to the fundamentals of what a teacher's job is all about. And from this perspective, the Federation is critical of its own efforts to mobilize its rank-and-file on larger professional and curriculum issues. Yes, OSSTF is currently saying to its members, we've done some very valuable professional and curriculum work over the years, but we now have "to take professional control of curriculum development" right across the province — to help shape all aspects of the curriculum and provide our members with the best available resources to teach it.[90]

OSSTF adds one final point to this second argument: Individual teacher representatives serving in an institution like the College of Teachers can easily be picked off by the bureaucracy, if they are unconnected to union structures supporting a strong curriculum development agenda. Good curriculum has to be fought for. The province is certainly not going to provide it. And teacher representatives have to be truly accountable to their peers for how they carry themselves in this battle. Only through the union can this this accountability be provided. And only through the union can the battle itself be joined.

Finally, OSSTF isn't just worried about the loss of control over teacher education and curriculum that will come with the College of Teachers. The Federation also understands that the College comes with a much more old-fashioned union-busting agenda. In setting out this agenda, the Commission is again surprisingly frank.

What the Commission wants to break, as all employers have traditionally sought to break, is the principle of due process applying when a teacher is threatened with firing. The Commission opens up its argument by noting that teachers' federations have "negotiated procedures that guarantee due process to teachers, ensure that teachers are given notice of problems, provided with assistance, and protected against arbitrary action on the part of school personnel." It then turns to the local boards' unhappiness with the current procedures for appraising teacher performance, and says that there are many additional sources for appraisal and for assistance to teachers in trouble which might be tapped. Then it's back to the problem of union contracts protecting, through due-process clauses, too many teachers who should be dismissed. "We believe," says the Commission, "that through collective agreements, the defence of teachers' rights may have overridden the need for students to be protected from incompetent or uncaring teachers, who may be unable or unwilling to do a good job." What to do? The Commission is not prepared to dot the i's and cross the t's on what a new set of arrangements might look like, but it is pretty clear about the direction in which the government should go. That direction doesn't take them anywhere near the teachers' federations to see if something more creative and helpful to everyone could be designed.

If there were real teacher control over the process, then OSSTF would join discussions about how to make it work. But the Commission has no interest in that level of democracy. The heavy hitters in the administration are going to save the day. "We believe," the Commission declares, "that leadership from the top is crucial: directors of education must communicate clearly that the system will make every effort to help teachers improve their performance if it is unsatisfactory, but that unless there is sufficient improvement after a reasonable time (within a year), principals will be held accountable for ensuring that appropriate action is taken." What happens then to contracts with "due process" clauses? The Commission doesn't say. It simply recommends that the federations, the Ministry and the boards "reach agreement on any changes required to ensure that policies and practices related to dismissal effectively balance the rights of teachers and the rights of students." The rest is, again, left up in the air. Are teachers now to wait, the Federation wonders, for provincial legislation that will wipe out their current due-process protection? OSSTF saw their collective agreements ripped up during the Social Contract process, and they know it could happen again.

Whatever is worked out to deal with teachers who are not doing their job, OSSTF argues, its members must never abandon the principle of due process: "Provision must be made," it says, "to protect individuals in instances where youth and inexperience might wrongly be equated with professional incompetence; where personality differences or poor relationships with administration might be met with charges of incompetence; where damage to reputation and career might result from unfair adverse reports from officials or colleagues; where the workload or other conditions of service militate against effective performance; and in other cases where mental or physical health or unsettling personal circumstances might account for less than professional performance. Even where incompetence seems to be clearly indicated, individuals must be accorded the due process of law to which they are entitled in natural justice."[91]

At the same time, says OSSTF, there are lots of ways to protect our students and to ensure they get a good education. It is to this issue — the building of a strong and purposeful curriculum that takes student interests to heart — that I now turn.

FOOTNOTES

1 *Report of the Royal Commission on Learning, Volume 4*, cited above, p. 128.

2 *Report of the Royal Commission on Learning, Volume 4*, cited above, p. 132.

3 See the section entitled "Religious minorities," *Report of the Royal Commission on Learning, Volume 4*, cited above, pp. 88–89.

4 OSSTF, *Submission to the Ontario Fair Tax Commission*, "Fair Taxation for Responsible Education: Report of the Funding Initiatives and New Directions Committee," September 22, 1992, pp. 20–22.

5 OSSTF, *Adequacy, Equity, and Democracy: A Proposal For Education Funding in Ontario*, January 1993.

6 *Report of the Royal Commission on Learning, Volume 4*, cited above, p. 7.

7 *Report of the Royal Commission on Learning, Volume 4*, cited above, p. 136.

8 For the following paragraphs, see Recommendations 4, 5, 10, 11, 15, 23, 26, 29, *Report of the Royal Commission on Learning, Volume 4*, cited above, pp.167–169.

9 Recommendation # 14, *Report of the Royal Commission on Learning, Volume 4*, cited above, p. 168.

10 In line with prevailing policy, the two bureaucrats who recently were appointed to head the Ministry's curriculum renewal agenda have no background as educators. David Walker, the former Executive Assistant to Deputy Minister, Charles Pascal, comes from the Ministry of Community

and Social Services. Marjorie Mercer, a career civil servant who, until recently, headed the policy research department within the Ministry of Education and Training, also has no teaching experience.

11 Recommendation #93, *Report of the Royal Commission on Learning, Volume 4*, cited above, p.24.

12 *Report of the Royal Commission on Learning, Volume 4*, cited above, pp. 7–8.

13 *Report of the Royal Commission on Learning, Volume 4*, cited above, p. 10.

14 *Report of the Royal Commission on Learning, Volume 4*, cited above, p. 6.

15 *Report of the Royal Commission on Learning, Volume 4*, cited above, p. 10.

16 Livingstone, David, "The Uses of Computer Literacy: Critical Reflections on the Royal Commission on Learning," *Orbit*, May, 1995. See also Noble, Douglas, *The Classroom Arsenal: Military Research, Information Technology and Public Education*, Falmer Press, New York, 1991.

17 *Report of the Royal Commission on Learning, Volume 4*, cited above, pp. 27–28.

18 Livingstone, David, "The Uses of Computer Literacy: Critical Reflections on the Royal Commission on Learning," *Orbit*, May 1995.

19 Education Ministry sources tell me that computer-labelled funds were already available for such programs and were considerable. Partly, it seems, this program simply involved a transfer of monies from one computer-related category to another.

20 Ministry of Education and Training, "Backgrounder: Information Technology in Our Schools," February 1995.

21 Ministry of Education and Training, "Backgrounder: Information Technology in Our Schools," February 1995.

22 Roberts & Associates, "Ontario Education as a Model User of Information Technology," February 27, 1995. This background document was used as a focus document for a Technology Visioning Project symposium held by the Ministry of Education and Training, March 27–28, 1995.

23 *Report of the Royal Commission on Learning, Volume 4*, cited above, p. 25.

24 The following discussion is taken from OSSTF Provincial Executive, "Public Education — In the Public Interest: The theme for OSSTF's 1995–96 Priorities and Program," *Update*, vol. 22, no. 5, March 1995, pp. 13–16.

25 *Report of the Royal Commission on Learning, Volume 4*, cited above, p. 102.

26 See for example, Cameron, David, *Schools For Ontario*, University of

Toronto Press, Toronto, 1972; Curtis, Bruce, *Building the Educational State: Canada West, 1836–71*, The Falmer Press, Barcombe, U.K., 1988; Curtis, Bruce, Livingstone, David, Smaller, Harry, *Stacking the Deck: The Streaming of Working-Class Kids in Ontario Schools*, Our Schools/Our Selves, Toronto, 1992; Gidney, R.D. and Millar, W.P.J., I*nventing Secondary Education: The Rise of the High School in Nineteenth Century Ontario*, McGill-Queen's University Press, Montreal, 1990; Katz, Michael, and Mattingly, Paul, ed., *Education and Social Change: Themes from Ontario's Past*, New York University Press, New York, 1975; Lind, Loren, *The Learning Machine: A Hard Look at Toronto Schools*, Anansi, Toronto, 1974; McDonald, Neil and Chaiton, Alf, ed., *Egerton Ryerson and His Times*, Macmillan, Toronto, 1978; Prentice, Alison, *The School Promoters: Education and Social Class in Mid-Nineteenth Century Ontario*, McClelland and Stewart, Toronto, 1977; Prentice, Alison and Houston, Susan, *Family School and Society*, Oxford University Press, Toronto, 1975, and *Schooling and Scholars in Nineteenth Century Ontario*, University of Toronto Press, Toronto, 1988.

27 *Report of the Royal Commission on Learning, Volume 4*, cited above, p. 102.

28 *Report of the Royal Commission on Learning, Volume 4*, cited above, p. 117.

29 Lind, Loren, *The Learning Machine: A Hard Look At Toronto Schools*, Anansi, Toronto 1974, pp. 205-06.

30 *Report of the Royal Commission on Learning, Volume 4*, cited above, p. 117.

31 *Report of the Royal Commission on Learning, Volume 4*, cited above, p. 117–118.

32 *Report of the Royal Commission on Learning, Volume 4*, cited above, p. 114. See also Platiel, Rudy, "Ontario to detail school-board amalgamations," *Globe and Mail*, February 22,1995.

33 *Report of the Royal Commission on Learning, Volume 4*, cited above, p. 113.

34 *Report of the Royal Commission on Learning, Volume 4*, cited above, pp. 116–117. See particularly Recommendation #156.

35 *Report of the Royal Commission on Learning, Volume 4*, cited above, p. 112.

36 See Ontario Ministry of Education and Training, *News Release*, "Government to Reduce School Boards and Cut Administrative Costs," February 24, 1995; *New Foundations for Ontario Education*, "Ontario School Board Reduction Task Force — Terms of Reference," and "Governance: Questions and Answers," February 23, 1995. See also Toughill, Kelly, "Cooke vows 50% chop in trustees, salary cap," *Toronto Star*, February 25, 1995, and Lewington, Jennifer, "Ontario to slash number of school boards by up to half," *Globe and Mail*, February 25, 1995.

37 See OSSTF, *Submission to the Ontario Fair Tax Commission*, "Fair Taxation for Responsible Education: Report of the Funding Initiatives and New Directions Committee," September 22, 1992, pp. 12–17.

38 OSSTF, *Queen's Park*, "School Board Amalgamation," March 1, 1995, p.1.

39 *Report of the Royal Commission on Learning, Volume 4*, Recommendations #143–148, cited above, pp. 103–104.

40 *Report of the Royal Commission on Learning, Volume 1*, cited above, p. 37.

41 See, for example, Livingstone, D.W., Hart D., Davie, L.E., P*ublic Attitudes Towards Education in Ontario, 1994: The Tenth OISE Survey*, Toronto, 1995, pp. 14–17. This survey reports that most parents want more participation in school governance than they have at present.

42 *Report of the Royal Commission on Learning, Volume 4*, cited above, pp. 106–108.

43 *Report of the Royal Commission on Learning, Volume 4*, cited above, p. 44.

44 *Report of the Royal Commission on Learning, Volume 4*, cited above, p. 108.

45 *Report of the Royal Commission on Learning, Volume 4*, cited above, p. 104.

46 *See Report of the Royal Commission on Learning, Volume 4*, cited above, pp. 44–45; Ontario Ministry of Education and Training, *News Release*, "Government Makes School Councils Mandatory," February 10, 1995, pp. 1–2, and Backgrounder, "School Councils," February 10, 1995, pp. 1–2; OSSTF, *Queen's Park*, "Government Makes School Councils Mandatory," February 13, 1995, p. 1.

47 *Report of the Royal Commission on Learning, Volume 4*, cited above, p. 107.

48 *Report of the Royal Commission on Learning, Volume 4*, cited above, p. 113.

49 *Report of the Royal Commission on Learning, Volume 4*, cited above, p. 44.

50 *Report of the Royal Commission on Learning, Volume 4*, cited above, p. 45.

51 *Report of the Royal Commission on Learning, Volume 4*, cited above, p. 37.

52 *Report of the Royal Commission on Learning, Volume 4*, cited above, pp. 42–43.

53 *Report of the Royal Commission on Learning, Volume 4*, cited above, p. 105.

54 *Report of the Royal Commission on Learning, Volume 4*, cited above, p.

106. See also Recommendation #86, *Volume 3*, p. 47.

55 *Report of the Royal Commission on Learning, Volume 4*, cited above, p. 42.

56 *Report of the Royal Commission on Learning, Volume 4*, cited above, p. 48.

57 *Report of the Royal Commission on Learning, Volume 4*, cited above, p. 48, Recommendation #112.

58 *Report of the Royal Commission on Learning, Volume 4*, cited above, p. 42.

59 In conversation with John Sewell, here is how Don Richmond describes the process of centralizing provincial social services. Richmond was Metro Toronto Community Services commissioner for the past five years and is now chair of the board and chief executive officer for the Metro Toronto Housing Authority. He was one of the major defenders of a municipally oriented social services system.

> "I came to Metro [from the province]," he told Sewell, as he was quitting his job in Community Services, "because I believed in local government. I'm leaving because I'm worried it has no meaningful future. I watched the Association of Municipalities in Ontario move from the small-town position of 'let the province do it' to the position 'If you're not in the business of human services delivery, then you aren't giving good local government.' And I've seen Metro go exactly the other way. Now debates about infrastructure and garbage dominate the local scene...."

The real problem, says Richmond, has emerged from local politicians acquiescing in the "creeping provincial delivery system."

> The province, he notes, "has now passed legislation that removes long-term care from social agencies and municipalities and puts it squarely in the control of provincial bureaucrats. In child care, as the province puts in money, it insists on control and management."

It is a change in responsibility from the municipality to the province, Richmond argues, that has been happening across the board in health and in social services.

In a related article, Sewell elaborates on this growing "provincial imperialism" over local services.

> The Rae government, he says, seemed, "bent on taking over every municipal function it can, thinking it can do better than municipal councils. His government has taken over responsibility for long-term nursing care, child care, welfare, a large part of education and where Metro is to put its garbage. Why shouldn't it take over transit as well?"

Certainly the premier's forceful role in pushing for extensions to Metro Toronto subways was premised on his willingness to extend provincial authority in this area, though in this instance, with a provincial election in the offing, it was to spend more money rather than less. See Sewell, John,

"Metro loses municipal social services defender," *Now*, March 2–8, 1995 and "Subway primes suburbanism," *Now*, March 2–8, 1995.

60 *Report of the Royal Commission on Learning, Volume 4*, cited above, p. 34.

61 *Report of the Royal Commission on Learning, Volume 4*, cited above, p. 39.

62 Little, Doug, "Pizza Panned," *Now*, April 6–12, 1995.

63 *Report of the Royal Commission on Learning, Volume 4*, cited above, p. 106, Recommendation #149.

64 *Report of the Royal Commission on Learning, Volume 4*, cited above, p. 45.

65 For a thorough list of practical suggestions on this front see OSSTF, Report of the Future of Education Task Force, "The Future of Public Education, " March 1995, pp. 26–28.

66 OSSTF Provincial Executive, *Public Education: Retracing our path, An examination of the goals of public education, its role in society and directions for reform, A Brief to the Royal Commission on Learning*, December 1993, p. 1.

67 OSSTF Provincial Executive, *Public Education: Retracing our path*, cited above, p. 1.

68 OSSTF Provincial Executive, *Public Education: Retracing our path*, cited above, p. 48. See also OSSTF Response to the Royal Commission on Learning, *Factsheet No. 6*, "School Community Council," p. 49.

69 OSSTF Provincial Executive, *Public Education: Retracing our path*, cited above, p. 50.

70 OSSTF Provincial Executive, *Public Education: Retracing our path*, cited above, p. 49.

71 OSSTF, Report of the Future of Education Task Force, "The Future of Public Education, " March 1995, p. 27.

72 OSSTF Response to the Royal Commission on Learning, *Factsheet No. 6*, "School Community Council," pp. 48–49.

73 OSSTF Response to the Royal Commission on Learning, *Factsheet No. 6*, "School Community Council," p. 2.

74 OSSTF Response to the Royal Commission on Learning, *Factsheet No. 6*, "School Community Council," p. 3.

75 Clandfield, David, "Notes on the Royal Commission on Learning," unpublished, p. 2.

76 OSSTF Provincial Executive, *Public Education: Retracing our path, An examination of the goals of public education, its role in society and directions for reform, A Brief to the Royal Commission on Learning*, December 1993, pp. 28–29.

77 OSSTF Provincial Executive, *Public Education: Retracing our path*, cited above, p. 28.

78 OSSTF Response to the Royal Commission on Learning, *Factsheet No. 6*, "School Community Council," p. 2.

79 OSSTF Response to the Royal Commission on Learning, *Factsheet No. 7*, "Staffing," p. 2.

80 OSSTF Provincial Executive, *Public Education: Retracing our path*, cited above, pp. 12–13.

81 *Report of the Royal Commission on Learning, Volume 3*, cited above, p. 11.

82 Barkley, Liz, "Where we stand: The Royal Commission on Learning," *OSSTF Education Forum*, Spring 1995, p. 6.

83 Barkley, Liz, "Where we stand: The Royal Commission on Learning," *OSSTF Education Forum*, Spring 1995, p. 6.

84 *Report of the Royal Commission on Learning, Volume 3*, cited above, p. 23.

85 *Report of the Royal Commission on Learning, Volume 3*, cited above, p. 33.

86 *Report of the Royal Commission on Learning, Volume 3*, cited above, p. 33. Recommendation #75.

87 *Report of the Royal Commission on Learning, Volume 3*, cited above, p. 39. Recommendation #81.

88 *Report of the Royal Commission on Learning, Volume 3*, cited above, p. 10.

89 *Report of the Royal Commission on Learning, Volume 3*, cited above, p. 9.

90 OSSTF, "Public Education in the Public Interest: The Theme for OSSTF's 1995–96 Priorities and Program," AMPA Update, March 1995, p. 11. See also Barkley, Liz, "Where we stand: The Royal Commission on Learning," OSSTF Education Forum, Spring 1995, p. 6, and OSSTF Response to the Royal Commission, *Factsheet: Anti-Unionism*, p. 1.

91 OSSTF Provincial Executive, *Public Education: Retracing our path*, cited above, p. 43.

Chapter Six

The Struggle For Curriculum

At a public meeting in March of 1995, Gerry Caplan, one of the co-chairs of the Royal Commission, is reported to have denounced the idea that a corporate agenda is active in Canadian education. In response to a questioner who suggested a major corporate influence in his report, an outraged Caplan assured his audience that this was a shallow and slanderous interpretation, promoted by a tiny minority of malcontents, like Jim Turk, the Education Director of the Ontario Federation of Labour. The corporate agenda in education, he declared, was just an American phenomenon, and it was certainly nowhere near his thoughts, or those of his fellow commissioners, as they drafted their recommendations.

On hearing this, a fellow leaned over to *Now* reporter Doug Little, who was covering the meeting, and said, "Jeez, Doug, what was all that NAFTA stuff about anyway?"[1]

Caplan's statement is contradicted by his own Commission's report, whose text makes plain a substantial corporate interest in our schools. It is also pretty obvious that there are major aspects of the Commission's Report — like the anti-democratic downsizing of public schools and children's services, the indiscriminate bulk-buying of computers, or the building of school-community "alliances" with business —

which are unequivocally corporate in their inspiration.

It is possible that Gerry Caplan didn't notice. Or maybe he believes that such arrangements are good government and would have happened anyway, as part of a normal administrative process, beyond the world of corporate pressure. But perhaps there may be another answer. Or at least a partial answer.

Maybe Gerry Caplan thinks that such policy proposals, whether corporate-inspired or not, lie at the periphery of his report. And that at its core — in its vision of a new curriculum and classroom structure for students — is a set of recommendations which are entirely outside the realm of narrow corporate interest and are somehow universal in their application. He may believe that for the things that really count for kids, the corporations really haven't called the tune, and the Commissioners' honour is safe.

It is possible he thinks this. Intellectuals who serve the corporate world needn't be all that conscious of their role, especially if they retain some of the ideological trappings of their social democratic past. The commissioners and the bureaucrats who researched and wrote for them may honestly believe that they have offered us a program of "excellence," unconnected to corporate power and to the oppression of working people. They are mistaken. But the determination that comes from this mistaken belief — perhaps like Bob Rae's determination to change the face of the Ontario Public Sector — is ominous.

It is difficult, of course, to estimate the strength of belief among the recently converted. In the case of a Bob Rae or a Gerry Caplan, their extraordinary sensitivity to the charge that they have dishonoured their socialist past should also tell us something.

At any rate, the Royal Commission seems to have taken pains to try to separate itself from the corporate agenda on curriculum as preparation for the workplace (or lack of one), on the streaming arrangements in which that curriculum takes place ("the hidden curriculum"), and on the assessment procedures through which students are placed in these streams.

In this section, I want to get hold of the Commission's critique of the old system and at the same time open up the territory in which its proposals do, in fact, link with a corporate agenda (both old and new). What we are watching, it seems, is a significant shift in a corporate-bureaucratic strategy for Ontario education, and it may give us a better idea of what a neo-conservative future in our schools will look like, and not just in Ontario. OSSTF has yet to respond fully to this shift in strategy, but what it has done so far appears to offer a number of important bases from which this new strategy can be resisted.

Shifting The Corporate Connection

The Commission takes particular pains to let us know that it does not intend to put forward any run-of-the-mill far-right nostrums for school reform based on the idea that improvement in student skill and attitude will bring about direct improvement in the economy. Such a link, it tells us, is "problematic." What the Commission proposes instead is that we consider two points of view on the relationship between education and the economy: "The first and currently most dominant, is that education drives the economy — that our economic well-being is dependent on a well-educated workforce able to compete in the 'new global economy.' The other view rests on a different assumption: that economic health is not primarily dependent on the skills and knowledge of the workforce, but economic health does help create educational opportunities."[2] There is, of course, a third view which says that a good educational system and a sound economy are thoroughly interrelated and that the building of a democratic and socially purposeful order in either one assists in the building of such an order in the other. This view — linking democracy, creative work in school and on the job, and the effective production of wealth — is not within the Commission's terms of reference.

What the Commission goes on to offer us are "different economic futures" that have somehow emerged from the different points of view it presents. "According to the Conference Board of Canada's Employability Skills Index," the Commission says, "most future jobs will require the kinds of high-level skills and knowledge that were once necessary only for a few, high-end positions. But others see a 'pear shaped' economy in which the mass of jobs are in the low-level part of the service sector ('McJobs'), or in which many people will simply be unemployed."

What it comes down to, it seems, is whether most of our kids are going to have a bright future in well-paid high-tech jobs or whether most will end up with badly paid no-nothing jobs, or no jobs at all?

This is a question the Commission seems uneasy about answering. It tells us that we are losing our well-paid jobs. Between February 1990 and February 1991, for example, "approximately 260,000 jobs were lost in Ontario, many in the manufacturing sector." In 1992, "more than 10 percent of Ontario's adult population was receiving unemployment insurance or social assistance." Younger workers were especially hard hit. "For the first time in our collective memory, families no longer anticipate that their children will be better off than they are, and stories of the educated unemployed haunt both parents and children." As many as 1.4 million Ontario residents (14 percent of the population) can now be considered poor. In the same context, the Commission reports the growth of the low-paid service sector in Ontario from 65 percent of workers in 1981 to 72 percent in 1991. Much of the increase was in part-time work." "Paradoxically," it notes, "current Canadian research suggests that the greatest potential for growth is ... both in well-paying professional occupations requiring few people with high levels of education and in poorly paying service occupations requiring low levels of education and employing large numbers of people."

What this seems to mean, then, is a future with a few high-tech jobs for the privileged and a lot of unskilled jobs or welfare for the masses.

So what are the educational implications?

Let's return to the Commission report: "Some researchers and policy analysts (Henry Levin in the United States, for example) suggest that unless a person has considerable education — at least at the university graduate level with some post-graduate work — schooling is not related to increased income. Already, the growing number of people who have degrees has begun to devalue university credentials as a step to employment. Clearly, the educational system does not cause economic crises, and it cannot cure them."

Now we know that with only a few well-paid complex jobs available, the credentials hunt is intensified.

Where does this point take us?

"On the basis of research and policy analysis, we have concluded," says the Commission, "that predictions about educational ties to the economic future are uncertain at best; it is difficult, if not impossible, to be sure which jobs will be available and which specific skills will be required. Although it seems reasonable to suggest that an increasing number of positions will require high-level technical and scientific training, it is entirely possible that the number of such jobs created by these new positions will be small."

We are now back, with a little less clarity, to stage one of the argument. The number of high-tech jobs is still likely to be small. No serious research suggests otherwise.

What do we do about education?

"Henry Levin's review of American research concludes," the Commission responds, "that overall educational requirements in the year 2000 are likely to be quite similar to those today."

What does that mean?

Unfortunately, the Commission doesn't tell us. There are, it seems, other realities at work. And it is to these the Commission turns its full attention.

Levin's voice, it appears, "is not the dominant voice being heard in either the U.S. or Canada. Although no-one can demonstrate how it would work in practice, many insist that school reform must be based on the needs of the economy — whatever those turn out to be in a future that seems even harder to predict than usual."

Here the argument ends, in a whimper, with education still in the hands of those who think school reform must be based on corporate need, whatever that need turns out to be.

These are also the hands in which education will stay, if the Royal Commission has anything to do with it.

In responding to sections like this in the Commission's report, David Livingstone makes the forceful argument that the

Commission has simply refused to face up to the fact that most people won't be using "advanced symbolic skills in running computerized workplaces."[3]

"The current workplace reality," he argues, "is starkly different. In 1990, the U.S. Commission on Workforce Skills found that less than 10 percent of American corporations were of this sort, with the most still running in a hierarchical, mass production model. According to the most recent extensive Canadian survey, the vast majority of our workplaces are similarly organized; less than 20 percent yet have any sort of self-directed work teams, a defining feature of the high-tech ideal."

At the same time, Livingstone says, "employers *are* demanding higher formal educational entry requirements. The proportion of jobs requiring a high school diploma nearly doubled in Ontario during the 1980s. But potential employees continue to get more formal schooling faster than employers inflate their credential requirements." Livingstone notes that university graduates make up more than 10 percent of food bank users in Toronto. He cites a recent OISE Survey that found 41 percent of the Ontario workforce say they have skills they would like to use but can't use in their present job. This includes about half of all employed workers under 35 and about half of those with post-secondary schooling. "Over 20 percent of the employed workforce is technically underemployed, in the sense of having at least one certificate more than their job requires, and most of these people actually feel overqualified for their jobs. Most other employees, regardless of their formal schooling, feel that their combination of experience and tacit knowledge makes them adequately qualified for their jobs." The survey found less than 5 percent who felt underqualified; most of these were upgrading specific credentials. On average, Ontario workers reported spending over 200 hours of unpaid time on job-related learning in 1994.

"The general picture that emerges here," Livingstone concludes, "is of a population that is already educated significantly beyond both the formal and actual requirements of current workplaces. It is not more computers in the classroom that are urgently needed, so much as the *genuine restructuring of our workplaces so that our available labour force can more fully use its existing levels of formal schooling, tacit knowledge of work and computer literacy*." Livingstone finds support for this view in the 84 percent of employees who favour employee participation in the management of workplaces. Livingstone does not fault the Commission for failing to address workplace restructuring, which goes beyond its mandate, but he does blame its "uncritical acceptance" of the "paradigm shift" rhetoric concerning information technology that "left the commissioners with no recourse but to blame teachers and the schools for an education-jobs gap that is largely not of their making."

Following this analysis, another question immediately arises.

If what we are looking at is a future of unskilled work or unemployment for the vast majority of Canadians, what is the Commission up to with all its stress on "excellence" in the curriculum and the need for a provincially controlled curriculum to ensure this excellence, this "love of learning?" It is a question linked to the present-day corporate insistence on more schooling for workers than their jobs demand.

The Commission has told us that it has to listen to those who insist that schools prepare their students for the needs of the economy. Yet the economy doesn't seem to need much in the way of complex or creative thinking on the part of its workers. Isn't this dangerous territory for big corporations? Already, as Livingstone notes, there are a great many workers who are deeply dissatisfied with the low-skill level of their jobs. Won't they be a lot angrier if they get an even better education and want more power on the job and more money for doing it? Yet still the Commission insists it wants a better education for all our children, and it says that this is also a point of view held by the big players in the economy, who have made educational reform a top priority "not just in Ontario but across the country and around the world."[4]

Here is how the Commission puts its position on the role of the school in preparing students for employment: "While we cannot predict in any precise sense which jobs will be available, or which jobs students might prefer, or what the characteristics of jobs will be over a long working life, we would argue that it is best to provide every student with a strong general education and an ability to adapt to changing conditions." Even "if most available jobs are low-level, requiring few if any skills," schools can't be "excused from providing high-quality programs to all students." The "first priority" of our educational system is to "intellectually nurture" all its students so as to prepare them for "life in a modern democratic society."[5]

How is it possible, you must be thinking, for corporations like Nabisco, Imperial Oil and IBM to support a program like this? Such a "learning partnership" (to borrow Metro Toronto's current label) surely goes against the grain of their best interests. Real democracy for their workers, on or off the plant and office floor, is the last thing such corporations need to squeeze profits from a domestic workforce or to build political support for the movement of international capital and the oppression of a third-world workforce.

As in most contradictions of this sort, there is really a very simple resolution. The "excellence" of the curriculum being proposed by the Commission turns out, in the end, to have very little to do with what most of us understand as high academic standards. Calling what it proposes for a school program "intellectual nurturance" is a bit like calling Coke "the real thing." Indeed, what we are looking at here can well be described as a junk-food curriculum, hyped by its makers, like most junk-food products, hurting working people most of all, while doing the better-defended middle class no good either (except, setting aside the metaphor, to keep some of their children at their present position on the social class ladder.) As it emerges in practice, this is a program especially responsive to corporate requirements for a few well-paid employees at the top and a lot more, with a lot less money, on the bottom. In this respect it merely extends that aspect of the system which focuses on the ideological and social control of students and which the current corporate elite thinks is valuable enough already to count as serious job preparation.

The program the Commission supports is called "Learning Outcomes." I want to turn to it now.

"Corporate Outcomes"

The generic title for "Learning Outcomes" is Outcomes Based Education (OBE). It has won broad support among centre-to-right education bureaucrats and the corporate sector.

Researchers from OSSTF District 15 note that OBE is being promoted by the Toronto Board of Education (through its Curriculum Planning Committee), the York Board's Outcomes Based Education Committee, the Ministry of Education's *Common Curriculum*, and the Royal Commission on Learning. "Corporations have shown interest in OBE as well. The Conference Board of Canada, which includes such stellar corporate citizens as IBM, Royal Bank, Imperial Oil and Inco, has produced what it calls an 'Employability Skills Profile,' a list of critical skills developed by the Corporate Council on Education. The list of desired graduate outcomes agrees generally with the outcomes list provided by Benchmarks, a Toronto Board project that has embraced OBE. Toronto's model school for the twenty-first century, the Ursula Franklin Academy, advertises itself by boasting that its outcomes are identical to those of the Conference Board."[6]

At the core of the "learning outcomes" envisaged by these educational and corporate "partners" is something the Royal Commission calls "foundation skills." "Curriculum guidelines," the Commission says, "should recognize the primacy of certain skills, and ... teachers, in the early grades especially, should emphasize and carefully monitor the acquisition by all students of these foundation skills, within the context of an integrated curriculum." These skills must lie at the centre of a common curriculum stretching from early childhood education to Grade 9. As defined by the report these foundation skills are "literacy/communication skills, numeracy/problem solving, group learning and interpersonal skills and values, scientific literacy, and computer literacy. While these foundation skills are represented in particular subjects within the common curriculum such as English/Français, mathematics and science," the Commission continues, "they are also fundamental in most other subject areas."[7]

These skills, I want to argue, are understood in such a way as to be largely dissociated from the logic of the subject material in which they are to function. It is the dissociation of these skills from the substance of a curriculum that gives the end result of this program its "junk food" quality: form without content. Such an approach to curriculum permits neither exploration nor "passionate understanding" of society, community, history, morality, the self, or the natural world.

There is a moment when the Commission makes an attempt to argue that it does not intend such dissociation. "We are not suggesting," it says "that these skills be taught without context, or that context is not important to the learning." But once it moves beyond this sentence, the Commission seems to have no serious concept of the interrelationship between form and content, between skill and human purpose. It continues by saying that "basic skills" and "thinking skills" ought to be taught simultaneously, meaning that subjects like reading and arithmetic ought to be intelligible. "If the word makes no sense in the sentence, or the answer does not fit the problem, the child must question it and try again. Teaching children how to estimate answers in arithmetic is an example of teaching for meaning, and of giving students the skill to question, and if appropriate, correct a specific response."[8] There are no human purposes here to be considered or complexities of life to be grappled with. There is only the shallow, one-dimensional logic of immediate intelligibility. It is in this sense, following a current neo-conservative line, that the Commission argues for "a balanced reading program" that includes "both phonics and 'whole language' or meaning-based approaches."[9] What it cannot grasp is that good whole language teachers don't "balance" phonics, they integrate this technique, without fuss, into a meaningful literacy program, where kids learn to read and write because they have something important to read and write about. OSSTF calls the Commission's approach to curriculum "minimalist." An old right-wing focus used to rest on "minimal competencies." Now the Commission stresses "higher-order thinking skills" as well. But at its centre is still a minimal understanding of what education is all about.

Fundamental learning outcomes are simply descriptions of "foundation skills" as they are expected to be known at various levels of the educational system. Thus what matters initially is that these skill outcomes are clearly and simply described for all levels of the system, right up to the completion of secondary school. These clear and simple outcomes, the Commission insists, must also "be linked with the work of the College Standards and Accreditation Council, as well as universities; and ... clearly written standards, similar in intent to those available in mathematics and language (numeracy and literacy), also [must] be developed in the other three areas."[10] The problem, however, with the skill descriptions available in mathematics and language, says the Commission, is that they aren't clearly and simply enough defined. They are to be found in the Ministry's *Common Curriculum*, and "many people," the Commission reports, "find them too numerous and too vague" to communicate "the actual and concrete expectations of learners they imply." Thus, while the Commission thinks it is "dangerous to insist on outcomes that are easily measured, at the expense of highly valued but less easily-gauged results," fewer and clearer descriptions are nevertheless understood to be an improvement. At the end of the day, "major outcomes should be presented to parents as a fairly brief descriptive list, which could appear on a report card, to give concrete indicators of a student's progress so that a 'satisfactory' in reading, for example, is broken down to tell the parent something about the particular reading activities and skills the student shows competence in."[11]

Learning outcomes are, furthermore, not limited to school-age students. These Ministry standards should also apply to younger children, especially those who "show signs of learning or interpersonal problems...." Following up *The Common Curriculum* for Grades 1 to 9, the Commission argues, "the Ministry could usefully develop a similar set of desired learning outcomes for Early Childhood Education in literacy, numeracy, and interpersonal and group-learning skills." In addition to these skills, the Report continues, "a developmental continuum that indicates stages of cognitive and social growth for children from birth to adolescence ... outlining desirable and expectable learner outcomes ... would be a real asset to all parents, teachers, and child-care workers, and would promote continuity and consistency among the home, daycare, and school."[12]

These clear and simple skill definitions, from birth to adolescence, are to serve "as a basis of curriculum design." Within this design, the Ministry must also "indicate which major areas, topics, or skills might be emphasized in an annual program, in a way that is not restrictive, but permissive and helpful in choosing priorities among alternatives." At this level of discussion, the actual content of the subject being taught doesn't much matter. What teachers "want and need" is "some guidance about the elements of a subject to be addressed in order to achieve the learner outcomes, described at three-year intervals. To argue backwards: if, by the end of Grade 3, a larger number of children are unable to use such features as tables of contents, indices, etc., how will Grade 1, 2, and 3 teachers know how to improve the lessons to meet that target?"

That the example given here, like so many in this report, involves such a high level of dissociated skill learning is significant. There is simply no particular curriculum substance to be considered. "What is missing" in Ontario, the Commission continues, "is a set of curriculum guidelines that describe at least some of the sequences. Without such common guidelines, there is no assurance of consistency in or between schools in what is taught and learned. Curriculum guidelines are frameworks within which specific programs can be elaborated in each school or class. Existing provincial guidelines below Grade 10 level are not congruent with *The Common Curriculum* and must be redesigned ... [on the basis] of its learning outcomes." This "will help teachers understand what they are expected to teach and what students are expected to learn each year. Such documents should encourage continuity from year to year, and avoid unnecessary duplication of effort at both the planning and delivery levels, and should help to create consistency both vertically (from Grades 1 to 9) and horizontally (within and across schools and boards)."[13]

What is being proposed here, then, is simply a linked framework of consistent and continuous "skill" development, largely dissociated from any particular content. And that is all it is. For some students this means complex skill development. For a majority it means less complex skill development. But for neither group will it mean a curriculum that matters to them, except in the sense that employers are more likely to hire those who get good grades in the various standardized tests that will measure these skills. Other than climbing a social class ladder or maintaining your spot on that ladder, there are no other reasons for mastering such a curriculum. It has no inherent human interest or purpose. It is to be driven entirely by a student's will for economic success. As such, it will be particularly hard on those students who have not been brought up for this kind of success — on those who have not been taught at home and in their neighbourhood to dissociate their personal feelings or sense of purpose from the work of the mind. A capacity for such dissociation is passed on, in different ways, almost entirely within the realm of upper-class and professional middle-class socialization. For most children of working people, however, even if they clearly understand its economic payoff, this sort of skill development is a deeply offensive form of learning, and they do not do well at it. Calling such an approach "minimalist" is the kindest possible description.

For an alternative approach, readers would do well to consider Ken Osborne's curriculum proposals in *Educating Citizens*. Osborne's curriculum doesn't hive off "academic" from "non-academic" concerns. Instead, intellectual work is suffused with social purpose and linked to action. "First," he says, "students, not just those who are thought to be 'academic' in orientation, must be exposed to the fullest range of human knowledge. Second, this knowledge is not an end in itself, but is important for the light it sheds both on current concerns and persisting human issues and for its ability to enrich and empower students. Third, the curriculum is to embody the values of cooperation, justice, freedom, equality, community and empowerment: it is directed to the development of active, socially committed citizens, not passive spectators or armchair theorists. Fourth, knowledge and action must be linked so that students learn how to refine, extend and apply their knowledge through action in the real world."[14]

Osborne also argues a position on what is important to teach kids — the actual substance of the curriculum — with the understanding that his position is one among many and that what actually gets to be taught must be worked out collectively at different levels of the school system. Following Osborne's example, it would have been much more valuable if the Commission had actually said to us, having consulted widely, what it believed should be the substance of our school programs, and then offered some well-worked-out suggestions for the structure in which these programs should be taught. Teachers, parents and other interested citizens could then decide, at our board and local school level, if they thought they had been given good advice or not. They could get back to the Commission or another similar body with their response. After that, more dialogue, in different forms, would undoubtedly be necessary. Such an extended conversation has to be carefully structured to ensure that clear decisions at all levels of the school system do in fact get made at the end of the day, but it is quite possible to set up these arrangements and for them to function effectively. That is what educational leadership is all about.

This view of democratic leadership was obviously not in the cards with this Royal Commission. Or, more accurately, it had no chance of survival inside the much more authoritarian, Ministry-led framework of "learner outcomes."

But why should corporations be so interested in the dissociated skills measured by these learner outcomes? Why put so much time and effort into making Outcomes Based Education central to a core curriculum for our public schools?

There are three main reasons, and all of them are rooted in corporate principles of profitability and long-term security of profits.

First, it is important for corporations, as they currently operate, to have their employees conditioned to detach their intellectual work (called "skills") from personal meaning and a larger sense of social purpose; to separate thinking on the job from thinking about other more human questions; to blinker the mind and then focus it on company interests. This kind of separation is important at all levels of the corporate hierarchy. If top management (with its "complex" skills) starts thinking of workers as human beings, rather than as manipulable extensions of machines, the company won't be "lean and mean" and the bottom line will suffer. At the base of the work pyramid, it is just as important that deskilled or low-skilled employees (often called multi-skilled) learn to "work smart." Much of what they may be asked to do is mindless, but it requires that their minds (and their bodies) be finely attuned to the job at hand — whether dictated by numbers on a computer screen or the symbols of a McDonald's cash register. The more such "skills" can be dissociated from the person involved, the corporations believe, the more efficient a worker or manager that person will be — the closer to a machine he or she will have become.

It is neo-taylorism for the 21st century.

The Commission calls it "love of learning": the love of process, floating free from the substance of what is to be understood and what is to be done. Actually, very few of us love this kind of learning, which is often boring and abstract. It is in understanding and in action that love can take hold, as well as sorrow and defeat. At least Hall-Dennis, for all its covering up of bureaucratic centralization and class-biased streaming, thought schools should be about "living" not just "learning."

The second thing about Outcomes Based Education that the corporations like is that it has the right attitude. Attitude (the "right" attitude, that is) is everywhere in Outcomes Based Education and nowhere more than in the Royal Commission, where it is central to one of the fundamental "foundation skills" to be hammered home as an "outcome" at every grade level — an area called "group learning and interpersonal skills and values." Here even values are now categorized as skills, which is how the corporations, in fact, understand them. Company values (or "corporate cultures") have little to do with what we understand as human morality, rooted in our experience of life. They are truly separate from society. Employees are constantly pressured to separate themselves from personal or community ideas of right and wrong and to give over the power to make moral decisions — on the job or in their communities — to those above them in board rooms and senior management. It is much the same process by which craft-based skills (rooted in a community of workers who controlled much of their own time and space) have been stripped from those who owned them and have been brought into a framework of management-controlled skills, thoroughly detached from these workers and their community.

The Commission expresses a fair amount of fuzzy feeling about "group learning and interpersonal skills and values" in its report, but when it gets down to what it has in mind the Commission puts forward a deeply conservative understanding of this category. This area of skill training, to be "shared" by corporate and agency partners, is to ensure "that students develop flexibility, eagerness to learn, and the ability to work in teams ... citizenship, social responsibility, leadership and initiative, and coping with change."[15] The education director for Chrysler or Bell Canada would have no trouble with that list. It is exactly the list he'd be using himself to make good corporate citizens of his company's workforce. There is no support for troublemakers here. No space for those who resist changes they see as deeply harmful to human kind and to our natural environment. There is no room for those who are not eager to learn flexibility in a society where a tough commitment to justice and decency is essential for survival, for those who do not want to be team-players in a corporate game to impoverish and disenfranchise a nation's citizenry. And there is no scope, either, for those who want to build a loving society, because that too implies what the Commission cannot accept: that there is something fundamentally wrong with what is happening now in the society and in the world at large and that it has to be made right. Instead, what our kids have to learn is to be flexible with the status quo and learn to cope — eagerly and responsibly.

Finally, just as the learning of dissociated "academic" skills is especially hard on working-class kids, so also is the learning of the "non-academic" skills of group and interpersonal relations. These kids are the least flexible and eager to cope. Most are far too angry about what the world has handed them. Cool or disruptive, they can only be reached if they see that what they do in school can help them change the world they experience. Their resistance may often be self-destructive — throwing out the baby of good intellectual work with the bathwater of such official programs like Outcomes Based Education — but it is surprisingly consistent, running deepest among children from very poor families. Resistance is also there among those, usually from better-off homes, who have learned to fake it (even to themselves) and to establish the kind of cheerful good citizenship the commissioners trust will be the result of their efforts. The "hidden injuries of class" never fully disappear, at least not in the space of one generation. And when we look at the streaming system — the practical social class division in our schools — which emerges from the Commission's Outcomes Based Education program, it is clear that such disappearance is the last thing the commissioners had on their minds, in spite of all their rhetoric to the contrary.

The third thing the corporations like about Learning Outcomes is in many ways deeply interconnected with the first two: separating skills from content (at many levels of complexity and across all grades) and developing the right attitude for a future workforce. And in the discussion above I made this third point quite explicit. But it is important, I think, to deal with it in isolation for a moment.

This is the "outcome" — supported by the Commission as it has been supported by generations of "school promoters" — that students should emerge from school without explicit political or social purposes, without, in other words, a conscious ideology. Implicit purposes and informally learned ideologies (the socialization of the hidden curriculum) have always been on the table for those who have constructed our school system, and they have always mattered a lot. They still matter. But those who have had the most say in our schools have always judged an explicit conservative or pro-business curriculum too explosive a proposal to put before a potentially unruly populace. Such a curriculum would have to be slipped in unobtrusively, when that was possible, or at particular moments when the tide was running favourably. Otherwise one must trust in broader social norms, brought forward by church, state and media, to shape the creation of local curricula and the manner in which they are taught. But under no circumstances was an alternative social vision to be taught. This position has been consistently resisted by many teachers and parents and community activists, but it has largely carried the day over many generations of curriculum development and many forms of "progressive" reworking of old texts and old pedagogies. Official school curriculum has come to be imbued with a conservative aversion to social critique tempered with a liberal rhetoric of individuality. Largely, this is the Commission's view of how it should remain.

As I noted above, the Royal Commission has taken great pains to divide "academic" and "non-academic" skills, "primary" and "secondary" ("shared") school purposes, as part of a process which separates intellectual work from any kind of larger social meaning or critical ideology.

The school's "secondary" social purposes are limited to the development of "healthy relationships." And the schools are to take on this role with partners such as "families, community agencies, youth groups, religious organizations ... with families probably playing the biggest role."[16]

It is interesting to note in passing here that while the Commission thinks of families as part of an official social services delivery system, managed by the school, it never articulates an actual place for them, a specific institutional role. It is the other agencies and groups that actually count as operational partners. And that makes sense, because however much they have been hurt, however much they may function as institutions of social control, families still do not act like social service agencies. Spare a moment to think about the families you know actually functioning as part of "a broad spectrum of ... groups and agencies," which are to be "brokered" by a principal as part of a delivery system to children. What is implied here is an unconscionable level of manipulation of intimate family relations, which, thankfully, is not yet possible, and thus not structured into the Commission's report. But who knows what the future will bring?

Having stressed the "pivotal role" of the principal in such brokering, the Commission goes on to make what it believes is "a necessary distinction between what schools and teachers are responsible for. Teachers we believe are essentially responsible for the primary purpose of the school, namely learning [or learning outcomes]." And while the Commission makes "healthy relationships" a task to be shared — teachers are allowed to show some "care and compassion" — social purposes don't enter their job description whatsoever.[17]

Indeed, the Commission goes on to approvingly quote the Stormont Dundas and Glengarry County Board of Education: "Schools cannot continually assume the responsibilities of society and hope to attain the high standards and expectations set by that same society in ... relationship to educational goals." And, as before, the Commission understands these goals as learning "basic skills as well as information technology, analysis of data, and thinking skills."[18]

It is in this context that the Commission's assault on Liberal Arts subjects is so meaningful. The Liberal Arts raise the larger questions of social purpose alongside a consideration and expression of the complexities of life and of "making history."

In the Commission's recommended diploma requirements for Grades 10 to 12, it is the more technically minded subjects that are given priority. There will be one fewer compulsory English/Communications courses (only three will remain). The Commission did nothing to improve the status of History, for which there is only one compulsory secondary school course — a situation widely regarded as scandalous. Its recommendations now allow a student to pass through high school having taken no Geography course, while overall Social Science has been downgraded from a required three to two courses. There is also a reasonable worry that we will end up with more "Communication" than "English," in the three courses remaining in this area. Moreover, if the Commission has its way, Ontario high schools will also demand two Maths instead of one, and two Sciences instead of one. And in place of one compulsory Arts, Physical Education or Technical course, there will now be one compulsory Arts or Physical Education course, two compulsory Language courses (French/anglais or one international), and one compulsory Business and Technical course. This leaves only seven electives in the Commission's program compared to fourteen in the present system. It is in the electives, of course, that many of the Liberal Arts programs are taken, and when this decline is combined with more compulsory practical or technical courses, the proposal will take a very big bite out of these programs.[19]

It is also important to recognize that in the new lower stream being proposed by the Commission (the Ontario Applied Courses), the official Liberal Arts program will be delivered "with an emphasis on application."[20] Such an emphasis is not quite what Plato or Shakespeare, Freud or Marx, Stephen Hawking or Margaret Laurence had in mind for the subjects on which they wrote, at least in the first instance. As I read these names my heart sinks for the students in this "applied" stream; they won't get so much as a brief look at what such authors have to say. In fact, their fellow students in the proposed "academic" courses will be lucky if they do such reading and get a chance to take it seriously. What is before us in this Royal Commission is worlds apart from Ken Osborne's emphasis on all kids experiencing "the fullest range of human knowledge."

Even in the academic courses for university preparation there is a technologizing and vocationalizing of the Liberal Arts program. For the university-bound we are now to have "packages of courses organized around such subject or career areas as math/science/technology, health-related occupations, communications, international languages, and finance."[21]

Finally, it is clear that as the Commission understands the future integration of curriculum, the spirit of the Liberal Arts will be seriously diminished. There is to be no real interdisciplinarity where teachers bring together the special knowledge of their subject areas and integrate it within a broader program, while keeping what's most valuable from the different disciplines they represent. Instead, such integration will be a top-down Ministry exercise, using a learner-outcomes "menu." "While a great deal of extremely valuable professional development may occur when teachers in a school work together to build an intelligently and thoroughly integrated curriculum," the Commission says, "it is unrealistic to expect that the time necessary for this process is available in many or most schools. In order to integrate subjects, teachers need an extensive menu of topics or themes keyed to the learner outcomes in the subjects to be integrated, sequenced appropriately."[22]

Perhaps this gutting of human substance from curriculum is most evident in the Commission's cheerleading for information technology. We saw earlier its willingness to consider the possibility that the joy of relating to a machine might come to equal the joy of human communication found in books. Machines can somehow come to replace human beings, not just in factories, but in our hearts and souls. It is a theme the Commission seems anxious to extend. Computers, it tells us, in and of themselves, make students feel "relevant" and as such "reinvent" education. With these tools, "students are challenged with complex, authentic tasks ... [which] are completed for reasons beyond a grade." The commissioners go on to quote positively, and entirely uncritically, from a 1990 project of the University of British Columbia and the Educational Technology Centre of British Columbia, to integrate computer-related technologies into twelve provincial schools. "There was a feeling," the project officers reported, "that the motivational aspect of the computer encouraged the students to spend more time at the computer, which led to developing skills in critical thinking, creative thinking and problem-solving."[23]

What is missing in all of this, as the Ontario Federation of Labour's Jim Turk has put it, is the understanding that "learning is an interactional activity in which learners' responses shape what is achieved as much as the teacher. The move to outcomes-based education is a move away from the recognition of the interactional nature of learning — a nature that makes the learning process always changing, always different at different times with different students, always shaped by the immediate social environment of the teacher and the student."[24]

The severing of social relationships from curriculum does not, of course, result in any kind of curriculum vacuum. What kids are to learn in school may be empty of purpose, but it is heavy with "information," with "data," with "learner outcomes" possessing, as we have seen, only the most limited intelligibility. In the end, it seems ironic that with all the corporate/bureaucratic posturing on this front, the "real stuff" of the curriculum has so little substance. It is so mind-blowingly dull. But perhaps such dullness is appropriate for a business class that thinks it is now coming to the end of history and ideology, and that its technology — driven by fewer and fewer human beings who will increasingly think and act like machines — will soon conquer all areas of human experience and endeavour. The sterility of such a vision could hardly produce anything more than this mouse of a program.

If any doubt remains about the shallow quality of this corporate/bureaucratic curriculum, let us now consider the new standardized framework in which, according to both the Commission and the Ministry, its fruits will be measured.

Corporate/Bureaucratic Standardization

As in its initial approach to curriculum, the Royal Commission appears to take a somewhat progressive line on standardized testing.

Indeed, when Education Minister Dave Cooke announced "a very extensive provincial testing agenda for grade 3, 6, 9, and 11, well beyond what the Commission recommended,"[25] the Commission's co-chair, Gerry Caplan, took issue with him. "The minister," he declared, "took the wrong emphasis out of our report and seems to be proud to talk publicly in quantitative terms." Caplan "worries," *The Globe and Mail* reported, "that Canada will copy the dubious record of the United States on testing." He went on to say that "Americans test more than anyone else in the world and it hasn't done a damn thing to improve the situation. Testing by itself is not worth a nickel."[26]

I'm certainly prepared to cheer Caplan on in this battle. My only hesitation stems from the fact that I couldn't find much of this attitude in the report he and his fellow commissioners prepared.

The Commission may not have been "proud to talk publicly in quantitative terms," but it certainly laid the groundwork so that no other kind of public talk about testing was really possible. (Needless to say, the Ministry had no particular plans to approach the subject differently.)

Not the least of this groundbreaking work was was the emphasis the Commission placed on dissociated skills in its "learner-outcome" framework for Ontario education. Once a skill is removed from the context or subject in which it functions and takes its meaning, its capacity to be measured in a standardized form is assured. Once skills are understood as free-floating (and skills are generally so understood within the Ministry) their assessment can then be packaged into tests, offering questions for which mechanical choices are possible and quantifiable in a one-dimensional fashion. If skills aren't separated in this way, such tests aren't possible. So, for example, the skills needed for a good physicist involve the use of mathematics to describe what can be seen or what can be imagined in the physical world. The mathematics cannot be divorced from the seeing and the imagining and cannot be tested outside this context. On the other hand, when the Ministry, through its provincial reviews, tests the level of Grade 12 Physics among Ontario students, it provides them with questions containing quantitative information and expects them to fit this information into formulas they have already memorized. This is, of course, a very low level of skill testing, but the important thing to recognize is that it is thoroughly divorced from the seeing and imagining we expect of real physicists. It is quantified skill testing entirely out of context.

But even in the text of its report, the Commission was not all that hostile to quantifying what students learn. My impression, in fact, is that the Commission was surprisingly supportive of this approach.

"Parents," the Commission insists, "want to know how their children are progressing in terms of acceptable and universal standards which, until recently, had not been established. Now that they have begun to be established, standardized assessment is possible — as long as teachers are equipped to carry it out."[27]

What is essential, say the commissioners, is the "creation of a provincial report card, an Ontario Student Achievement Report (OSAR) based on the outcomes and standards expected in each grade and each subject. In addition to a global mark for each subject or interdisciplinary area (e.g. maths or arts), students should be rated on a set of specific outcomes, derived from the common curriculum and provincial standards documents. In the first and second terms, the report should indicate the extent to which the student is (or is not) making good progress toward the achievement of each of the several outcomes related to the particular subject and, at the end of the school year, has or has not achieved that outcome at a satisfactory level."[28]

Caplan may not be proud of such quantification, but his Commission is certainly public about it. And there's more to come.

The Commission does take some time to worry about the dangers of province-wide quantitative testing, but then it goes right ahead and proposes such testing anyway. Whatever public opinion surveys may say,[29] the Commission insists that an unsophisticated public demands it. "While we want to be very clear about our lack of enthusiasm for extensive, expensive, universal testing, as opposed to sample-based assessment," the Commission declares, "we recognize the public's need for some measure of basic student achievement that is applied in the same way to every student at a few points in time. That is why we are recommending two province-wide assessments to be given to all students relatively early in their schooling, with the understanding that educators (most especially school principals) will make it clear that the results of such assessment are to be used by teachers, individually and collectively, for purposes of diagnosing and remediating the individual student's difficulties or gaps in learning. In addition, the tests are to enhance reporting to parents and for examining the content and delivery of curriculum. Test results are, more emphatically, not be used to place or sort students for any reason."[30]

The conclusion, then, is that we should be moderate on "universal testing" (unlike the province, it seems, which went much further and added tests at two additional grade levels) and we should stress "sample-based assessment" to let us know generally how we are doing. At the same time, however, there is nothing here that says quantitative, out-of-context skill testing ought not to be taking place across the board. Quite the contrary. That is what both universal and sample-based testing are all about in a "learner-outcomes" framework. Indeed, the Commission expects standardized tests to be used for "diagnosing and remediating" students' learning problems. Furthermore, to say that these test results ought not be used "to place or sort students" isn't to say that students should not be placed and sorted through similar tests — like "challenge" exams or the regular classroom variety — that have at their base an understanding of learning as the mastery of dissociated skills, which can be assessed quantitatively.

In responding to the Royal Commission's recommendations on this subject, the Minister of Education did not, it seems to me, deny their spirit in any way, in spite of the fact, that as Dave Cooke proudly put it, he was "introducing the most extensive testing program in Canada," in which all students in Grades 3, 6, 9, and 11 would be tested in "reading, writing and mathematics." His ministry was doing this testing, Cooke said, because "we want to make sure that if a student needs help in a particular area, we find that out as soon as possible." These tests "will let every student know whether they are meeting the standards we have set. They will ensure that parents and teachers know where the student stands and what needs to be done to ensure improvement...." It is almost the exact language used by the Commission to justify the tests it recommended. Furthermore, Cooke argued, following the Commission's bias, that "these are tests that are based on curriculum; tests that can describe what students know; tests that can show why improvement is necessary; tests that provide relevant information that can be shared with parents and the public." "We intend," the minister continued, "to build on our experience with the Grade 9 Reading and Writing Test [which] was spread over several classroom periods and was part of a unit of work. It gave students an opportunity to demonstrate their knowledge and understanding in a way less sophisticated testing would not."[31] The Commission, in fact, described this Grade 9 test as "a very good test," and concluded it "was a genuine assessment of performance." Consistent teacher reports, based on clear learner outcomes over nine years, would be better, the Commission judged, and the test itself should differentiate students from particular immigrant (and linguistic) backgrounds. Still, it "gave us valuable data on how well Ontario Grade 9 students understand what they read and whether they can write clearly, expressively and to the point." The only real worry expressed, as before, was that administrators would use such tests to place and sort their students.[32]

The only place the Commission seems to take a strong stand against quantitative testing where it deals with what might be described as the far-right of the testing spectrum: the quickie tests needing short-answer and multiple choice questions. But even these tests, the Commission reports, can "measure certain important abilities we expect all students to have." The only problem with them is that they can't measure all these abilities or even a representative sample of them. They are not complex enough, in other words, but there is nothing wrong with them in principle. Thus when financial pressures move the province in the direction of such tests, and that is very likely in the next few years, there will be little from the Royal Commission to hold them back.

It is only the complexity that matters, and, as we shall see later on, only for some kids.

"Experiments," the Commission tells us, "have revealed the importance of meta-cognitive strategies — thinking about thinking — as a way of taking learners to more complex levels of comprehension and competence." Thus, "the education system must give high priority to doing precisely that. The results of provincial, national, and international testing show that Ontario students do reasonably well on measures of basic or lower-order skills and knowledge — in math, for example, facts about numbers and simple arithmetical operations — but appear to do less well on measures of higher-level skills, such as estimating and problem-solving. Similarly, in tests of literacy, students in Ontario and other provinces tend to perform fairly strongly when decoding text and answering simple recall/comprehension questions, but many fall short in being able to synthesize, to infer, or to extend what they have read."[33]

What is supposed to motivate kids is the mastery of these complex (and dissociated) skills. That alone. Once more, there are no social or human purposes to be considered. "Nothing is more motivating than competence," says the Commission, "and increasing competence is the essence of schooling. As students acquire competence, they perceive the power of knowledge, and are motivated to stretch themselves even more."[34] What our schools must accept, therefore, is that the testing of such complexity must itself be "complex and costly."[35] "Accurately evaluating more complex thinking skills in the classroom demands careful training, extensive supervised practice, and the development of skills that are seriously neglected in teacher education.... [To] the extent that we can teach teachers to evaluate complex thinking skills well and consistently, we build the capacity to measure well what matters most."[36]

The Commission also adds a few standardized tests of its own, which the Ministry has yet to comment on. There is to be a Grade 11 literacy test, which students, if they fail, can repeat in Grade 12. They must, however, pass this test before receiving their secondary school diploma.[37] There are also to be a great number of what the Commission calls "challenge" exams, which we will turn to when we examine the new streaming arrangements it proposes.

In conclusion, the Commission demands a major new provincial initiative in testing to ensure that its proposed new program of skill-outcomes (which have begun to be described in *The Common Curriculum*) be accurately measured. It recommends that "the Ministry continue to be involved in and to support national and international assessments." Furthermore, the Ministry must develop "detailed, multi-year plans for large-scale assessments (program reviews, examination monitoring), which establish the data to be collected and the way implementation will be monitored, and report the results publicly, and provide for the interpretation and use of results to educators and to the public." Finally, as it begins this initiative "and for a five- to seven-year period, until the process is well-established in the school system and in the public consciousness, an independent accountability agency be charged with implementing and reporting the Grades 3 and 11 universal student assessments...."[38]

The Commission will undoubtedly be pleased at the speed with which the Ministry responded to its recommendation for "an independent accountability agency." The Commission had hardly caught its breath from its report, when the Minister announced it had set up a full-blown Education Quality and Accountability Office (EQAO) to "conduct province-wide testing," to "manage the province's participation in national and international tests," and to prepare an annual report on the system that analyses not only provincial test results, but also examines graduate and drop out numbers, post-secondary placements, and the percentage of education expenditures that end up in classrooms. The EQAO would also "conduct program reviews of school boards to ensure high quality instruction is happening throughout the province." The board of this organization includes the president of General Motors of Canada, a dean of engineering, the recently resigned president of the CBC, a former director of the Toronto's French-language public school board, a former Tory Minister of Education, and one pro-NDP union leader. Its chief executive officer is a former director of the Toronto Board of Education. Both the assistant deputy minister responsible for this initiative and the coordinator for implementation are Ministry civil servants who have no background in the school system. Sadly and surprisingly, the chair of this institution is Richard Johnston, who once stood against Bob Rae for party leadership. Johnston used to believe that education was about character and understanding and purpose — light years away from the world of standardized tests — and it is hard to imagine him chairing this collection of "educators."

The Streaming Shift

In much the same fashion as it attempted to distance itself from a right-wing agenda in curriculum development and testing, the Commission tells us that it has no intention of supporting an unjust streaming system, with its biases against poor and minority students. It then goes about doing just that.

The Commission seems to make no bones about it. It doesn't want our schools producing "young women and men who are mostly characterized by deference, docility, passivity, or submissiveness. We want schools to develop students — all students — who are feisty, questioning, creative, imaginative, autonomous, and independent." Everyone is to be treated equally, to have "the same opportunity to make the most of the challenging schools we envisage." Furthermore, the Commission argues, we don't want schools "reinforc[ing] the belief that success in school is a relatively simple matter of merit … [and that students who] don't make it have only their own moral and intellectual inadequacies to blame." The Commission recognizes that school success is largely dependent on a student's economic status. "Students," it says, "who are streamed into the basic- and general-level high school programs … are disproportionately from non-professional backgrounds." They are presented with far fewer academic challenges than the better-off students placed in the advanced program. For the students in each of these streams their placement and program become "a self-fulfilling prophecy."[39]

The Commission even goes so far as to lend its support to the research that says that destreaming does not disadvantage "the most and least able students."[40] This research is a key plank in a destreaming program and its implications are far-reaching, undercutting most of the arguments against destreaming. The Commission then goes on to back George Radwanski's 1987 report on school drop outs in its overall critique of the streaming system: "As long as there are different streams, students from less advantaged circumstances, or students who are handicapped by unfair assumptions and social and racial bias, will always be disproportionately represented in the least demanding courses, and will obtain a lower quality and quantity of formal education, to their long-term economic and social disadvantage. [Radwanski] offers abundant evidence," the Commission continues, "to show that these disparities are not primarily related to students' ability to learn, but to such non-academic factors as family income and parental education level. (The 25-year longitudinal study also found that the stream or level in which the student was placed bore more relation to that student's subsequent academic success, or lack thereof, than did measured intelligence or elementary school marks.)"[41]

So, we should get rid of class-biased streaming. Right?

Wrong, says the Commission, even though that was, in fact, Radwanski's conclusion.

Why is it wrong?

Well, says the Commission, there is an awful lot of political flak involved in such a move. The Ministry under the Liberals, the Commission reports, "would not accept Radwanski's recommendation 'that the current policy of streaming high school students into academic, general and basic courses of study be abolished and replaced by provision of a single and undifferentiated high-quality educational stream for all students.'" They just wouldn't do it. There was also "a negative response" from teachers, students, university people, and from "many parents of students in the advanced-level stream." As a result of this opposition, the Ministry, which had been considering destreaming in Grades 9 and 10 and was now under the NDP, "proceeded with the destreaming of Grade 9 only, and gave schools three years, from September 1993 to June 1996, to complete this change." By the time the Royal Commission got under way, there was still "considerable opposition to be heard, but the response was mixed, and there were an increasing number of reports about schools and teachers who felt they were making a success of the destreamed Grade 9 program."[42]

What was the Commission to do?

We are left with the impression that it was not prepared to rush in where Ministry angels feared to tread.

The Commission doesn't put it this way initially. What it does is to shift gears immediately after this last remark, and turn our attention to the fact that Grades 7 to 9 are treated as a three-year block in *The Common Curriculum*'s structure of learner outcomes. The Commission says it now wants to build on this structure. "Because we see curriculum as a continuum, rather than as a dichotomy, instead of referring to an elementary and a secondary curriculum, we prefer to think in terms of a common core curriculum from Grades 1 to 9 (which includes some options for local specialization) and a specialized curriculum after Grade 9, which nonetheless has considerable room for common courses." Having made this point, it then turns back to the issue of extending the common curriculum to the end of Grade 10 and to the question of political flak. It notes "that many educators have found the decision to destream Grade 9 traumatic, and they have told us they feel beleaguered by the pace of educational reform in the last decade: they have not had time to implement one change before another is upon them." As a result, the Commission concludes, it should not "recommend the extension of the common curriculum to the end of Grade 10," even though they are "convinced" that "a common core curriculum could be offered through Grade 10, as is done in British Columbia and Quebec."[43] By this time, it has forgotten Radwanski's recommendation that there should be "a single and undifferentiated high-quality educational stream for all students" throughout their high school years. There is also no response to OSSTF's proposal for a systematic "protocol for change," in which policies like destreaming could be effectively worked out.[44]

At this point in the discussion, it appears as if the Commission has folded its tent on the issue of high school destreaming and that old Ministry policies will simply continue under some new rubric.

Appearances, in this case, are deceiving.

What the Commission ends up proposing as its "specialized program" — building on a continuum of "learner outcomes" from *The Common Curriculum* — is a much harder and well-defined streaming system than currently exists. It will also be much tougher on working-class kids, and particularly on those from poor families.

The primary problem for the Commission seems to be the shaping of a university-bound stream that won't be cluttered up with students who don't actually end up at university.

As it describes the problem, because "two-thirds of students entering secondary school want to go to university, they therefore choose all or almost all their courses at the advanced level.... Only about one in three who follow this sequence from Grade 9 to graduation actually enter university (because of the limited number of university spaces); some go to college, others to different kinds of private post-secondary training or directly to work. About 88 percent of students who begin Grade 9 in advanced-level courses complete their OSSD, although some switch and take some or almost all their courses at the general level before they graduate." On the other hand, "just over one in four students begin Grade 9 taking general-level courses, and another 5 percent taking mainly basic-level courses. In both categories there is an over-representation of children from working-class parents, while the children of professional and managerial parents are under-represented. (Many students in basic-level courses have not graduated from Grade 8, and have been transferred rather than promoted to secondary school.) The non-completion (drop-out) rate for students from general level courses is 58 percent, and for those from basic-level courses is 65 percent — about six times higher than for those in the advanced level. The difference in both selection and retention rates makes it clear that the three levels are not equally appealing or equally satisfying. There is general agreement that one cause of the high drop-out rate among those enrolled in general- and basic-level courses is that they recognize that these courses do not lead anywhere," and are not expected to lead anywhere.[45]

What has been happening here is a de facto destreaming process. Students are voting with their feet and ending up in the advanced program, although how many actually expect to go to university is another matter. Clearly a substantial number expect to end up in a community college, because that is now a well-established pattern. So why not formalize such a process, which seems to be operating smoothly enough? Teachers are not seriously complaining. Middle-class parents aren't mobilizing. Why not structure in more booster programs of one sort or another so that more bottom-stream students can enter the advanced program? The advanced stream is now the program of a large majority of our students, and with a completion rate of 88 percent, it is functioning with surprising effectiveness. And its expansion needn't mean a weakening of its curriculum, if the booster programs are solid and its basis of support is not undercut. Indeed, why not take this as an opportunity to strengthen the quality of the advanced program itself as the basis of a quality academic program for all? Why not fit technical courses within its structures? (In this context, something also has to be done about accessibility to community college and university programs. These programs are currently closed to far too many students, who must then turn to a continuing — and increasingly privatized — series of short term and inadequate training programs.)

These are not questions the Commission chooses to consider. What the Commission has in mind moves it in a very different direction. What it proposes, instead, is to get rid of the small basic-level program and "boost"[46] its students into a vastly increased general-level stream, which will now be called an "applied" program. In the process, the advanced stream, now referred to as an "academic" program, will be sufficiently shaken down to include, as much as possible, only those students who will actually end up on university rolls. The "applied" program will now be more formally tied to the community college system.[47]

The Commission's "specialized program" for Grades 10 to 12 is thus broken down into two main streams. One of these will focus on courses called Ontario Academic Courses, or OAcCs, which will "be offered with an academic emphasis." These will be required for university entrance, and may be "packaged" for different faculties. The other stream will focus on courses called Ontario Applied Courses, or OApCs. These will be offered "with an emphasis on application," and will be linked to community college entrance requirements. Other courses —Family Studies, Physical Education, Life Skills, Drama, Visual Arts, and most Business courses — will be set up as "common courses, blending academic and applied approaches, and with no special designation."[48]

The Commission admits that in developing and expanding its Applied stream it will be difficult "to provide an attractive and realistic alternative" to the Academic program. The problem of such vocational streaming, it notes, "is deep-seated in a culture that values and rewards academic and professional skills more than applied skills. In spite of the fact that we lament the lack of skilled craftspeople, and despite our chronic dependence on immigrants with these skills, we do not pay or honour skilled workers as we do those who have a university degree and professional training. University is the gateway to higher earnings and status, and is likely to remain so. We tend to equate general intelligence with academic intelligence, so that academic success and academic credentials become the major evidence of individual excellence and employability. As a consequence, courses or course sequences that do not lead to university eligibility will probably remain less desirable."[49]

What we have to accept is that "no matter how the curriculum is altered, there can be little doubt that students from disadvantaged homes and neighbourhoods will continue to be under-represented among those admitted to university. But a more successful multi-stream system should enable more of them to complete their diploma — which is itself a measure of increasing equity."[50]

But aren't we back now to the Commission's concern about high drop-out rates in the current general- and basic-level programs? Why shouldn't students continue to vote with their feet and choose the Academic Program over the Applied?

The Commission seems to hope there will be two answers to this problem. The first is that since the Applied Program will link directly with the community colleges, those who actually expect a community college education will be more likely to go this route. There is something in this argument, although it is hard to believe the community colleges will turn down Academic stream applicants or refuse to put them at the top of their lists. Without regulatory legislation — which the Commission doesn't seem to promote — I can see no reason why these formal links should break the present pattern now evident in Academic stream applications to college. Our society's refusal to "honour" skilled workers, not to mention its firing or deskilling them in droves, is surely not going to disappear in the near future. Nor is it likely that middle-class parents will give up the "soft-landing" of a community college placement for their kids, if they fail to win a university spot from the Academic stream.

The other answer also seems doomed to failure, encouraging, I suspect, as much resistance as it will compliance. It involves, however, a much more aggressive hands-on process for keeping working-class kids in their place. The Commission calls this process "career counselling." It is to start in the first years of a child's life at school.

"The curriculum we recommend," the Commission says, "would begin building connections between the school and the community very early, starting with a focus on community and career awareness in ECE/kindergarten, and continuing with a Cumulative Educational Plan (CEP) starting in Grade 7. But it is in the specialized curriculum that actual participation in extended, as well as brief, work experiences occurs, and the crucial links to work, career, and full-time employment are made — whether that employment begins for the learner at age 18 or earlier, or later, after post-secondary education. Starting in Grade 10, serious attention must be given to building links between curriculum and work applications."[51]

What the Commission has in mind is a systematic push to ensure that broad "career" paths are chosen early in school, and are then nailed down in Grade 10 with its "specialized program" of streamed "learner outcomes."

In a school system desperate for spare cash, the Commission insists on a major infusion of new "career" personnel to insure that such choosing will actually take place. It recommends "that all elementary school teachers have regular access to a 'community career co-ordinator' responsible for co-ordinating the school's community-based career-awareness curriculum, and working with teachers and community members to build and support the program." Furthermore, "in order to support the Cumulative Evaluation Plan (CEP) and the career-education-related curriculum beginning in Grade 7, we believe," says the Commission, "that students and their teacher-advisors must have access to a career-education specialist who knows about education, training and work opportunities, about secondary and post-secondary educational programs, and who is able to provide students with assessment and counselling as well as job and career information. We want schools, beginning no later than Grade 7, to have career-education personnel who are professionally trained to organize, co-ordinate, and deliver educational and career information, planning, and counselling, with differing emphases according to the age and needs of the student...."[52]

This may also involve a plan to remove a number of well-paid teachers from their current guidance function, in addition to the introduction of a new approach to job-slot counselling. "Teacher training," the Commission notes, "is not the essential component [for these new personnel]; training as a career educator/counsellor is. To the extent that the function will continue to be carried out by existing staff for some time, they must be retrained; people entering the field must also be trained, whether or not they are teachers; the result may be a mixture of teachers and non-teachers doing this work."[53]

At the centre of the career counsellor's work is the Cumulative Education Plan, beginning in Grade 7. This plan, which "includes the student's academic and other learning experiences, is understood to be the major planning tool for the student's secondary and post-secondary education, and is reviewed semi-annually by the student, parents, and by the teacher who has a continuing relation with and responsibility for that student as along as she or he remains in the school."[54]

If the student is failing to succeed in the appropriate learner outcomes, the Cumulative Education Plan will be increasingly shaped to direct the student to the Applied program in high school. Such students are to learn early on that they must abandon false hopes for worldly success. And if by any chance some of these students still manage to stumble into the Academic program, the Commission takes special pains to make certain that even fewer of them will succeed in their inappropriate passage to university. To do this, the Commission insists that unless they do very well on their immediate entry into Grade 10, they cannot expect to make up for poor performances as they mature. In high school there will be no second chances for the main prize. The Commission caps the number of courses that can be taken in Grades 10 to 12 at 24, three courses beyond the required 21. And it further recommends "that all courses in which the student has enrolled — whether completed or incomplete, passed or failed — be recorded on that student's transcript."[55]

The Commission notes that it is "not restricting the length of time students may take to finish the equivalent of three years of full-time schooling."[56] But in the real world, it knows perfectly well that many students will plunge into courses they are not ready for. Hoping to do well, they find they do badly. That is part of being young. Even more so, it is part of being young *and* working class, and carrying, not all that consciously, a large burden of resistance to schooling. Overcoming that resistance (even for short-term goals) requires an enormous output of will and, in some ways, a quite unrealistic, if life-giving, faith in the future. Both this will and this faith are the product of growing up. As things stand now, high school students are still permitted a little room to grow up. They can do badly in a few courses, even quite a few courses, and make them up later, and it won't show on the transcript. All the university registrar will see are the credits in which a student has done her best. In its way, it is one of the few forms we have of affirmative action for working-class kids in school, or for alienated kids generally. Ambitious middle-class parents, however, whose offspring have kept their shoulders to the wheel, feel quite grumpy about it. They want to keep their children's proper place in the university line, established over many years of responsible and successful behaviour. "Isn't this a competitive system?" they ask. "Our children played by the rules of the game. Surely, these rules can't be changed at the last minute."

The Commission's recommendations here are a direct response to this grumpiness. And as OSSTF understands them, they are "a direct challenge to universality of access: The proposed restrictions will limit the opportunity for picking up failed credits, remediation, successfully completing the compulsories in the compressed three years of specialization, pursuing a broad range of subject areas, including co-op ed, participating in a broad range of extracurricular activities during the three year period, upgrading to meet university entrance requirements, [and] meeting the special needs of adult learners...."[57]

At the core of these restrictions is the idea that students must be rewarded for their success within certain time limits, whatever the Commission's qualifications. How well a student does in a certain number of courses within a certain amount of time will be the key factor in university access. Even now there are means by which universities reward those who finish their programs in four years flat rather than slipping over into a fifth year. With all courses registered (and presumably dated) on a student's transcript, how quickly the student has proceeded will clearly be balanced with how well she has done.

The idea of time limits, in fact, pervades this report, and it is fundamental to the way the Commission has rethought and restructured the streaming system as part and parcel of a "learner-outcomes" education.

Let us follow the main points of an argument in a section called "Outcomes and Time."[58] It is written within the chapter on *The Common Curriculum* for Grades 1 to 9, but it also applies to the "specialized" years.

First, the Commission says, it wants to make time "a variable rather than a constant," and that a "learner-outcomes" program lets it do that. "Focusing on learner outcomes," it says, "makes it possible to abandon the strict number of days or hours as a measure of 'product' and allow for the reality that people learn at different rates." Leaving aside the objection that even the worst of schools measure product by product produced as well as by time, the important starting point is that learner outcomes provide a framework in which people learn at different rates.

Second, learner-outcomes, it appears, offers another mode by which we can describe how learners differ — "not categorically but along a continuum according to the rate of learning, and that these rates vary by subject matter." Some students learn more quickly in some subjects than in others. Some learn more quickly in most subjects, if not all subjects. That is how they should be described.

Third, given more time, we can expect that most of those who have not learned quickly or well will eventually learn what is expected as an average outcome for an average grade level. Others who do learn quickly and well will need less time to move through the curriculum and will achieve higher grades in this process. None of these students will have to repeat a program. They will simply proceed at their own speed — and in high school within their own stream — learning outcome after outcome at different levels of proficiency, but hopefully, says the Commission, with different time frames available, there will be less of a gap between these levels of proficiency.

Finally, in all of this, the best thing a student can do is to go as fast as he or she can. Not only does this save the school system money, but it also sorts out the winners and losers with remarkable clarity for university registrars and future employers. Thus the Commission recommends year-round schooling to provide more time for slow learners and a fast-track for the ambitious and the already successful. And for elementary students "who can move more quickly through one or several subjects," the Commission goes on to recommend "that exams similar to the challenge exams at the secondary level should be available. A student who shows, on such an exam, that she is ready to move ahead to the next level should be helped to do so, whether or not the eventual result is acceleration (skipping a grade)." In high school there should be even more flexibility for such fast-tracking. "One way," says the Commission, "is to design units or modules, either within courses of the traditional length (one semester or one year), or as partial credits in themselves. In either case, the idea is that students could progress through a sequence of modules at different paces, with those needing more support able to get it, and those capable of accelerating doing so. Another form of acceleration is by prior learning assessment: to the extent that courses are broken into modules, or that partial credits are offered, it becomes increasingly plausible to give students the option of 'testing out' through a challenge exam and moving to a higher level."[59]

Given the initial resistance to school among working-class kids, the unwelcoming reality that learner-outcomes-based education presents to them, the deepening of formal secondary streams and their "career" infrastructure, this new breathless path to school success and university placement is a final nail in the coffin for social class equity in Ontario schools. I'm inclined to call these new structures "time streams."[60] The name might appeal to the Commission's high-tech vision of the future. The capacity to "manage" time and to produce ones' own individual "time and motion" persona is perhaps the most treasured aspect of middle- and upper-class cultural capital. Working-class kids are babes in the woods when it comes to this territory. Such discipline they understand may be necessary to survival, even effectiveness, on the job, but it has nothing to do with finding any kind of happiness. Whenever you get a chance to shuck it off, you do. How else are you going to live? Later, these kids learn, that a working life, in all its complexities and responsibilities, offers few chances for such freedom, and maybe they would have done better to rethink their management of time, whatever the downside of such management might be. Indeed, the growing involvement of working people in what has been described as a "continuous learning culture" — various forms of night school, on-the-job training and education for the unemployed — reflects this rethinking process, and it runs directly against the notion that the timing of knowledge should make any difference in the status of the learner.

With its "learner-outcome time-streams" in place, and with firmer "academic" and "applied" channels through which students must eventually run, it is no wonder the Commission is prepared to take on the labels of the old streaming system and some of its more expensive bottom-stream structures.

Since students will now be defined along a "rate-of-learning continuum," the Commission argues, much of the entire category of "handicapped" will increasingly be unnecessary, along with its various sub-categories. In the past, it says "we have tried, usually with little success, to create different, often separate, learning programs for each of these groups." Now, with learner outcomes, the slow learner can simply take her place within the continuum, proceeding at her own speed. And "rather than putting her in a different program with a different and less challenging curriculum, where she has no chance of completing the same work as her peers, her best chances for success will probably come from being in that same program, with support and assistance, so that she can move with them. In some cases, additional catch-up time can be made available in the summer."[61]

Picking up the left critique of Special Education — a critique that has been active over the last 30 years — the Commission argues that the various definitions and diagnoses describing and separating the Learning Disabled, the Learning Disadvantaged, and Slow Learners are largely meaningless in themselves and irrelevant in determining the proper program for students so labelled. The programs are also stigmatizing and ineffective. What we really have here, for a great many of their students, says the Commission in an unexpected flash of irony, is "an instructional deficit disorder." And the learner-outcomes-time-stream approach will do the trick as an over-all cure. "Some people," it concludes, "learn some things faster or more slowly than do other people. School emphasizes certain kinds of learning, and rewards certain kinds of intelligence. Children who continue to have difficulty learning from print, or who continue to need to move systematically from the concrete to the abstract, or who need more or different examples or experiences to understand or to internalize a concept may need not just a greater variety of teaching and learning modes, but more time to master the same curriculum. Providing more variety pedagogically and more flexibility in learning time is probably simpler — *and is certainly more cost-effective and easily justified* [my italics] — than going through a lengthy process that ends in a label ('slow learner' or 'learning disabled') that may be stigmatizing and that is in itself no guarantee of receiving effective help."[62]

The Commission makes much the same point about "socio-emotional or behavioural disabilities." For many of the kids so categorized, it says, the labels are also false and destructive, while the programs themselves stigmatize, lower expectations, and generally fail to help. For such students, the best solution is often a teacher well trained and well supported in learner outcomes and in conflict-resolution techniques, with perhaps some additional adult help in the regular classroom.[63]

The Commission doesn't go so far as to actually recommend getting rid of any of these labels or programs, though it does make it more difficult to be categorized as Learning Disabled.[64] While it may encourage a more efficient (more high-tech) steaming system, that doesn't mean the old system should be immediately abandoned. The old structure is safe until a new structure has been solidly prepared. As the report puts it, "while integration should be the norm, school boards [should] continue to provide a continuum of services for students whose needs would, in the opinion of parents and educators, be best served in other settings."[65] But the word is out: These expensive bottom-streams — with their very low pupil-teacher ratios and very high percentage of students from poor families — should increasingly be shelved. There is a better and cheaper way to dump these kids. And the optics are right.

It is worth noting at this juncture that our current bottom-stream Special Education curriculum has largely been of the learner-outcome variety anyway, with quite a fierce devotion to separating "basic" skills from any particular content. What the Royal Commission recommends for the regular classroom is simply a more complex version of these skills, which are to be handled over longer periods of time. Instead of "basic skills," integrated students will get "higher-level cognitive processing" and a slower time-stream.[66]

As I've indicated earlier, what these students actually require is not more time to complete their tasks, but more real tasks to complete. They need a much tougher and richer curriculum that both encourages and supports their developing a clear view of the world, powerfully expressing that view, and seeing the possibility of translating their ideas into action. These students do not need to be bored to death. None of our students do.

When it comes to the privileged streams for "able, advanced, and fast learners," the Commission opts for a kinder, gentler approach. It is especially concerned with full-time programs for the gifted, which are increasingly being demanded in middle-class communities and which are very costly. The Commission suggests that the category "gifted" might best be narrowed to apply to those students "who would be at a substantial disadvantage in any class not tailored to their very special individual talents" — for example, in music or math, which "cannot be met by any teacher in the school." For the "larger group of quick or advanced learners," the Commission recommends instead a process of "acceleration," through teacher assessment and challenge exams. Acceleration, it says, has "a very strong and positive record," better than "enrichment," and with little prospect of harming the student socially. Learner outcomes will allow them to learn "faster and better," and no serious gaps will emerge through skipping a grade. "Time is not the problem," it says, "especially for the quick." The Commission assures its readers, however, that it is "not suggesting that enrichment and special gifted programs cease to exist." Not at all. It is merely "question[ing] the idea that this is the best strategy for quick learners, and reiterat[ing] that acceleration is a highly effective, greatly under-used, and extremely cost-effective alternative for students who are fast learners."[67] For the ambitious middle-class parent, this is a finely calculated pitch. Acceleration could well get their kid to the front of the university line. Maybe the prestige of the gifted classroom isn't worth it?

There is one further dimension to the Commission's new and improved streaming system for Ontario schools. It is what David Livingstone understands as "the nurturing of a technological elite" within middle-class neighbourhoods.

Livingstone makes the point that the Commission "conveniently ignores the fact that the demonstration school projects to which private corporations have devoted themselves [and which the Commission has set up as models] have typically been in affluent suburban areas. It is not just coincidental," he argues, "that Apple selected River Oaks in Oakville, historically one of the richest census areas in the country, for its major project in this country. The intent here appears to be nurturing of a technological elite in a largely middle class community, with lucrative spinoff profits to boot. Class affinities and cost-benefit calculus make it unlikely that many private corporations will offer comparable support to such projects in our inner city areas, such as Regent Park or the Jane-Finch corridor. The most consistent of all findings in the OISE Surveys since 1978 has been the strong majority opposition of corporate executives to increased funding for public education, an opposition which has grown in the context of definite majority support for increased funding during the past 10 years. Of course, there are serious public funding constraints. But for the Commission to put its faith in the private corporate sector to voluntarily offer substantial sustained resource support to schools in general, let alone with a serious preference for overcoming inequities in poorer and immediately less profitable communities, seems quite naive."[68]

From the all corporate/bureaucratic territory we have covered so far, "naive" is perhaps a more benign description than any others which immediately spring to mind.

OSSTF And The Curriculum: Finding Its Own Voice

OSSTF knows that its concern for decent school funding and for honest democracy must finally rest on how it thinks that funding and democracy will be used to provide a good education for the students in Ontario schools.

With the new corporate/bureaucratic agenda on streaming, standardized tests and Outcomes Based Education coming on like gangbusters — the Royal Commission on Learning functioning as just one of its many vehicles — the Federation must now, as never before, face up to what it believes students should experience as the core of their curriculum.

It must say unequivocally what a solid school program has to be about. And it must be willing to fight for that program.

As I've argued earlier, this is the toughest area for Federation policy-making and organizing.

It is here that the biggest ideological guns of the society's rulers are trained, both from inside and outside the school system. From a broad range of corporate, government, media, social agency and educational sources, teachers are told in no uncertain terms that the basic ideas they see in the Royal Commission report and in the government announcements which followed are what they are going to have to live with. There are no alternatives. This is what is necessary for our schools to link with the realities of global capitalism, to make our future workers and citizens effective competitors in the international marketplace. It is hard, but we have to bite the bullet on this one.

OSSTF knows perfectly well, at all levels of its leadership, that it is not only a lie, but a very destructive lie. This kind of education has little to do with real efficiency and almost everything to do with social control. It brings with it, as I've indicated, a curriculum policy that will prove extraordinarily damaging to both students and teachers, subjecting them to an increasingly limited and purposeless program of studies.

OSSTF also knows that it is a lie that runs deep in the society — in the public at large and among its own membership. It isn't that people so much believe it is true, but rather that they cannot find the words to say why it is false. They cannot find the means to express an alternative that appears realistic, that is rooted in the good things done at public school, that makes sense to the reforming instincts of classroom teachers, and that can carry broad public support.

OSSTF, alongside its sister teacher unions, has to create that alternative.

It must find its own voice, stronger and clearer than any it has yet achieved. This is not the voice of the teacher on the picket line, however true and necessary that voice may be. It is the voice of the teacher at his or her place of work. It is the voice of a person who has not forgotten what young people think about and care about and why that matters to us as individuals and to the society as a whole.

I think OSSTF has begun to find that voice.

To start with perhaps the most immediate and contentious problem in this area, the Federation understands it has to develop a detailed policy on destreaming. The current streaming system is obviously unjust and cannot be seriously defended. That it continues to be routinely supported at many levels of the Federation is the result of two factors. First, there is a vocal minority which honestly believes poor kids and minority kids are inferior beings either for genetic or environmental reasons. As one of its more prominent spokesmen said a number of years back, "You can't race donkeys against horses." They also believe that children in the upper streams of the system are inherently superior to those beneath them. These teachers give solid leadership to the anti-destreaming lobby. But theirs is very much a minority position.

The second factor is much more significant. A substantial majority of teachers understand destreaming as a government policy designed to load their classes with hard-to-handle kids, offering little or no help with programs or discipline, and with the very strong possibility that their class size will actually increase in the process. They know it is "politically correct" to be against streaming, but they also judge that their classroom work will suffer and suffer badly. They don't give a damn what the research says about the virtues of destreaming, because they think that the conditions under which destreaming in their school will take place won't match the conditions under which the research was done. They know what administrators do with well-meaning programs developed by politicians. They've been there before. Most of these teachers are also aware that their high schools have been doing their own brand of destreaming through the expansion of the advanced level program, and that this seems to be working reasonably well. So they would mostly like to be left alone in dealing with this problem. The present logic of the system should be allowed to take its own course. However, if there are to be additional destreaming initiatives, these must not only be properly supported, but their implementation must also be left to the good judgement of teachers and parents in their local school. They want no more reform via government fiat.

It is in this context that OSSTF's Provincial Executive, in its submission to the Royal Commission, insisted on a "properly tested and developed destreaming plan," which would itself be part of a larger "protocol for change." The Executive put particular stress on an educational structure and program that would focus on the vast majority of our students, rather than "providing special attention for the gifted and the disadvantaged." A great many students who do badly in school, they argued, "do not have learning disabilities or any intellectual reason for their lack of mastery of basic understanding." Tough economic and social conditions and family stress are much more to blame. We should not be meeting these students with a rigid set of high school streams. Instead, we should opt for the kind of structure that allows "easy passage from one level of study to a higher order of study." This would not be difficult, their submission argues, if only the Ministry "re-introduce[d] the open credit, removed under OSIS, and introduce[d] a series of up-grading credits in the areas of mathematics, English and science." What is fundamental to making this internal destreaming work, they concluded, are solid "remediation and bridging loops." These are "absolutely essential if opportunities for transfer between career paths are to exist."[69]

Throughout the school system as a whole, OSSTF argues, we should continue to minimize the divisions between our students. "It is impossible in society for the winners ever to be disconnected from the losers," the Federation argues. "We have public schools because we learned long ago that education cannot be an enclave of one class or ethnic group. It is a public responsibility essential to democratic society and our economy. It cannot be left to whim. It is society, not the individual or family, that benefits most from education. It therefore must be the responsibility of society and not individual or private groups. The current debates about education only underscore the fact that there is no more important decision in a democracy than the kind of education we want for all our children — what knowledge, what values, what skills. Answers to those questions shape the future of our society. The answers require a collective response, not an individual response, if democratic society is to be upheld."[70]

On the issue of standardizing education, in curriculum and

in testing, OSSTF stands clearly against the main thrust of the Royal Commission's recommendations.

"The obsession of reformers with standardized and computerized tests is disturbing," OSSTF's Provincial Executive declared to the commissioners. While "OSSTF does not oppose more thorough testing and changes that make student learning more accountable to parents," it refuses to support a "minimalist" emphasis on "information memorizing," which lies at the centre of so much learner-outcome "skill" testing. "The quantification obsession," its brief continues, "trivializes and marginalizes curriculum changes demanded by changes in science, the fight for Canadian independence, sensitivity to the environment, immigration and perceptions about race and gender."[71] What OSSTF wants instead is what it calls "meaningful standards for education achievement in Ontario. To the greatest extent possible, standards for public education in Ontario should be developed based on sound educational research and judgements of what is worth knowing and doing."[72] Such standards are to be built in direct opposition to a "system that is driven by standardized tests and the one correct answer, that fails to recognize multiple intelligences, creativity, and the spirit of inquiry and lifelong learning."[73]

Finally, OSSTF remains solidly committed to the idea that education cannot be divorced from the social purposes that link us as citizens.

The Federation believes, its Executive insists, "that education is fundamentally a public good rather than a commodity for individual consumption. Public education, like public health care, is a cornerstone of Canadian democracy. Democratic government and society rely on public schools as an essential civic resource to provide an informed, well-educated citizenry and to give it strength and substance."[74]

This is a very long way from the practice of Outcomes Based Education.

OSSTF has just begun to train its sights on this particular form of the corporate agenda in education. When it appeared initially, OBE seemed not much more than a bland and clumsy expression of goals and therefore not especially worrisome. That view has changed. At its last Provincial Assembly there was a clear feeling in the room — though it was too late to find adequate expression in official motions — that the OBE approach to program and testing will require much more critical investigation and a well worked out action plan to deal with its implications. As OSSTF's Toronto District 15 put it, this is a program that "provides the appearance of standards without the substance," and does so, as we noted above, with major corporate and board sponsorship.

What these local activists suggest is that "OSSTF has to come up with its own restructuring plan, one that emphasizes Public Education as a distinct, though not necessarily exclusive, field from job-training. The organizations necessary for this plan already exist. Subject councils consist, for the most part, of teachers who feel passionately about their subject and try to transfer that passion to the students. Subject council control of OSSTF educational policy will put power into the hands of those people who best represent public education: classroom teachers."[75]

This stress on subjects and subject councils is a fundamental one for OSSTF. For it is here that the Federation expresses most clearly its understanding that skills cannot be divorced from the real stuff of the curriculum. In its submission to the Royal Commission, OSSTF's Provincial Executive took particular care to stress the importance of subjects as a curriculum framework and to insist that an "integrated" program respect subject integrity rather than operate with too dominant an emphasis on detached skill development. "Extreme proponents of this concept [of integration]," says the Executive, "suggest the elimination of subject areas in favour of an integrated curriculum totally focused on skills education. OSSTF continues to believe that the delivery of education should continue to be organized around credits based on subject disciplines. The segmented nature of education finds its cause in the failure of educators to teach the relationship of subjects to each other and how these subjects connect to each other. Correcting this shortcoming is easy if the school asks educators to emphasize the connection of their subject area to other areas of study. Accomplishing further integration would examine the possibility of teaching courses cooperatively in various disciplines at the same level. Natural connections appear to be mathematics and science; history, English and art; art, drama and music. Increased flexibility in allowing schools to package courses would go a long way to achieving greater integration in education in Ontario."[76]

In many respects, this is a call to arms for a renewal (and a rethinking) of the Liberal Arts, which have taken a substantial pounding in the Commission's Report. As District 15 puts it, "the OSSTF curriculum, if it is to have a clear and distinct voice, must also promote a core curriculum that has been present since civilizations began. Although choices should be allowed for the student, the student should receive an obligatory education in the humanities (art, literature, history), mathematics and science. This is not a reactionary or an atavistic idea. The notion of training all students in these areas once reserved for the elite is radical and profoundly democratic.... If OSSTF were to come up with such a plan and promote it, public sympathy would be on our side. With OSSTF describing their vision of a solid education in humanities, mathematics and science, along with a large variety of electives, and [with] the Boards pushing Outcomes Based Education, which few parents understand and fewer like, the public will surely be on the side of the teachers. When this happens, when people see that it is the classroom teacher who is fighting for genuine public education, teachers will regain their prominent position in society and our other battles with the board will become easier to win."[77]

If a Liberal Arts program is to be appropriate for students for all social classes, it must also incorporate a serious commitment to equality for all students. The Federation's Race Relations Task Force made this very clear in its submission to the Royal Commission. "The essence of antiracist education," it said, "is the creation of a learning environment in which each child is valued and differences celebrated. It taps into a rich vein of cultural, ethnic and racial diversity and, by validating the individual, improves education for all. This can only be achieved through a public education system which provides access for all, equity for all and opportunity for all. It can only flourish within a learning environment which provides value for all and allows achievement for all."[78]

But not only are students on the line with Outcomes Based Education; OSSTF members are increasingly aware that they too are under the gun.

As District 15 argues, "... the wages of teachers will be cut and the profession deskilled."[79] As this form of education "removes power from the classroom teacher and gives it to an outside department responsible for setting the 'outcomes'," it will also devalue "the skilled and knowledgeable classroom teacher." Subject expertise will "fade in importance," and there will be "little need for teachers with university degrees. In other countries," District 15 continues, "teachers are being hired with only high school degrees after, at best, a short training period in the bells and whistles of current pedagogy theory. Under an OBE education system, it will become increasingly difficult to maintain the teaching qualification that comes in the form of subject-area academic degrees or professional expertise."

District 15 goes on to stress the tight interrelationship between teacher subject knowledge and economic security, between teachers' material interests and the quality of their program. It is another dimension of the "natural alliance" between parents and teachers. "As long as we must have an academic degree to teach our subjects," District 15 argues, "we can much better fight the ongoing attack on our wages. Without subject specialty, teachers become much more vulnerable to cost-cutting. Our strength is our knowledge: to teach a subject, one must know a subject is a phase on which we must insist. Otherwise, teachers will need only a teaching certificate of some kind because a university degree will be irrelevant if subject competence is de-emphasized. The labour pool grows, teachers are less skilled and our wages are cut."

It is all part of the fight against what OSSTF has chosen to call "the minimalist" approach to public schooling. This approach, like that expressed in the Royal Commission, "would strictly circumscribe the services offered by schools and make public education into a smaller system serving fewer people for fewer years. [It] would limit curriculum, knowledge, skills and the values school teaches."[80]

What OSSTF wants is a lot more — a program rooted in the

best intellectual traditions of the society and at the same time directly relevant to the present and future lives of Ontario students. This means, to return to the argument with which we opened this chapter, that the Federation continues to insist in the area of curriculum — just as it has on issues of finance and decision-making — that people have to come first. There can be no place in an education system, it argues, for mechanical job-slotting, either in skills or attitudes. Schools must not be directly at the service of Canadian business and its needs in a global economy, although job-related abilities are rightfully part of education's mandate. Whatever the larger patterns in the subjects its members teach, these must be interwoven with the life-patterns of those who learn. Such interweaving has always been at the heart and soul of the Liberal Arts, as OSSTF has long understood. As these subjects are reshaped and rethought for the modern world, they must continue to reflect and to hold together both our private and our public values. That the tension between private and public worlds is now very great makes it even more important that teachers and students struggle to come to grips with the integration of social reality.

More Than A Blunt Instrument

Let me close with some comments from my old friend Bob Davis, a Scarborough high school teacher and a long-time OSSTF activist. For a number of years Davis has decried the current "skills mania" in our schools which has been so prominently featured in the Royal Commission on Learning. He notes that education has always had an important vocational emphasis, but he is convinced that something very different has been happening in the past decade or so. His analysis is much the same as the one that has run though this book.

"The new twist," he says, "is that the vocational idea has taken over the liberal arts program itself. Vocational used to mean tech wings and commercial programs. When it worked best, you learned how to type or you learned how to be a tool and dye maker, then in history and English class you learned what the world was like — or at least what the authorities wanted you to think the world was like. But now the education cutting edge says that in those mainstream courses you should also be learning vocational. We cannot afford to teach content any more, they say. Content is both something you forget very fast and something that becomes obsolete very fast. So what we have to do in the new education is to teach people not to learn but how to learn. This should start off with basic skills, numbers and words, but should eventually move on to something called generic skills, especially thinking skills." At the same time as this academic "skills mania" hit the schools, Davis discovered an increased corporate and administrative emphasis on "collaborative activities" or "teamwork" for student learning. Increasingly, it didn't matter much what students learned though these groups by way of content. It was only the process — operating within firm guidelines set by school authorities — that mattered. And functioning in this process, it turned out, was also a skill. As in the corporate workplace, this skill was further subdivided into various interpersonal work skills, framed by management, and mostly described in terms of attitude. Proper attitude was now knowledge, while the larger issues of production (or content) remained outside the student-worker's competence.[81]

This "skills mania" has been increasingly "pressed on students," Davis continues, "by the system of authority, the general school milieu, the evaluation and grading systems, the specialization, the streaming, the scientific management jargon, accountability schemes, the slant of the text books and the confident labelling of different kinds of students." As a result, Davis argues, students have more and more come to see school as "simply a competitive labelling system" they should "take advantage of for a well-paid job. There is nothing [they say] worth learning here or anywhere else."

In the face of such a powerful curriculum thrust, what is a teacher to do? "How do we face up," Davis asks, "to the challenge of the skills/outcomes curriculum here in Canada?" His answer has two parts.

First, he says, we must recognize that the "core approaches to education — conservative, liberal and radical — which were formerly at war, now appear, when contrasted with the technocratic skills approach, to have more that unites them than separates them." It is in the union of these traditions that

Davis sees the basis of a common curriculum focused on excellence and purpose. From the conservative tradition he stresses "the passing of a legacy" and the need to "teach and debate roots." From liberalism come ideas of "individual and minority liberties" and the need to teach and debate the meaning of freedom — "civil liberty, toleration, and rights." From the tradition of radical thought comes "the challenge of equality and the building of a new society." This vision must also be taught and debated. "Conservatives, liberals and radicals of the non-technocratic kind must come to see their common interests in education and contribute in their own ways to building this curriculum. To put this perspective another way," Davis concludes, "while taking on the issues of freedom and justice — issues of class, race, gender, peace and the environment — a common curriculum must also deal with love and community, with the real lives we live together."

Davis' second point focuses on the need to combat undue scepticism and shallow "bias-detecting" techniques — approaches which still pass as critical thinking in our schools. In their stead, it is the deeper thoughts and feelings of teachers and students which must be front and centre in our classrooms. Davis is especially conscious of students floundering on the most elemental level of understanding, "unsure of what they believe about the most basic human and political ideas." These students, he says, are searching for something much more fundamental than "different points of view." It is the business of the schools — whatever the skills enthusiasts may say — to deal with fundamental issues of belief and understanding. Working with minds is not simply working with "thinking skills." But it is not indoctrination, either. It is, instead, helping to root a student's knowledge in herself and in her deepest experience of the world. It is assisting in the development of a person who will not be "malleable in the hands of dogmatic governments and advertising executives." It is part of the creation of honest citizens.

And it is something else, too.

It is the linking of our ideas and our actions in the world to a larger sense of our humanity and of our life's meaning. However much technique we may master to shape our human and natural environment, it cannot be dissociated from our humanity. "All means," Davis quotes Albert Einstein as saying, "prove but a blunt instrument if they have not behind them a living spirit." It is "the living spirit behind the curriculum," Davis argues, that must underlie our work as teachers. If we accept a curriculum based on mechanical "outcomes" for corporate job slots, however complex those outcomes may be, our public schools will simply die — in boredom and despair.[82]

My hunch is that most of Davis' colleagues in the end share this perspective, however much it may get lost in the daily grind of our schools. And when push comes to shove, with a Mike Harris government or with his successors, I think we'll find that out. In action, if not in words.

I also have a hunch that District 15 is right. If OSSTF has the courage to stand and fight for a strong and revitalized Liberal Arts program — one that captures the "living spirit" of the present age for Ontario and for Canada and sees in it a powerful platform for school reform — then the public will stand with them.

It will be the real beginning of a new education politics.

FOOTNOTES

1 Interview with Doug Little, March 15, 1995. The public meeting, which Caplan attended — an Ontario Institute for Studies in Education Forum on the Royal Commission's Report — was held on March, 1995. Little's story was superseded by other news, and it didn't make the paper. He kept his notes, however.

2 Quotations in the following pages are taken from the *Report of the Royal Commission on Learning, Volume I*, cited above, pp. 24–27.

3 Livingstone's response, quoted in the following pages, is found in Livingstone, David, "The Uses of Computer Literacy: Critical Reflections on the Royal Commission on Learning," *Orbit*, May 1995.

4 *Report of the Royal Commission on Learning, Volume 1*, cited above, pp. 36–37.

5 *Report of the Royal Commission on Learning, Volume 1*, cited above, p. 55.

6 District 15 Toronto PAC Educational Issues Subcommittee, "Outcomes-Based Education and Classroom Teachers: Backgrounder on District 15 AMPA motions MAC 235 and 236," Annual Meeting Provincial Assembly, March 11, 1995.

7 *Report of the Royal Commission on Learning, Volume 2*, cited above, pp. 25–26.

8 *Report of the Royal Commission on Learning, Volume 2*, cited above, p. 26.

9 *Report of the Royal Commission on Learning, Volume 2*, cited above, p. 29. For an example of the neo-conservative use of this strategy see the Joel Friedman and Mark Holmes video *Failing Grades*.

10 *Report of the Royal Commission on Learning, Volume 2*, cited above, p. 27. Recommendation #5.

11 *Report of the Royal Commission on Learning, Volume 2*, cited above, p. 55.

12 *Report of the Royal Commission on Learning, Volume 2*, cited above, pp 20–21.

13 *Report of the Royal Commission on Learning, Volume 2*, cited above, p. 56.

14 Osborne, Ken, *Educating Citizens: A Democratic Socialist Agenda for Canadian Education*, Our Schools/Our Selves, Toronto, 1988, p. 27.

15 *Report of the Royal Commission on Learning, Volume 1*, cited above, p. 57.

16 *Report of the Royal Commission on Learning, Volume 1*, cited above, pp. 56–57.

17 *Report of the Royal Commission on Learning, Volume 1*, cited above, p. 57.

18 *Report of the Royal Commission on Learning, Volume 1*, cited above, p. 57.

19 OSSTF, *Response to the Royal Commission on Learning, Factsheet No. 1*, "Specialization Years and Compression," pp. 2–3.

20 *Report of the Royal Commission on Learning, Volume 2*, cited above, p. 78. Recommendation #18.

21 *Report of the Royal Commission on Learning, Volume 2*, cited above, p. 79.

22 *Report of the Royal Commission on Learning, Volume 2*, cited above, p. 61.

23 *Report of the Royal Commission on Learning, Volume 4*, cited above, p. 13–14.

24 Turk, James L., "Comments on *Report of The Royal Commission on Learning*," Ontario Federation of Labour, February 1995.

25 Charles Pascal, "Deputy Minister's Report," February 17, 1995, p. 1.

26 Lewington, Jennifer, "Province-wide tests yield 'real positives,'" *Globe and Mail*, March 31, 1995.

27 *Report of the Royal Commission on Learning, Volume 2*, cited above, pp. 140–141.

28 *Report of the Royal Commission on Learning, Volume 2*, cited above, p. 142.

29 OISE surveys point to the fact that most parents continue to insist that teachers' judgements remain central to student assessment, not the results of province-wide tests. See Livingstone, D.W., Hart, D., Davie, L.E., *Public Attitudes Towards Education in Ontario, 1994: The Tenth OISE Survey*, Toronto, 1995.

30 *Report of the Royal Commission on Learning, Volume 2*, cited above, p. 150.

31 Cooke, Dave, "Speaking notes on Testing and Accountability Initiatives," Queen's Park, February 17, 1995, p. 2.

32 *Report of the Royal Commission on Learning, Volume 2*, cited above, p. 149.

33 *Report of the Royal Commission on Learning, Volume 1*, cited above, p. 65.

34 *Report of the Royal Commission on Learning, Volume 1*, cited above, p. 68.

35 *Report of the Royal Commission on Learning, Volume 2*, cited above, p. 131.

36 *Report of the Royal Commission on Learning, Volume 2*, cited above, pp. 138–139.

37 *Report of the Royal Commission on Learning, Volume 2*, cited above, p. 151.

38 *Report of the Royal Commission on Learning, Volume 2*, cited above, p. 187. Recommendations #53, 54, 55.

39 *Report of the Royal Commission on Learning, Volume 1*, cited above, pp. 59-60.

40 *Report of the Royal Commission on Learning, Volume 2*, cited above, p. 73.

41 *Report of the Royal Commission on Learning, Volume 2*, cited above, p. 72.

42 *Report of the Royal Commission on Learning, Volume 2*, cited above, pp. 72–73.

43 *Report of the Royal Commission on Learning, Volume 2*, cited above, pp. 73–74.

44 OSSTF Provincial Executive, *Public Education: Retracing Our Path, An examination of the goals of public education, its role in society and directions for reform, A Brief to the Royal Commission on Learning*, Toronto, December 1993, pp. 52–53.

45 *Report of the Royal Commission on Learning, Volume 2*, cited above, pp. 69, 76.

46 *Report of the Royal Commission on Learning, Volume 2*, cited above, p. 78.

47 *Report of the Royal Commission on Learning, Volume 2*, cited above, pp. 76–78. See Recommendation #17.

48 *Report of the Royal Commission on Learning, Volume 2*, cited above, p. 78. Recommendation #18. Also pp. 83–84.

49 *Report of the Royal Commission on Learning, Volume 2*, cited above, p. 77.

50 *Report of the Royal Commission on Learning, Volume 2*, cited above, p. 78.

51 *Report of the Royal Commission on Learning, Volume 2*, cited above, p. 91.

52 *Report of the Royal Commission on Learning, Volume 2*, cited above, p. 111. Recommendation #40.

53 *Report of the Royal Commission on Learning, Volume 2*, cited above, p. 111. See Recommendation #41.

54 *Report of the Royal Commission on Learning, Volume 2*, cited above, p. 52. See Recommendation #10.

55 *Report of the Royal Commission on Learning, Volume 2*, cited above, p. 78. Recommendation #16.

56 *Report of the Royal Commission on Learning, Volume 2*, cited above, p. 75.

57 OSSTF, *Response to the Royal Commission on Learning, Fact Sheet No. 2*, "Specialization Years and Compression," p. 1.

58 *Report of the Royal Commission on Learning, Volume 2*, cited above, pp. 58–60.

59 *Report of the Royal Commission on Learning, Volume 2*, cited above, p. 85.

60 It is worth noting American educator Herb Kohl's point about Outcomes Based Education propaganda insisting that everyone would advance in school at their own speed. In practice, Kohl says, the ones who take a long time to pass their outcomes test end up in a separate group, functioning as a lower stream, just as they did in the old system. Interview, Community Radio, Rochester, Minnesota, 1991.

61 *Report of the Royal Commission on Learning, Volume 2*, cited above, pp. 58–59.

62 *Report of the Royal Commission on Learning, Volume 2*, cited above, pp. 111–114.

63 *Report of the Royal Commission on Learning, Volume 2*, cited above, pp. 115–116.

64 *Report of the Royal Commission on Learning, Volume 2*, cited above, p.

111. Recommendation #33.

65 *Report of the Royal Commission on Learning, Volume 2*, cited above, p. 119. Recommendation #39.

66 *Report of the Royal Commission on Learning, Volume 2*, cited above, p. 113.

67. *Report of the Royal Commission on Learning, Volume 2*, cited above, p. 118. See Recommendation #34.

68 Livingstone, David, "The Uses of Computer Literacy: Critical Reflections on the Royal Commission on Learning," *Orbit*, May 1995.

69 OSSTF Provincial Executive, *Public Education: Retracing our path*, cited above, pp. 7–8, 16–17.

70 OSSTF Provincial Executive, *Public Education: Retracing our path*, cited above, pp. 10–11.

71 OSSTF Provincial Executive, *Public Education: Retracing our path*, cited above, p. 8.

72 OSSTF Provincial Executive, *Public Education: Retracing our path*, cited above, p. 2

73 OSSTF Provincial Executive, *Public Education: Retracing our path*, cited above, p. 41.

74 OSSTF Provincial Executive, *Public Education: Retracing our path*, cited above, p. 3.

75 District 15 Toronto PAC Educational Issues Subcommittee, "Outcomes-Based Education and Classroom Teachers: Backgrounder on District 15 AMPA motions MAC 235 and 236," Annual Meeting Provincial Assembly, March 11, 1995.

76 OSSTF Provincial Executive, *Public Education: Retracing our path*, cited above, p. 17.

77 District 15 Toronto PAC Educational Issues Subcommittee, "Outcomes-Based Education and Classroom Teachers: Backgrounder on District 15 AMPA motions MAC 235 and 236," Annual Meeting Provincial Assembly, March 11, 1995.

78 OSSTF Provincial Executive, *Public Education: Retracing our path*, cited above, p. 33.

79 District 15 Toronto PAC Educational Issues Subcommittee, "Outcomes-Based Education and Classroom Teachers: Backgrounder on District 15 AMPA motions MAC 235 and 236," Annual Meeting Provincial Assembly, March 11, 1995.

80 OSSTF Provincial Executive, *Public Education: Retracing our path*, cited above, p.6.

81 Davis, Bob, "Mentally Skilled But Mindless?" *Our Schools/Our Selves*, May-June, 1993.

82 Davis, Bob, *What Our High Schools Could Be*, Our Schools/Our Selves, Toronto, 1990, pp. 13–21.

Join The Debate On What Should Happen In Canada's Schools. You Can Still Get Your Own Copy Of Each Of These Issues Of Our Schools/Our Selves.

Double Issue #40-41: Whatever Happened To High School History? Burying the Political Memory of Youth: Ontario 1945-1995 by Bob Davis. A passionate and probing book about the decline of history as a secondary school subject. With the narrative of progress and British civilization gone, and the contemporary cult of content-free "skills" offering no basis for understanding the past, how can history teachers help today's students make sense of their world and their future, Davis asks. Being an experienced teacher as well as a scholar and a theorist, Davis is in a unique position to pose this question and to propose new directions and new hope. A "must read" for teachers, parents and university students concerned with where our curriculum is going.

Issue #39: (Journal) Capitalism Goes to Napanee High ... Student Demonstrations in France ... Insight into Gender, Identity, Equity ... Gender Studies in the English 12 Classroom ... No Answers on Grade Nine Reading and Writing Tests ... Education Roundup ... Parents Save a School in Nova Scotia ... Cooperative/Competitive Athletics ... Reviews of Barlow, Nikiforuk, Walcom ...

Issue #38: In Defence of History: Teaching The Past And The Meaning Of Democratic Citizenship by Ken Osborne. In the neo-conservative economic and political climate of the 1990's, history is fast becoming an endangered species. Ken Osborne, who has been teaching history for some thirty years, argues that the subject is unlike any other in the school cirriculum. How we see and interpret the world, how we understand the problems that face us on the local, national and global level, how we treat each other, our very values are largely the result of how we understand our past or fail to understand it. Besides offering a cogent argument for the importance of history, Osborne's book also provides many strategies for developing a liberating, egalitarian pedagogy, which stresses critical awareness among students, healthy scepticism about "official versions" of the past, and active student involvement in the production of socially relevant history.

Issue #37: (Journal) Globalization, NAFTA and Education ... A Year of Education Politics in France ... Teacher Morale ... View from the Classroom ... Winnipeg General Strike ... Beware of the Penguins ... What Facts, Whose Arguments? ... Going Beyond School-Based Management Before We've Even Got There ... Education Roundup ... Name One Female Inventor ... Ethics and the Corporate Classroom ... Canada/Us Border Project ... Buying In But Not Sold Out.

Issue #36: Sex In Schools edited by Susan Prentice. This anthology offers insights into how Canadian schools have sought to regulate and discipline sexuality — through sexual education classes, in teacher-student relationships, in curriculum and pedagogy, and every-day practices. The authors explore the links between sexual regulation and other forms of social organization: especially gender, sexual orientation, age, class and race.

Sex in Schools starts from the perspective that sexuality is socially constructed and is shaped by power relations. Contributors show how "normal" sexuality is created, reproduced and struggled over. From historical to contemporary examples, this anthology explores over a 150 years of Canadian education and sexual regulation.

Issue #35: (Journal) The Toronto Board Takes The Pepsi Challenge ... And Loses ... School Board NDP Failure Leads To Possible Demise ... Bombers, Kids, And Kites ... The Turkey Vulture Who Lived His Literature ... The Best and Wisest For All: A Look At Gifted Programs ... Vouchers: Will They Cure Our Schools? ... The Myth Of The "Model Minority" Rethinking The Education Of Asian Canadians ... Class Warfare: The Assault On Canada's Schools ... A Good Idea And Its Enemies Part 2: The Best Kept Secrets Of North American Education ... Education Roundup ... A Sad Time To Be A Teacher ... Slash and Burn in Alberta Schools ... A School-leaving Literacy Test Is Not Going To

Make Schools Accountable ... Teaching For Social Justice ... Neo-Conservatism In South American Education ... A Passionate Journey Into Canadian History.

Issue #34: Don't Tell Us It Can't Be Done! Alternative Classrooms In Canada And Abroad edited by Chuck Chamberlin. A remarkable collection of essays — covering a social action project in Red Deer, Alberta, a progressive school in Maryland, student governance in Sweden, the Tvind Schools of Denmark, Freinet pedagogy in France, a Piagestian school in Spain, as well as Montessori and Waldorf School programs.

Issue #33: (Journal) "Children Are Not Meant To Be Studied ..." ... Curriculum And Teaching In Canada: The Missing Centre ... More Training For What? The Canadian Labour Force Development Strategy, Saskatchewan Style ... The Regime Of Technology In Education ... Teacher Unions And Social Responsibility ... You Might Enjoy The Humble Pie At Pete's, Mr Coren ... Like Small Streams That Feed The Mississippi: Resistance In America Education ... The Lament Of A Passer-by ... Lies, Dammed Lies, And Statistics: Drop-outs, Literacy & Tests ... Education Roundup ... To Stream Or Not To Stream In Manitoba ... Getting Off The Track: Classroom Examples For An Anti-tracking Pedagogy ... Speaking Of Our World.

Issue #32: Rethinking Vocationalism edited by Rebecca Priegert Coulter and Ivor Goodson. Returns us to some of the "old questions" about education — who controls it?, and whose interests are served by it?— as they examine the "reconfiguration" of vocational education in a period of global restructuring. Other authors include Christopher J. Anstead, Jean Barman, Catherine Casey, Kari Dehli, Jane Gaskell, Madeleine R. Grumet, Nancy Jackson, Jeffry Piker and Jim Turk.

Issue #31: (Journal) The NDP and Education: What Happened In Ontario, B.C., Saskatchewan, and Manitoba? ... N.B.'s Strategy For Post-Secondary Education ... Gender Equity: A Personal Journey ... American Racism, Canadian Surrender: More Reflections On "To Kill A Mockingbird" ... A Letter From Siberia ... All The News That's Fit For Business: YNN Zereos In On The Canadian Classroom ...

Speak It! From The Heart Of Black Nova Scotia ... Educating The English.

Issue #30: Pandora's Box: Corporate Power, Free Trade and Canadian Education by John Calvert and Larry Kuehn. The authors lay bare the real story behind corporate interest in education and show, via a detailed analysis of the NAFTA text and political and economic trends throughout North America, how NAFTA is being used by Corporate Canada in their attempts to commercialize and privatize public education.

Issue #29: (Journal) Teaching Mi'kmaq: Living A Language ... TV And The Dene ... Turning A Blind Eye To Linguistic Genocide ... After 1492–1992: A Post-Colonial Supplement For The Canadian Curriculum ..., The Emerging Corporate Agenda For Canadian High Schools ... A Critical Look At The Skills Mania ... Show Boat: Reflections On The Passage Of A Racist Icon ... The Ninth OISE Survey: The Public Mood In Tough Times ... A New Vision For Bilingual Education.

Issue #28: Schools And Social Justice by R.W. Connell. Throughout this broad analysis, which spans the educational systems of Europe, North America and Australia, Connell argues that the issue of social justice is fundamental to what good education is about. If the school system deals unjustly with some of its pupils, the quality of education for all of the others is degraded. He calls for "curricular justice," which opens out the perspective of the least advantaged, roots itself in a democratic context, and moves toward the creation of a more equalitarian society.

Issue #27: (Journal) NAFTA's Destruction Of Canadian Education ... The Corporate Hijacking Of Canada's Universities .... Lining Up Gender In Elementary School ... Totems and Taboos In Bilingual Education ... Teaching Outside The Mainstream ... The Nuclear Agenda In Saskatchewan's Schools ... The Anti-Racist Uses Of To Kill A Mockingbird ... New Brunswick Reading Circles ... John Dewey And American Democracy ... Surveying Canada's Teens ... Educating For Change.

Issue #26: Training For What? Labour Perspectives On Job Training by Nancy Jackson et al. In this book a number of union activists analyze the corporate training agenda in Canada and open up a labour alternative. They let us see training as a tool of political struggle in the workplace, which can contribute to skill recognition, to safe and satisfying working conditions, to career progression and to building a more democratic vision of working life.

Issue #25: (Journal) The Meaning Of Yonge Street ... What Should The NDP Do? ... New Brunswick's Plunge Into 'Excellence' ... Bargaining For Childcare ... Denmark's Efterskoles ... Reader Response And Postmodern Literacy ... Against Skills ... Slash And Burn In Nova Scotia Schools.

Issue #24: Stacking The Deck: The Streaming Of Working Class Kids In Ontario Schools by Bruce Curtis, D.W. Livingstone & Harry Smaller. This book examines the history and structure of class bias in Ontario education. It looks at both elementary and secondary schooling and proposes a new deal for working class children. The evidence is taken from the Ontario system, but the ideas and analysis can be extended to every school in Canada.

Subscribe Now!

In One Year
You'll Receive
3 Journals And 3 Books.

It's Not Only
A Great Read,
It's A Great Deal.

Here's What's Coming In Future Issues Of Our Schools/Our Selves

Articles On:

Labour Studies At The Toronto Board — What Do We Tell Our Kids About Canada — Science And Standardized Testing — Environmental Activism — Unionizing ESL Teachers — A Winnipeg Inner City School — CUPE's Fight For Parental Leave — The World Of Teenage Girls — Labour, Education And The Arts — Sex In Upper Canada's Classrooms — Young Women In Trades — Inside The Labelling Process — Schools And Museums — Whatever Happened To York University?

You'll get three journals and three books a year for each subscription.

Books On:

A Socialist-Feminist Approach To Phys Ed — Native Control Of White Education — Whatever Happened To High School History? — Assessment And Evaluation — Australian Education Activism — What's Basic? A Teachers' Union Response To Bob Rae's Assault On Ontario Schools — Racism and Education — Where Is The US Left In Education? — What Do People Really Think About Our Schools? — An Anti-Racist Curriculum For Nova Scotia — The Canadian Intellectual Tradition — A People's History of Canada

It's a great bargain, as much as 50% off the newsstand price.